An original work

THE GRE... ....
P L A N

A THREEFOLD CELESTIAL PROGRAM TO RETRIEVE URANTIA FROM THE SINFUL LEGACIES OF THE LUCIFER REBELLION

JOSEPH E. JEAN-PHILLIPPE

Announcing a New Era of Spiritual Enlightenment

Vol. 1

The Great Correcting Time Plan is a cosmic undertaking to restore the will of God on earth and 36 other inhabited planets that were severely affected by the outbreak of the Lucifer rebellion around 250,000 years ago. The diverse components of this endeavor were specifically designed and tailored to address the issues and deal with the local condition of each world. It was initiated on earth by Christ Michael, the Creator Son of this universe during his human bestowal as Jesus. Today, it is being implemented here by three supernal programs known as the Urantia Book, the Teaching Mission, and the Magisterial Mission.

~

Abomaly—the disembodied personality with whom we interfaced to obtain this information, is essentially the main voice of this text. He was himself a former mortal from another inhabited realm thousands of years prior to his present status as an Ascended Master.

~

In this volume, he describes some of the primordial [celestial and global] events that challenged the original plan of God for this world and drastically altered the course of human evolution. Moreover, he depicts the major problems that beset the world and their current exacerbation by a dark cabal for a sinister purpose, which emphatically demonstrates why it is vital to bring this correction on the planet through divine intervention at this time.

paradisePress

— Promoting Transcendental Consciousness —

THE GREAT CORRECTING TIME PLAN

A Threefold Celestial Program to Retrieve Urantia from the Sinful Legacies of the Lucifer Rebellion

~

JOSEPH E. JEAN-PHILLIPPE

...An Original Work of Channeling with a Celestial Personality

Announcing a New Era of Spiritual Enlightenment

ParadisePresS

Spiritself1st@aol.com

ParadisePress

Promoting Transcendental Consciousness

THE GREAT CORRECTING TIME PLAN
A Threefold Celestial Program to Retrieve Urantia from the Sinful Legacies of the Lucifer Rebellion

...An Original Work of Channeling with a Celestial Personality

Published by Joseph E. Jean-Phillippe for ParadisePress
Spiritself1st@aol.com

Formatting: Jean-Phillippe
Cover design: Jean-Phillippe
Picture: Khaalid Yaqoub
Proofread: Marcia Lewis

Please visit our sites on the World Wide Web.

www. ParadisePress.com – www. Lagrandevue.org

Printers' errors—perhaps this will make the book more valuable, just as a misprint in a stamp make it more valuable!

ISBN   978-312-72042-8

First printed, paperback version with index, 2014

Table of Contents

Part 1

Part 2

Parts of the book

Part 1

THE LUCIFER REBELLION WITH ITS FAR-REACHING AND WIDESPREAD CONSEQUENCES: *the Dark Cabal that secretly rules the world*

Part 2

THE ACTIVITIES OF THE CORRECTING TIME PLAN: *Its three major celestial programs to restore the Creator's will on earth*

Special Dedications

—This book is especially dedicated to humanity's spiritual liberation, healing, and transfiguration. It is a selfless act to foster a greater consciousness of the depth and limitlessness of our True Selves as sentient, will-endowed Personalities. —

—It is also to those wonderful souls with whom I am currently sharing this journey, particularly my lovely daughter, Havona.—

Foreword

"After over 250,000 years in cosmic quarantine, Urantia [planet earth] has been finally reinstated into the fold of the universe's normal evolving worlds. It was declared ready by divine decree to break off with the sinful legacies of the Lucifer rebellion following the recent adjudication and execution of the latter. Thus, now all existential authorities that beset and hamper humanity's progress are being scrutinized and evaluated either for rectification or for eventual annihilation. Our assignment is essentially focused on disclosing the primordial celestial events that distorted the natural order of this world with the present supernal plan to heal and correct it. The diverse co-creative transmissions must expose the principal adversaries of God, the astronomical consequences of their cosmic insurrection, and the Creator's correctional programs that will help transition this realm to a golden age of awakening and spiritual enlightenment.

Symbolically, this book is 'a small voice in the wilderness' that is announcing the dawn of a '*spiritual renaissance*' with the arrival of a New Era of peace, justice, harmony and goodwill on earth. Although it is a unique voice, it is not alone in the deserts. It belongs to a large and growing global choir of Lightworkers—pioneer and devoted truth-seekers, who are actively engaged in the promulgation of this great news. This emerging multitude of truth-emissaries in the world is neither a coincidence of time nor the result of human efforts only. It is rather the gathering body of the '*new church of real Jesusonians,*' who are inspired, rehearsed and ably assisted by their celestial caretakers. Today, this group is generally serving in many different capacities, each member according to personal talents, devotion, and ability to cooperate with their unseen friends in a co-creative process to bring about peace, equity, and right-mindedness in the collective consciousness of humanity."

Celestial Teacher – Ahmezdy

THIS BOOK IS AN ORIGINAL, co-creative work of channeling with a disembodied personality—Abomaly. It is a glimpse into the primal events that thwarted the Creator's plan for the evolution of man, and the current transcendental efforts to restore it. At the onset, these unfortunate circumstances, which altered the initial programs of God for human temporal development and Paradise ascension, are defined. Abomaly exposes the perfidious celestial personalities who distorted the earth's natural order, implanted a rebellious mindset on it, and disconnected man from the source of creation. This, as it was intended, has poisoned humanity's relationships for the past two hundred and fifty thousand years.

In addition, he explains how these wicked entities operate in this realm, using a few strains of *hybrid bloodlines* as their conduits and agents. The callous nature of these selected individuals, which he referred to as the *"dark cabal"* in the text, is emphatically denounced as he unveils their secret conspiracy to orchestrate world conflicts, decimate the planet's population, and impose a fascistic global dictatorship.

Additionally, the most urgent political, socioeconomic and spiritual challenges the world is facing presently are delineated. The roots of all international problems are identified and connected to the cabal's agelong merciless systematic control of global affairs.

Prologue

The techniques use to mislead and enslave the world are revealed, and information to help humanity redeem itself are also provided.

Furthermore, Abomaly describes the existence of a *"Divine Correction Plan,"* with three major programs designed by the Creator to liberate our species from the sinful legacies of the Lucifer rebellion. The fundamental activities and methods that are being utilized to execute this cosmic project are also duly explained.

Lastly, he announces the coming of a *New Era of Spiritual Enlightenment* with the prospect of many future celestial visitations, such as the bestowal of a Magisterial Son, the return of Christ Michael and Machiventa Melkisedek, and the reincarnation of Adam and Eve. The three final sessions [Papers] treat the recent direct intervention of the Prime Creator on earth; the expansion of consciousness through communion with the indwelt *God-Presence;* and the inherent power of the human personality to create experiential reality.

Those who shall peruse these lines are kindly advised to recognize the *factuality* of their indwelling divinity; to transcend mind and follow their heart's intuitions; to find their own truths, purpose and destiny within themselves. Abomaly encourages us to be faithful to God and ourselves, and to contribute to the activities of the Correcting Time enterprise in order to help heal the world for the temporal as well as the spiritual betterment of all mankind.

The volume is comprised of two parts with eighteen varied Transcriptions or Papers:

Part 1: **The Lucifer rebellion with its far-reaching and widespread consequences:** [1] describes the archenemies of the universe with the historical tragedies and current legacies of their sinful revolt against God; [2] exposes the evil ones that furtively maintain their ungodly mindset on earth, their control system, the extensiveness of their operations and their ultimate infernal agenda; [3] outlines society's critical problems, discusses the values and flaws of human government.

Part 2: **The Activities of the Correcting Time Plan:** [1] reveals the Master Architect and Senior Executives of this extraordinary cosmic endeavor; [2] describes the three different major programs that are being implemented to heal, sanctify, and retrieve this planet from the impurities and isolation of sin.

Nature & Objectives of this Book

Overall, this book is both a prehistoric as well as a contemporary work. For it not only probes into the furthest conceivable past moments in time and uncover the supernatural causes of existing global problems, but it also reveals the present celestial undertaking to salvage the world from these ills.

Essentially, it was conceived with four main objectives in mind, which constitute the central theme of its narratives:

- [1] Reveal the primordial events with the principal celestial beings that revolted against the government of God, which plunged the world into spiritual confusion and moral decadence at the earliest stages of human development.

- [2] Expose their terrestrial syndicate of minions and agents whom they secretly entrusted to manipulate and control humanity for an unspeakably cruel and sinister final design.

- [3] Disclose the divine correction plan and its three major programs, which are being currently executed to help liberate mankind from the domination of this dark cabal, and salvage the world from its prolonged history of strife, division, suffering, and irreverence.

- [4] Announce the coming of the fifth Epochal Dispensation, which will commence a New Era of peace, goodwill, tolerance, impartiality, and spiritual enlightenment on earth.

In other words, ultimately, this original co-creative channeling work is kindly intended to help you, the truth-seeker:

- [1] Identify the major celestial adversaries of creation, their statuses and functions before and after apostasy; their tragic systemic rebellion and its disastrous consequences upon this planet.

- [2] Discover the secret cabal that represents and prosecutes their nefarious agenda on earth.

- [3] Recognize the pervasive control system, which is used to compel humanity to remain complacent and support their parasitic and unsustainable empire.

- [4] Learn about the many correcting steps that are being undertaken by the Creator to rekindle the light of Truth in the hearts of men.

- [5] Prepare for the forthcoming age of a spiritual renaissance.

- [6] Discern the unusual implications and the decisiveness of many current geopolitical events and actualities.

- [7] Realize and embrace the sublime truth of your affiliation to divinity and indissoluble connection to God—the only One and all that exist.

Preliminary Discourse

Celestial Teacher: Ahonualy - Channeled: Joseph Elie - 09-12-2012

NOWADAYS, IT IS UNNECESSARY TO persuade anyone that this world is gravely ill. Most of you know that it is facing extraordinary challenges, and it is in serious need of salvation and healing. If we ask, practically all sensible persons would concede that these are exceptional times of enormous troubles and uncertainties. With ever-increasing geopolitical frictions, socioeconomic disparities, rampant institutional corruptions, sectarian conflicts, famine and pandemics, the dangerous and desperate situations on this planet are frightening, imposing, and overarching. Many countries are plunging into utter chaos and lawlessness, while tensions between the rival major powers are intensifying. Instead of collaborating to resolve the issues, the few potent self-appointed nations that are supposed to guarantee international peace, security and stability are deeply divided and mutually suspicious, and thus, are headed on a collision course.

On our dimension, there is virtually a universal consensus concerning the uniqueness and the urgency of this moment on your planet. In effect, the future of the present global socioeconomic order is not clear even to its most dedicated champions and supporters. The nations are bewildered, perturbed, and paralyzed by fear. A peculiar sense of hope mixed with despair has overtaken the peoples of your world. Some are simply waiting for a fatal end, while others somehow are trying to prepare for the eventualities ahead. Many are desperately seeking for new political alternatives to the established authoritarian systems of government. Through science, metaphysics, philosophy and spirituality, scores of sagacious souls are eagerly seeking to transcend the boundaries of this paradigm and expand their consciousnesses beyond the material shores of the realm.

These critical developments are in no wise way normal or accidental events. Today, a dynamic momentum for humanity to seek earnestly for transcendental knowledge and discover your cosmic identities is emerging as a global phenomenon. Man's moral self, which is deeply peaceful, kind and benevolent, is awakening from its age-long slumber of temporal illusions and spiritual ignorance. Thus, now virtually all right-minded souls on earth are asking for change—are demanding a reckoning from those who have held absolute dominion here for millennia. Every receptive individual reacts to this new liberating spirit, *uniquely*. Some use it for matters of purely political and social nature. Many apply it for personal self-improvement, while others strictly commit themselves to share the truths, the liberties, and the joys it brings. But irrespective of the different applications of this *spiritual power*, as in all decisive times, the perceptive inhabitants of the world who receive it are intuitively motivated to ensure the survival of the species through the fluctuations of this precarious transitioning period.

By virtue of God's decree, justice and mercy shall be ministered to the inhabitants of this world without partiality. We on the spiritual realms may be a bit more patient than most of you on the physical plane, but we are nonetheless, equally motivated and eager to see the final days of your total liberation from the unjust rules and restrictions of the dark ones. Those who have covertly manipulated global affairs for centuries in prosecution of their own self-seeking wicked agenda to impose upon you a despotic control system that operates above all laws designed to guide the conduct of nations on the planet must now acknowledge the imminent termination of their reign. Their corrupt order has exhausted its potentials and relevance. They were judged and found wanting on the balance of divine justice on high since the initial announcement of the Creator's Correction Plan on Urantia. Thus, their organization is at this point insolvent and incapable of transitioning into the future, for it has reached the end of its time mandate.

Truth be told, the many centuries of their brutal rule are the main cause why this world stands in such a desperate need for direct celestial intervention now. This is not just for the spiritual upliftment of its inhabitants. But also, to cleanse it from the impurities of ages of cosmic quarantine, systematic abuses, and neglects. Accordingly, in order to accomplish the ambitious goal we have set for ourselves in this co-creative assignment with you successfully, it is imperative that some of the primordial and decisive events of the four previous planetary dispensations with their continuing effects on existing global actualities are disclosed and clarified. By that, we do not intend to recount the entire anterior history of Urantia in a single volume, for this is not the purpose of our project. Rather, we wish to convey a compacted summary of these major past epochs with their lasting consequences on her today. In doing this, it is also our intention to accentuate the importance of knowing true history in order to decipher and understand present realities.

Civilizations never appear spontaneously; they are neither accidental nor magical. They initially spring from imagination and then evolve progressively in time. The concepts and ideals of a social order had to emerge in the human mind first before they could be embraced, developed, and materialized. Humanity is intrinsically an evolving species. The trends of time are a palpable proof of that. Beliefs and traditions do not manifest accidentally; they are never random. They are willfully invented and then slowly develop into conventions over long periods of time. Irrespective of their recent progresses and achievements, the foundational values and guiding principles of all civilizations are always rooted in their historical origins. Apart from God who is naturally eternal, there is no such thing as a "self-existent or causeless power." Therefore, the current world order, being finite and evolutionary in nature, its problems can never be fully understood unless their roots are unearthed, recognized and properly examined.

In reality, conceptually, human society remains quite limited to the olden customs and ideologies of immemorial time no matter the levels of its current technological and social developments. Thus, to comprehend the complexities of today's world, it is imperative to acknowledge the earliest events that altered its original evolving course, distorted its natural order, and reversed the process of life upon it. Some insights into the past four dispensations—way beyond the time-range of recorded history—are vital to grasp the present situations. To break free from the spell of planetary ignorance, one must become familiar with some of the most significant anterior events that transpired in the universe, which seriously affected this world and changed the direction of mankind's biological, intellectual, social, and spiritual evolution.

Indeed, many unique ancient supernatural incidences tremendously affected the direction of human development and the quality of life on your earth. However, none was as consequential and global than *the Lucifer Rebellion - the Caligastia Insurrection - the Adamic Default - the Incarnation of Machiventa Melkisedek - and the bestowal of Christ Michael as Jesus of Nazareth*. Hence, the transcriptions pertaining to these events must be outlined as transmitted following the sequences in which they occurred at the onset of this book. Together, they constitute the four major epochal shifts and cosmic revelations Urantia has experienced throughout her existence as an inhabited planet. For better or worse, each greatly influenced the general fabrics of society, revolutionized man's thinking processes, and changed the course of your history.

The Present Divine Intervention
Preparation for a New Paradigm

Today, Urantia is again experiencing another providential episode of celestial interference. But contrary to human opinions, this is not happening necessarily because of prophecies, politics, economics or even religious problems, though they are also pertinent to this decision. Rather, this novel shift was decreed on high because humanity has shown a readiness to transcend the current stage of your mental, social, and spiritual awareness. In fact, collectively, you are now moving ever faster into a higher dimension of reality that is motivated by a transcendent, heart-centered consciousness.

Gradually, a revolutionary, transformational, spirit-based paradigm, founded on the understanding and appreciation of the *Oneness of All Creations* is coming into view, living behind the dreadful circumstances of duality and separation. And, although most of you have not embraced this momentous change, it is nonetheless, quickly spreading, expanding and awakening many new souls everyday.

Presently, there is indeed a growing worldwide movement of truth-seeking and spirit-conscious individuals whose ideals and visions far exceed the ordinary boundaries and the existing range of common human perception. Since this new celestial intervention was called on high, a quiet but profound aspiration to know who they are spiritually transpired in the hearts of all rational and truth-seeking persons on your earth.

No other generation since the times of Atlantis was ever so inquisitive and excited to discover the transcendent mysteries of personality and its affiliation to the Primal Deity of creation. Nowadays, you are witnessing an extraordinary time of revelation and expression of the Infinite Creator-Father in His finite receptive evolutionary children. And... this phenomenon will continue unabated as the recovery programs of the Correcting Time Plan are implemented throughout the world.

There are many *profound and inspiring concepts* that recently surfaced in the collective awareness of truth seekers on this planet, which were nonexistent in previous generations. For example, *"We are One," "We create our reality," "Consciousness is eternal and infinite," "Star Seeds," "The Mighty I AM Presence," "The Higher Self," "Our galactic family," "God is everything,"* etcetera. This remarkable phenomenon is the commencement of an emergent massive global awakening. It is the beginning of an unprecedented spiritual renaissance that will release the human race from its current enslavement to all temporal institutions — be they secular or religious. Mankind's final liberation from all static, unprogressive mystical and socio-political traditions is the prime objective of this novel dispensation. Individually and collectively, the single most important task now is to realize *who you truly are spiritually* in contrast to the temporal human identity.

The powerful energetic frequencies from these latest supernal thoughts are transformational in quality. They will continue to energize and empower their faithful recipients to become genuine truth-seekers and peacemakers, for they are intended to help men *"turn their swords into plowshares,"* abolish warfare and create a more equitable global society. Thus, after the collapse of the current unjust "system of things" with the removal of the dark cabal, the superior collective mentality, which is being created from these expressions, will be the novel foundation for a better international order predicated on peace, tolerance, and harmony.

This political crash must transpire first before humanity can move fully into the New Era – and eventually unto the Ages of Light and Life.

An original, progressive, and balanced society is slowly emerging from this superb phenomenon of transcendental thinking and inspiration. As obscure this may be to most of you now, it is nonetheless, clear, and real to us. The planetary implications and consequences of this development are tremendous, to say the least. No one can predict what this astronomical shift will look like when everything is settled.

After eons of functioning from a physical and mind-dominated perception, the transformations that will occur when you change to a spiritual, heart, and love-motivated social consciousness will be so different and fascinating they cannot be accurately estimated at this point.

Wake Up!
Regain Control for a New Beginning

It is obvious to us why this world is in desperate need for serious changes in practically all domains of life upon it. But the roots of the problems and the dark ones who are manipulating and controlling society with their evermore cunning and sophisticated methods, are not always tangible—especially to those placid and complacent folks that refuse to open their minds and think for themselves. Hence, apart from exposing this ignoble cabal [without citing names] which is secretly ruling global society and feeding off humanity's blood and energy, we will also endeavor to reveal the great celestial plan that is unfolding to eradicate their satanic order and divest them of power for all time. They may have been allowed to prosecute their nefarious agenda for ages, but they were never given the license to maintain their control over the world forever. Now you are witnessing the gradual breakdown of their overarching matrix piece-by-piece, and that will continue apace without interruption. Once the dismantling process is finished, then the healing and the renewing phase of the globe shall begin in earnest. In due time, everything will be transformed and restored to the ideal conditions favorable to peace, solidarity and goodwill among men. War, division and hatred shall become obsolete.

A fresh global mindset grounded in the values of universal truths with an understanding leadership shall replace the arrogance and bellicose attitudes of today's supposed leaders who are, in fact, a college of reactionaries, hell-bent on enslaving and destroying the human race. No more will they be permitted to misguide and dominate society by creating false enemies and threats to submit the population to their demands. All nations will find it easier to appease their differences and co-exist peacefully after these usurpers and malefactors are deprived of authority over the earth.

Contrary to the present divisive and competitive social order, the emerging society will be peaceful, cooperative, tolerant, and impartial. Irrespective of race, nationality, or culture, diversity will be celebrated, and every living soul here will have the opportunity to find purpose for existence as this was intended by the Creator Son.

This magnificent future of benevolence and goodwill is possible, and within reach if all of you choose it now and take full control over your lives and destinies—period. The notion that you are hopelessly trapped in this mess, and nothing can be done about it, is sheer rubbish. This is just another sleazy tactic that is used to manipulate you into believing that you are powerless because you do not embrace their satanic agenda – like many spineless, subservient lackeys, who walk-on their knees executing orders. But far from that ruse, the energetic substance that empowers and sustains their tyrannical system stems from you. You are their source of energy. It is rather your pathetic ideological differences, which separate and divide you that allow them to compartmentalize society, and thus, secretly rule the world.

The entire history of the human experience and the traditional structure of authorities you are taught to respect and honor are actually a colossal deception. You have been terribly deceived and deliberately manipulated to remain ignorant of your true relationship to the universe and its Eternal Maker. And that extremely affected your creative ability to discover the *transcendent Truth of who you truly are* contrary to your perceived version of self-identity. Like a battery, you are used to energize a feudalistic dynasty that disguises itself under the societal establishments and slogans of a falsely so-called 'free-world.' Your lives are exploited to feed a *parasitic control system* that survives on your ignorance, hard labors, and sacrifices. The knowledge of the immortal nature of personality has been suppressed and kept from you. The facts of the existence of your inherent spiritual powers have been purposely concealed in order to keep you in perpetual material servitude. Most of the genuine informations about these subjects are either hidden from you, distorted, or substituted with ferry tales and speculative abstractions.

The fantastic historical narratives of your species' origin may differ in every culture, but all of them are profoundly rooted in the various myths and legends fabricated by the dark ones. The fact is the formal accounts of history are mainly artificial fabrications. *But the greatest deception ever contrived and perpetuated against you is the false definition and the systematic concealment of the knowledge of Self, of who you are as conscious, will-endowed personalities. The wisdom of mankind's spiritual identity and affiliation to Deity is essentially, the real 'Holy Grail' which is ferociously censored and hidden from you.*

This topic is also partially addressed in general terms in this first volume of the Correcting Time trilogy. We succinctly consider some of the innate creative powers of the human personality, such as thought, will, and imagination, coupled with its unique faculty to transcend time and make a gift to the Creator. But much more remain to be said about this broad and profound subject. Hence our plan to expound upon it in the second volume where other similar themes will be discussed.

We invite all genuine truth seekers to set aside their prejudices and read this book with an open mind and a kindred spirit. It is thoughtfully intended to inspire you to carry on your quest for wisdom to full spiritual enlightenment. The grand call to be of service that was made to humanity following the preliminary enactment of the Correcting Time Plan on this planet was broadcasted from Paradise—at the center of all things—to every breathing soul on earth. Thus, it is indeed your time to *'rise and shine,'* because you are the dear hearts that anchor the light and maintain the sacred flame of Truth on this strife-torn world.

This is Joseph: And now, before you proceed to the first part, please remember the numinous nature of this text. As with all of our channeling works, this is simply information gleaned from spirit, kindly offered for consideration to all who may peruse these lines. We are not trying to persuade anyone. This is obviously an original co-creative act, which is virtually in a league of its own. The entire book derived from ongoing communications with a disembodied personality– i.e. Abomaly – my personal celestial teacher.

Our sole intention is to stimulate your appetite for Truth, not to win you over. Therefore, whether or not you resonate with our narratives, we appreciate your critiques and respect your opinions. The idea here is to tax your mind and motivate your soul for the reception of transcendent informations beyond the scopes of the world's established paradigms.

Many unusual terms and concepts are cited throughout this book due to the transcendental source and nature of its contents. They are in no wise way intended to confuse the reader, but rather to provoke thought and project your imagination beyond the regular limits of time.

In all, besides its broad topics, this text was published mainly to convey one fundamental truth to its readers: *you are an enigma* – a unique personality, endowed with a creative mind, an evolving soul, and a divine spirit [*the very Presence of God*] that already knows and understands everything in perfection.

You were created complete in the image of the Eternal One, to be a temporal conduit of his love and light in this physical domain. You are not an ordinary Joe or Jane, but a divinely indwelt son or daughter of the Universal Creator. Accordingly, verifying the authenticity of the narratives in the succeeding Papers is absolutely a personal matter for every reader. And we do advise you to seek for confirmation through stillness and meditation in consultation with your *all-knowing indwelling spirit.*

Part 1

THE LUCIFER REBELLION WITH ITS FAR-REACHING AND WIDESPREAD CONSEQUENCES: *the Dark Cabal that secretly rules the world*

The following Papers [Channeled Transcriptions] relay a collection of diverse celestial and human issues that seriously affect this world. Concisely, they depict: [1] the archenemies of creation; [2] consequences of their cosmic revolt on earth; [3] their terrestrial representatives [the dark cabal]; [4] the use of the "doomsday prophecy" to manipulate society into self-destruction; [5] orchestration of international problems to bring about global chaos and wars; [6] the repressive nature of mortal authority; [7] the perilous condition of the current world order; [8] the universal existence of government; [9] the shortcomings and failure of human leadership.

These rather extensive revelational transcriptions were communicated during many channeling sessions through the intermediary of Joseph Elie Jean Phillippe by the celestial teacher—Abomaly. Although they have been edited and somewhat revised, all measures of precaution were taken to preserve the original communications.

Read on...

Paper 1

The Arch Enemies of the Universe

LUCIFER, SATAN, AND CALIGASTIA

The Systemic Luciferian Revolution

Celestial Teacher: Abonady - Channel: Joseph Elie 9-17-2012

A LITTLE OVER TWO HUNDRED and fifty thousand years ago, according to the linear time frequencies of Urantia—the cosmic name of your planet—the universe of Nebadon experienced one of the most tragic episodes of spiritual disloyalty in its history. It was the outbreak of a massive rebellion spearheaded by Lucifer—one of its powerful and brilliant executives. Since throughout the entire creation there was not a single situation favorable to an insurrection, the idea of defying the supremacy of God must have originated directly from his mind. At that time, Nebadon had no Sovereign Ruler. Christ Michael—the Creator Son—ruled as Vice-Gerent of the Universal Father.

For about three hundred thousand years prior to his revolt, Lucifer, a Primary Lanonandek Son of great brilliance, presided over Satania—a vast Planetary System of six hundred and seven inhabited worlds—as Sovereign Executive in the Constellation of

Norlatiadeck. He had as his immediate senior assistant and lieutenant—Satan, who was also a sagacious and experienced Lanonandek Son of the first order. Throughout their long careers as administrators, the pair had a very reputable record of desirable performances. They were highly respected and honored by all residents of the Local System. Their relations with the higher rulers of the universe such as the Most Highs, Gabriel, the Father Melkisedek, or the Creator Son himself, were always amicable and pleasant. Prior to their betrayal, save the Paradise Deities, we doubt anyone could have imagined or even slightly anticipated that such brilliant personalities of divine origin can be blinded by the illusions of self-pride, succumbed to the sophistries of their exalted egos and fall into spiritual darkness.

Nevertheless, about a hundred years before the fateful day of his manifesto, Immanuel, the Union of Days assigned to the universe of Nebadon, had communicated to some of his colleagues, including Christ Michael, that all was not well in Lucifer's mind. Upon this knowledge, many attempts were made to help him keep his divine balance. But in spite of these benign efforts, he harshly criticized and categorically rejected the sympathetic counsels under the pretext they were violating his prerogatives and liberty.

The Outbreak of Rebellion

Around 250,000 years ago, at a moment when everything was seemingly normal in Satania under Lucifer's jurisdiction, one day, during a periodic visit of Gabriel to the System's Capital, Jerusem, there was a sudden tumult throughout the sphere. For the first time since his tenure as System Sovereign and as a Lanonandek Son of God, Lucifer openly manifested his dissatisfaction with the universal administration of Christ Michael.

The event was so unusual and surprising it provoked a lot of consternation and confusions not just on the central headquarter, but also on all of its surrounding architectural satellites. A great suspense of uncertainty and apprehension concerning what would transpire next permeated the entire System, for such a brazen act of disloyalty was completely unexpected. But we did not have to wait for long. A few days later, Lucifer formally announced his decision to sever all relations with the higher rulers of the universal creation and reorganized the planets under his immediate authority according to the chatters of his new government. He appointed Satan as the governor general of his administration to promote his cause and oversee the affairs of what he called, *"the newly liberated worlds of Satania."*

Yes indeed, as the Apostle John noted in his revelation while in exile on the Island of Patmos, *"There was a war in heaven."* Rev. 12:7. The Dragon—symbolizing the three evil personages—fought against Michael and His loyal angels. But the rebels did not prevail; and they were emphatically cast-out of Jerusem.

Although the Creator Son Himself did not intervene in the conflict, but Gabriel, His first-born and the Chief Executive of Nebadon did effectively confront and vanquished the evil forces. Minus the barbaric scenes of human strife, that war was real, and with far greater consequences than any mortal clash. For in a physical combat only the temporal life vehicle is subjected to destruction, but it is the eternal survival and destiny of man's soul that is contested and endangered in a spiritual struggle.

The Lucifer Manifesto
His Major Deceptions

Like most egocentric, self-deluded tyrants, Lucifer had his own manifesto, which was propagated throughout Satania to defend his insurrection and organized his government under Satan's control. Essentially, the revolution was founded upon four main deceptive arguments: 1] *the nonexistence of God the Father;* 2] *equality and infallibility of all minds;* 3] *absolute liberty exclusive of all divine values and loyalty to Deity;* 4] *total rejection of the universal Ascension Plan for mortal men from time to eternity.* To persuade the lower orders of created intelligences to espouse his cause, especially the angels, the midwayers and mortals, Lucifer postulated that they must be allowed to determine their own cosmic destiny without any supervision, assistance, or guidance from the higher rulers of the universe.

It was indeed disheartening for a lot of loyal spirits in Nebadon to observe so many misguided souls fallen for his blatant lies, which he astutely enshrouded in many sophistries. From the narrow perspectives of those beings, his assertions and propositions were sound and enviable—even enlightening. With his evermore pretentious slogans of liberty and autonomy, Lucifer proclaimed himself *"the God of freedom—a friend of man and angels."* They trusted his intention and believed he had their best interests in mind. They were blinded by his exceptional charm and intelligence. Very few managed to withstand his cunning approaches, and practically none could discern that he was leading them to destruction.

However, today, as time has already proven to most of these naïve and bewildered spirits, the narcissistic and self-exalted philosophies of their sly master were misleading and dangerous. His exaggerated support of absolute autonomy for the lower orders of intelligences restricted of all supervisions from higher universe authorities was nothing but a ruse to disconnect them from the Creator for his own glory. Furthermore, his assertion of the universal equality of all minds; of the infallibility and sovereignty of the finite intellect over all creations without spiritual responsibilities and acknowledgment of subordination to Deity, were detrimental to angels and suicidal for mortals.

While there was hardly anything praiseworthy in his entire proposals, but to some of us personally, the most injurious and disgraceful of his deceptions were the negation of the Eternal Creator's existence and the vehement attacks against the divine plan for mortal ascension. Lucifer asserted that God the Father was not real, but rather a myth invented by the Creator Sons of the evolving universes to corrupt and maintain control over all creations while they are glorified and worshiped in the name of that fictitious Deity. He harshly criticized the ascension program for the mortal pilgrims of time, claiming the long period spend to train and educate human beings before reaching Paradise was another *"grotesque and unsavory stratagem"* of the Michaels to indoctrinate and co-opt those personalities into a system of mass deception. He derisively mocked the Father's perfection mandate to mankind and strongly rejected his eternal plan. He postulated the presence of some Paradise Finaliters on the evolving worlds of space as an indication that there was no higher destiny for man to attain, and that the whole cosmic event of mortal evolution and ascension from time to eternity was a "colossal hoax." He also lunched a vicious attack against the Ancients of Days—the supreme judiciary personnels of the superuniverse—describing them as "foreign potentates" who had no business interfering in the affairs of the local creations. Overall, his numerous contentious arguments were deceitful and blasphemous.

Casualties of the Rebellion

Lucifer's unexpected betrayal and momentous declaration of secession from the universe's administration were widespread throughout the Satania system. Early on, he urged the supernatural governments of the evolving worlds, particularly their Planetary Princes, to defy the will of God steadfastly, to counter the influences of all higher universal authorities, and to cancel the original programs that were previously implemented for the cultural, social, and spiritual developments of these realms according to the mandates of the Creator Son.

Moreover, he categorically rejected the Father's ascension plan and eternal commandment to mortal man, **"Be you perfect even as I AM Perfect."** His defiance was a flagrant attack not just on the sovereignty of Nebadon but also on all creations. He and his equally wicked assistant, Satan, painstakingly endeavored to confound the worlds under their immediate authority, and they were unfortunately successful in this nefarious enterprise on several newly evolving planets like your beloved mother Gaia.

Besides the vast number of celestials who joined the rebellion, scores of ascending mortals were also duped and erred from the light. Thirty-seven Planetary Princes, including the terrible Caligastia, who became the "devil" on your sphere, espoused Lucifer's cause and aligned their planets with his government.

They had even planned to infiltrate other nearby Local Systems of inhabited worlds. This uprising was not the first in Nebadon's history, but it was by far the most widespread and catastrophic. There had been two previous rebellions within this universe involving System Sovereigns, but Lucifer's exceeded the casualties of both combined. Unlike those earlier insurrections, which were confined to a few planets and less personal creatures participated, his was extensive—systemic. With his charming manners and sophisms, Lucifer succeeded in persuading vast numbers of personalities to espouse his cause—mainly among the lower orders of celestial and mortal intelligences.

The Present Status of the Revolt and the Rebels

Lucifer and his principal accomplices such as Satan, Caligastia and the other apostate Princes had been fallen Sons and deposed universe administrators after their tragic insurrection. Recently, they were tried and deprived of personality consciousness by a decree of the Ancients of Days on Uversa. Their disgraceful revolt was a severe setback to the spiritual economy of the Local System of Satania, and even to the entire universe of Nebadon. Nevertheless, it is encouraging to note that following the official inauguration of the Adamic dispensation in this world, it was recorded that the goodness resulted from the conflict had already exceeded its evil consequences threefold. And since then, the harvest of righteousness has steadily continued while the status of the outbreak has remained unchanged.

The dishonorable end of those unfaithful beings was a solemn warning of the fatal cost of deliberate, persistent, and wholehearted embracement of iniquity to all evolving creatures in Nebadon.

From our standpoint, technically, the revolt ended as a systemic crisis since the triumphant bestowal of Christ Michael as Jesus of Nazareth on Urantia. No more rebels were allowed on Jerusem after the Master's ascension to the right hand of the Holy Father on Paradise. Lucifer was apprehended and incarcerated following the Creator Son's return from his successful incarnation on earth. Satan, who arrogantly used to penetrate the sacred enclave and presented himself as the representative of the quarantine worlds in the council of the loyal Planetary Princes was also cast out and prevented from ever participating in these deliberations. Thus, after the seventh and last creature incarnation of Christ Michael, Lucifer's rebellion was, in principle, finished for the celestial universe.

However, the rebellious mindset persisted on the 37 gravely corrupt worlds that were thoroughly aligned with the Luciferian government, and, of course, that include your earth. Knowing full well that their fate was practically sealed after their shameful defeat by Joshua Ben Joseph here, the chief rebels were determined to bring about the destructions of all the planets they had under their control. He, [Lucifer] personally declared, *"If we cannot maintain these realms under our commands, then it is best to set them up for self-destruction."* That ominous attitude was also echoed by his two equally iniquitous acolytes. Therefore, though the rebellion had practically terminated in the System of Satania, nonetheless, there still existed on these troubled planets this horrific prospect. I said *existed* not to negate this existential threat, but to call attention to the programs of the Correcting Time, which are being implemented now to salvage the affected life-spheres.

With this ongoing development, that infernal design will not be allowed to manifest in reality...and we are confident of the final liberation of your world from this madness.

Because of its comprehensive scope, many of us believe that no matter how hard we try, we will never fully satisfactorily assess the myriad casualties and problems caused by the Lucifer rebellion in Satania. We have discovered from our research that it is virtually impossible to penetrate the depth and measure the scope of its innumerable consequences intellectually, though we do not believe this is impossible. Actually, the Melkisedeks have provided quite an extensive report explaining the manifold repercussions and the positive results surrounding this catastrophic insurrection. And it is always a refreshing experience to learn something new about the proceedings of this tragic upheaval – especially when the findings and evaluations are favorable to the light. However, much more remain to be debunked and clarified concerning the magnitude and the degree to which the universe of Nebadon was affected by this sinful revolt.

I will now take leave temporarily from you. Our assignment has just begun. Hence, you can expect a nudge from me soon to continue to mingle our energy signatures as we proceed to complete this work together—co-creatively. Thank you for your kind attention, good-bye for now.

Paper 2

Consequences Of The Rebellion On Earth

THE CALIGASTIA BETRAYAL AND THE ADAMIC DEFAULT

The Four Previous Dispensations

Celestial Teacher: Abomaly - Channel: Joseph Elie 9-20-2012

ONE OF THE GRAVEST AND far-reaching consequences of the Lucifer rebellion was the premeditated disloyalty of Caligastia—the ex-Planetary Prince of your world—whom most of your religions refer to as "*the devil or the evil One.*" Around 500,000 years prior to the outbreak of rebellion on Jerusem, humanity's first dispensation was opened. This secondary Lanonandek Son was commissioned by the Constellation Fathers as the cosmic ruler of your planet. After his appointment, Caligastia promptly arrived with his staff to take jurisdiction on earth and oversee the evolutionary development of mankind. For a time, everything pertaining to his mission appeared to be unfolding as planned, and quite satisfactorily. The material personnels of his staff were making serious progress helping early humanity to develop an intelligent culture and a peaceful global society. Significant advances were made in education, sanitation, social, and religious values, family life, science, recreation, trade, art, agriculture, animal husbandry, weaving, tool making, and many other early technologies. For several millennia during Caligastia's Dispensation, the future of your world looked so promising that the celestial hosts were excited to see how far you've come since Andon and Fonta. There were great expectations for your kind until that sad and tragic day of betrayal.

Satan Disclosed Lucifer's Plan to the Planetary Princes
Caligastia Prematurely Betrayed His Sacred Oath

A hundred years before he formerly announced his rebellion, Lucifer had dispatched Satan to inform the Planetary Princes of the worlds under his authority about the plan. He wanted to ensure their full supports once he declares his manifesto publicly. Most of them were mystified and disappointed to hear such terrible news. They could see where this was going already. Some could visualize the disastrous astronomical ramifications of such an event. These Sons listened with concerns but gave no formal reply. Others wished him luck and success. But Caligastia readily accepted to espouse the cause and aligned earth with the rebel forces prematurely. That was by far one of the most shocking and unexpected acts of betrayal ever committed by a being of supposed divine origin. Even Christ Michael was appalled and indignant by this faithless and unconscionable act of disloyalty.

Knowing he had made this choice a hundred years prior, it was not surprising when this traitorous Prince openly supported the Luciferian manifesto after it was announced, and quickly began to reorganize this world according to the directives of the latter. The consequences of this sudden and drastic change were enormous for the earth. Almost all the progresses that were made thus far were practically annulled. The whole program of planetary evolution to uplift humanity had to be completely revised. The world could no longer follow the regular course of cosmic events as do normal evolving spheres—it was quarantined. You were now isolated from the ordinary ascension plan of creation. There were a lot of turmoil, consternation and uncertainty here. Most of the celestial beings who were assigned in service on the planet could not truly believe what was happening. It took a while for everybody to settle and adapted to the new reality this upheaval created. *The war in heaven had literally reached the earth.*

However, the universal evolutionary ascension plan for the mortals on the inhabited worlds of space from time to eternity is designed and ordained by the three existential Paradise Deities. The irreverent attitudes and subversive acts of a few unruly creatures cannot abrogate or destroy it. Therefore, many centuries after the Caligastic revolt, a second planetary dispensation was duly inaugurated by the arrival of Adam and Eve on earth.

Adam and Eve as New Rulers of the Earth
The Second Dispensation

The arrival of Adam and Eve on earth around 38,000 years ago was truly a breath of fresh air and a blessing to those humans who were informed about this advent many decades before. After the Caligastic betrayal, there was a tremendous vacuum of spiritual authority on the planet. The loyal angels and mortals were bereft of good direction and longed for a new and worthy divine ruler.

The coming of the material son and daughter as new ruler was widely propagated and shared among all those beings who had remained loyal to Christ Michael and the Universal Father. For many years, preparations were made to receive the promised Messiah who would take back the jurisdiction of the earth from the unworthy traitor, Caligastia.

As you can imagine, for many humans, these times of qualms and waiting were hard, and quite often depressing. They were soul-searching moments that tested early man on every constitutive level of his being. Even some of the celestial personalities who were confined to the planet were sometimes perplexed and demoralized by the continuing blatant approaches of the devil to co-opt them and misguide humanity.

The Adamic Default

About a hundred and fifty years after their arrival on earth, Adam and Eve were making quite significant progress in their plans to up-step humanity, and they were moving forward despite that their programs and activities for human development were greatly challenged by Caligastia. They had an elaborate, superbly ordinate, and coordinated strategy to uplift human society, but the apostate Prince, who still technically had some control over world affairs, continued to be a formidable threat to their mission. Given the harsh circumstances and the hostile environments they were operating in, their works and achievements were extraordinary. Things were yet not as they had wished them to be, but overall the world's future looked quite promising.

Except, the traitorous Prince would not relent from the prosecution of his nefarious plan. Obsessed with his wicked agenda to control the destiny of Urantia, with clever ploys, he managed to outmaneuver the pair, and thus contributed to the disastrous default and failure of their world mission as biologic up-lifters and planetary leaders. Caligastia's power to influence humanity was significantly reduced subsequent to his declaration of sovereignty, but he was not yet officially divested of all authority on earth. In effect, theoretically, he was still regarded as the formal Planetary Prince of the world right up to the time of Christ Michael's incarnation in the flesh.

Through his numerous demonic agencies, Caligastia launched a fierce campaign of resistance against the administrative organizations and efforts of Adam and Eve. He persistently counteracted and challenged all their attempts to refine men culturally and spiritually. For some times, the couple effectively withstands his manifold seductive approaches, and managed to evade his deceptive ploys to thwart their mission. However, regrettably, they eventually succumbed to his evermore cunning and sophisticated plots to lead them into rebellion against Michael. Although he did not fully succeed in corrupting Adam and Eve, Caligastia did successfully hinder and virtually nullified their planetary programs and disqualified them to continue their world assignment.

Immediate Repercussions of these Events
The Severe Price of Disloyalty

The events following the Caligastia betrayal and the Adamic default plunged the celestial government of your world into extraordinary administrative difficulties. For a time, everything was chaotic. These terrible acts of disloyalty created a unique situation here, which offered the most testing and complex governmental challenges that were ever encountered on any evolving planet since the creation of Nebadon. The terrestrial program for the cosmic ascension of mankind had to be significantly modified and, in some cases, changed by the universe Rulers.

Soon after the disloyal Prince declared his sovereignty, your earth was immediately quarantined and severed from the universe's broadcasting circuitries. This decision, which was taken by the Constellation Rulers, was one of the most regrettable and costly results from this unjustified revolt against the supremacy of the Paradise Father and the rule of His Creator Son. Consequently, early humanity was completely deprived of the social and spiritual education of the first and most important age in the evolutionary journey of a life-planet. For it is vital to foster the development of a peaceful culture among the diverse indigenous mortal races, in preparation of the Adamic Dispensation.

The miscarriage of the Material Son mission, for its part, quickly precipitated the world into deeper spiritual confusions and administrative uncertainties. It completely deprived humanity of the priceless benefits of the superlative intellectual, social and religious educations of an Adamic Dispensation, which is indispensable for the realization of a unique and peaceful race—a harmonious global community.

The Incarnation of Machiventa Melkisedek
The Third Dispensation

Several ages following the tragic dispensational failure of Adam and Eve, the third one was opened with the incarnation of Machiventa Melkisedek on earth. This material bestowal of a Melkisedek Son as an emergency minister was by universe standard a rare and unusual event. For even when assigned in service of an evolving world, these Sons of divine origin do not normally engage in such planetary adventure in the likeness of material will-creatures. However, this was a serious emergency where the whole destiny of an evolutionary planet was in peril. Urantia's general condition presented such a horrible and uncertain prospect that this Son, who was then a member of a corps of twelve Melkisedeks assigned to the planet, deemed it necessary to incarnate in order to prevent a total spiritual collapse. Some of the basic values of divinity such as Truth, peace, humility and justice had to be restored in the hearts of men if the evolution of the human race was to continue – if ascension to the higher dimensions of reality was going to occur ever on earth.

It was indeed an extremely grim and critical time in the human experience on your planet, when spirituality was practically hibernating. The previous revelations of the universal reality of God and His kind nature were seriously and rigorously challenged by the relentless machinations of the apostate Prince to resist the divine plan of Christ Michael for the spiritualization and ascension of men. During that dark and decisive period, the concept of an eternal loving God and Father of all was nearly extinguished in the world. The ideals of divinity were rapidly fading and vanishing from the mortal intellect. Conscience—the basic sense of right and wrong— which constitutes the foundation of man's moral nature and understanding, was greatly suppressed and disappearing. Even though Melkisedek's work suffered many setbacks after his departure, he was quite successful in his diligent efforts to restore the veritable concepts of the One and only true living God in the minds of men. Some beings of my order maintain that had he incarnated on an older planet with a more mature human civilization; undoubtedly, Machiventa would have been more successful in winning more souls to the divine cause. His teachings would have been received with more enthusiasm and faith on a morally and spiritually adjusted inhabited sphere.

While this is technically accurate, but it is quite a redundant observation. For this Son of emergency-service voluntarily bestowed himself upon this world primarily because it was in spiritual decadence, not because it was favorable to his mission.

In taking the initiative to incarnate, Machiventa was not particularly interested in a planet with an advance human race that would be sympathetic to his teachings. He well knew the existing conditions on Urantia and was fully prepared to re-establish the Father's rule in the hearts of His mortal children.

Throughout his 94 years on earth, his loyalty to service and dedications to the bestowal purpose were well nigh superb, commanding, and inspiring. Machiventa did much to improve humanity's primitive concepts of Deity and rekindle the light of Truth in the hearts of men. He patiently, wisely but rigorously promoted the appreciation of spiritual communion with and worship of a unique God, which he denominated as "El Elyon."

In recognition of the stationary Vorondadek Son in supervising duty on the planet, Melkisedek limited his revelation of the living God to the Constellation Fathers. The successes of his bestowal mission paved the way for the incarnation of the Creator Son, almost two thousand years later as a man among men on earth, the most extraordinary event that will ever occur throughout the history of any evolutionary universe in time and space.

The Bestowal of Christ Michael as Jesus of Nazareth
The Fourth Dispensation

The miraculous mortal incarnation of Christ Michael as Jesus of Nazareth over 2000 years ago, marked the beginning period of the fourth dispensation on your planet. This mysterious event was also the first major step in a successive chain of developments that officially terminated the Lucifer rebellion in the Local System of Satania, and permanently deposed Caligastia as the recognized Planetary Prince of Urantia. Following the momentous and triumphant success of the Son of Man on earth, the traitors were completely divested of all authority over the 37 worlds that were supposedly aligned to their infernal government.

We were all delighted to witness that historic ending of the madness and upheavals these miscreants had provoked for so long throughout the System. The rebel chiefs were emphatically defeated and shamed before all natives of the universe.

But even better, that event was the overture of a greater plan in development. It was the forerunner of the Great Correcting Time—the cosmic undertaking to retrieve and heal the rebellion-affected planets of Satania. This extraordinary salvaging project was designed and tailored to be implemented on each world according to its specific situations and needs. On your sphere as you now know, it is comprised of three major programs: 1] the issuing and dissemination of the Fifth Epochal Revelation–known as the Urantia Book; 2] the Teaching Mission; 3] the Magisterial Mission. However, there are also many other events and different activities connected to that comprehensive enterprise that are not necessarily attached, or in any wise way limited to these three.

Simply put, the success of Christ Michael's earthly bestowal and eventual reception of Sovereignty from the Universal Father

had sealed the destinies of all the inhabited worlds of his universe--
including those that were lost and isolated because of sin.

In fact, he conceived and designed this plan to restore God's
will on the troubled planets in exclusive collaboration with his
closest associates immediately after the Luciferian manifesto. He
later finalized it following his resurrection and ascension to Paradise
after the termination of his mortal life on Urantia.

Now, since the last two planetary dispensations were
mainly corrective in nature due to the grave problems the two
previous had created; and because there is such a profound
connection between them, before we proceed with our final
observations on Michael's Dispensation, we deem it necessary to
mention some of the revolutionary transformations that occurred on
earth after the memorable incarnations of Machiventa Melkisedek
and Christ Michael as Jesus of Nazareth.

Exaltation of Urantia's Cosmic Status
Relation between Melkisedek's & Michael's Dispensations

Following the tragic dispensational failures of Caligastia
and Adam, Urantia was immensely blessed by two extremely rare
universal events: 1] the material incarnations of a Melkisedek Son; 2]
the bestowal of Christ Michael – the Creator Son Himself. This
world was cosmically exalted when it was chosen by Michael among
more than three million others as the realm whereon he would
experience the last bestowal mission required to achieve his fully
earned sovereignty over the universe.

Since the days of Adam, especially after the miscarriage of
his mission, which was followed by Michael's announcement of his
choice to incarnate on earth at some undisclosed future age, Urantia
became a question mark – a subject of great interest and curiosity to
all kinds of spirit intelligences in Nebadon.

After the Caligastia secession, conditions were such that
new and unprecedented measures had to be taken to reorganize

your celestial government. Urantia was quickly classified as one of the most troublesome and problematic spheres in the System of Satania – and later, in the entire universe of Nebadon. It was immediately placed in the catalogues of those problematic worlds that required special attention and tremendous celestial assistance in order to preserve the light of Truth in the hearts of their mortal inhabitants. It became [and still is] one of the most oddly governed evolving life-planet in this universe.

Nevertheless, subsequent to the dispensational incarnations of Melkisedek and Christ Michael, Urantia's status was suddenly exalted. It became the shrine of the Creator Son—the never-to-be-forgotten kingdom whereon he obtained his universe Sovereignty. Virtually, all aspects and personnels of its supernatural government were completely revolutionized. For instance, many agencies of power once exercised by the Planetary Prince with his staff of assistants were seized upon by the Constellation Fathers. They continued to be under the jurisdiction of the Most Highs up until recently, after the Father's direct intervention in the correction plan.

But these drastic reforms were not necessarily intended to eradicate the unfortunate consequences of the rebellion on the planet, at least not immediately. And... that is why even though mankind was delivered from the authority of the traitorous Prince after these momentous events, it was only a partial liberation. For despite that you were tremendously empowered to resist the sophistries of the heralds of darkness, the planet itself was still technically isolated from the universe's broadcasting circuitries up until the recent final adjudication of the Lucifer rebellion in 1985 of your time. The archenemies of the universe enormously delayed the temporal as well as the spiritual development of humanity. But they could not prevent the world and its inhabitants from attaining their ultimate destiny, which is the Ages of Light and life.

In fact, to the contrary, a number of later events subsequent to his insurrection actually insured the future and secured the cosmic fate of your world even more so. As we've said already, the incarnations of Machiventa Melkisedek and Christ Michael in the flesh practically sealed the destiny of this planet. Urantia became one of the most renowned inhabited evolutionary realms in the universe of Nebadon after these extraordinary personifications of divinity in humanity. Undoubtedly, these two exceptional events greatly altered the history and elevated the cosmic status of your world.

Yes, Machiventa and Michael's advents on earth were not ordinary universal events, for both carried tremendous implications pertaining to the revelation of *divinity* to your species. They significantly altered the course of your planetary history and Paradise destiny. Machiventa's incarnation as the *Sage of Salem* more than four thousand years ago marked the third dispensation of spiritual awakening to your sphere. He was to pave the way, to prepare the terrain for the eventual bestowal of the Creator Son. Michael opened the fourth dispensational era of divine grace and mercy, and the magisterial roll call for the mass resurrections of the deceased souls since the days of Adam took place after his crucifixion and ascension. Judging by universe standards, or in comparison to other great epochal transitions, there were hardly any special incidents attached to their physical manifestations.

Normally, dispensations are always complementary to one another. But these two were directly related; they occurred and functioned co-dependently. Actually, there is a handful of historical as well as spiritual facts that support this assertion. For example, during his sojourn here, Machiventa Melkisedek made a covenant with Abraham, the father of the Jews. He promised to increase his generation and bless his offspring if he, [Abraham] chose to renounce his military life as an army general to become a loyal servant of God. Mary, the mother of Jesus was a direct descendent of Abraham. In addition, during their bestowals, both Machiventa and Michael experienced their human lives indwelt by the same Thought Adjuster—a very unusual spiritual phenomenon in the universe. Moreover, remember, it has been said of Jesus, "*You are a priest according to the order of Melkisedek.*"

Overall, we believe there is solid evidence that strongly suggests that the dispensations of those two divine beings are interdependent in the universal affairs of this planet.

The Dragon Supported the Crucifixion
A Secret Pact with the World's Elite

By incarnating as a mortal creature, Christ Michael was not fulfilling His Father's wish to offer himself in sacrifice as ransom for the sin of men. This belief is the most erroneous of all the alleged meanings and purposes that are attached to the Creator Son's bestowal on your planet. Jesus was not a martyr to secure the forgiveness of God or to move humanity closer to the heavenly Father. Rather, the Son of Man was a revelation of the profound relationship of divinity with humanity – *of man's sonship with God.*

The crucifixion of Jesus was neither willed nor ordained by the Paradise Father. Such a deduction of what happened to the Creator Son on the cross at Golgotha is utterly absurd and fictitious. During the final days of his human incarnation, especially after his baptism and transfiguration, Christ Michael had made the personal decision to finish the remainder of his life on earth, as a man among men, just as he did prior to those momentous events after which he was fully conscious of his divinity. He declined to use any supernatural mean or power to assist or protect his physical personality. He wanted to finish his bestowal in the flesh as he had entered it, as any other human being must do. He was fully aware of the dangers of such a decision, for he knew about all the plots that were being formulated against him. But the Son of Man was fearless, faithful, and always dignified.

Upon learning about Jesus' decision not to use his powers for protection or to accept any supernatural assistance from the celestial realms, Lucifer, Satan, and Caligastia moved into full gear to provoke his ignominious death and destruction. They were particularly upset and wanted revenge against him after he had refused to be co-opted or persuaded, and especially upon their realization that he had effectively terminated their rebellion. Caligastia particularly was furious and sought the physical destruction of the Son of Man by all possible means when he recognized that he was finally officially dethroned as the Planetary Prince of Urantia, hearing the declaration from Jesus himself, "*Now the Prince of this world has been deposed and cast out from heaven*." He was enraged and totally beside yourself.

The situation was quite humiliating to say the least. The rebels could not stand it. Here are those highly conceited celestial personalities who had attacked the very source and purpose of creation, and who were allowed to prosecute their plans and set up their own government for eons of time, now were being deposed and removed from power by a single mortal peacefully and effectively. Something had to be done to account for this failure, or at least to feel better about this crushing defeat. Hence, they set out to work more closely with some rogue and bellicose elements within the political Kingdom of the Roman Empire while they also galvanized many of the Jewish religious authorities in Jerusalem to conspire and killed Jesus.

Subsequent to their defeat by Joshua Ben Joseph, Lucifer, Satan, and Caligastia knew that their days of existence were numbered. They recognized that soon or later the Ancient of Days on Uversa will demand a reckoning for their misdeeds, and that they stood no chance of keeping their identities if they are unwilling to accept Michael's mercy and apologize to the Universal Father. However, they had become too obstinate and intoxicated with pride to do such things even if that could prevent their annihilation. And so, they decided to throw their full weight with all they had left into the rebellion to produce as many upheavals as possible and make everything extremely difficult for the Creator Son and his loyal subjects. They were wicked before, but after that event, they practically became insane. Caligastia, particularly completely lost all personality balance; he was hopelessly confused and delusional.

Using some of the corrupt religious leaders in Palestine who were already at odds with Jesus and his Gospels, they conspired and strategized many plans to ensnare, discredit, humiliate, and destroy him. It was so pitiful to hear those spiritually blind mortals, which were being used by these iniquitous personages accusing the Son of Man of being in league with them. Putting Jesus to death in the most deplorable manner possible and formulating a pact with the world's powerful elite to maintain the rebellion mindset on earth became the prime focus and the main agenda of these celestial rebels.

Prior to their recent executions by the decree of the Ancient of Days on Uversa, they had since the crucifixion entrusted and empowered an exclusive group of planetary overlords to prosecute a plan to keep mankind in perpetual fear, ignorance, and spiritual darkness. Those miscreants that they used as conduits to impose their rebellious mindset upon the earth have had the heavy responsibility to rule the world in their stead by oppressing, demoralizing, and enslaving humanity. Although this small cartel of Luciferian wields great power over all global affairs, they have always made sure to maintain a secret profile, preferring to run things and rule over humanity as their subjects behind the scenes through proxy agencies and representatives. This mode of operation and control is analogous to how they are used by the Dragon as mortal liaisons and deputies. It is appropriate to say that these people are somewhat a different race within the human species as their blood types and genetics were altered to carry out specific information supporting the Luciferian insurrection on your planet. Many of the organic and cerebral fabrics that constitute a normal human being were dislodged and replaced with synthetic bio-chemical genes expressly created to uphold the rebellion mindset on earth. Several sentimental and moral qualities such as conscience, empathy, care, and love, which are integral features of the human species, were completely removed from their biological and intellectual system. This was done to detach them from all emotional consequences of any action they take against humanity, so they can easily carry out their tasks without hindrance or remorse, thereby ensuring their success.

This concludes our second transmission focusing on the diverse anterior cosmic events that gravely affected the normal course of evolution, on Urantia. In our next session, we will endeavor to expose those planetary miscreants that are responsible for maintaining the Luciferian mindset and agenda here.

By now, you should be aware of how I intend to conduct this co-creative assignment with you. I surmise you already know when I'm about to terminate the connection and bid you farewell. But I still feel like being formal, so good afternoon, my dear friend.

Paper 3

The Dark Cabal and The Rebellion Mindset

THE OVERARCHING GLOBAL CONTROL SYSTEM

The Three Pillars of the Cabal's Power Matrix

Celestial Teacher: Abominaly ~ Channel: Joseph Elie 9-22-2012

HAVING FAILED TO CORRUPT ANYMORE worlds after the 37 that were affected since the rebellion, Lucifer and his accomplices decided to use their minions and established agencies on these troubled planets to control and manipulate their inhabitants gradually toward self-annihilations. Being aware that their arrests and ultimate executions were imminent after Michael's bestowal on Urantia, in conjunction with their terrestrial conduits, they worked urgently to set up a "pervasive control network" on each of the quarantined realms to pursuit that nefarious design. Upon this fateful decision, the lower rebel chiefs convened on earth for a final oath of allegiance to Lucifer; vowing to defend his legacy at all cost. It was truly a surreal sight to behold this once Sovereign Executive of a vast system of more than six hundred inhabited worlds, duped by an exalted ego, now so fully engaged in planning their destructions. In fact, to him, as egregious as it was, the consequences of this defiant act against creation were irrelevant, for he had already chosen his own fate. Instead, this was done expressly to serve as a final tribute to himself and his willpower. This was to be the last statement to show that whether in life or in death, he could never be denied what belongs to him, which are essentially all the worlds along with their inhabitants who followed him into rebellion. Basically, to the deluded and blind ego of Lucifer, whatever that was right and good for him—including loss of existence and eternal oblivion—was also positive and best for everyone else in these creations.

During that special conference, a resolution was taken to strengthen their grip on the rebellion stricken worlds by establishing a secretive consortium of overlords on each to consolidate and centralize all authorities into a few hands. The rationale behind this action was that this would facilitate their mortal agents to more effectively control the populations of these realms. Given the sinful nature of their intention, it was unanimously decided to keep the plan confidential. Like this, the terrestrial miscreants who are prosecuting it could remain anonymous to ensure its successful execution.

It is important for Urantia mortals to understand that the obsessive tendency of some among you to control and dominate others is a Luciferian mentality. From our viewpoint, this is a grave psychological disorder. It is an egotistical, bigoted, self-deceiving complex of superiority, which is delusional, irrational and immoral. Such an unspiritual motivation springs from deep-seated prejudices, apprehensions and insecurities. When this vainglorious attitude dominates one's psyche, it strongly suppresses or destroys the ability to trust, care, or empathize, much less, to love. Thus, power and domination over others become an obsession— really the "main pursuit of life."

Those who are infected with this mind poison are naturally cynical, coldhearted and arrogant. Since they deliberately shunned from all values, they have completely lost the ability to express or relate to qualities such as compassion, integrity and love. They are unfit and incapable of experiencing or appreciating any spiritual relationship in this sort of inverted state of mind. Hence, they can never muster the level of faith or realize the wisdom necessary to experience the transcendental phenomenon true believers famously call, "*God-consciousness*."

Identifying the Dark Cabal
Why the Obsession with Secrecy?

As we indicated at the onset of the preliminary discourse, no sensible person would deny today that this world is at a critical juncture. The decisive and precarious nature of this moment is very clear everywhere one looks. Actually, as we saw, there is a vast host of severe global problems and challenges that greatly support this conclusion. From rampant greed, institutional corruptions, social unrests and disastrous wars, to famine, poverty, bigotry and excesses, the current issues are enormous and depressing. Most are highly detrimental to the stability of civilization here, to say the least. For example, to us, the continuing deterioration of the natural environment, the moral degradation of society, the machinations to world conflict etceteras, unequivocally exhibit and confirm the prevailing desperate condition on your planet.

However, almost none of these awful and perilous circumstances are necessarily normal occurrences of time. Most of them are deliberately planned and orchestrated events by a secretive cabal of callous individuals who are determined to execute Lucifer's evil plot against this realm. It is this rather exclusive group of miscreants that embody and maintain the Luciferian mentality over your world. Although they are relatively few in comparison to the rest of humanity, but through their vast networks of agencies and assets, they wield tremendous powers and influences over society. Now virtually nowhere on the earth is safe or immune from their tyrannical forces.

But strangely enough, although these people are used by the celestial rebels as portals and liaisons to access and influence the physical dimensions of your planet, they are inherently faithless, paranoid and insecure. Ironically, though they worship Lucifer, they trust no one but themselves and the power they wield over mankind. They are completely obsessed with the design to rule over all inhabitants on the planet without accountability. They are prisoners of their own sophistries and self-seeking ambitions. Contrary to the grandiose image they like to project, they are neither noble nor invincible. Instead, they are a college of cynical, arrogant, heartless, demonic, and highly insecure individuals. They are morally and spiritually bankrupt.

In effect, the true secret of their power depends on remaining *anonymous*, not by choice but by necessity. Comparatively to humanity, these few iniquitous characters with their entire global network of minions who are willfully provoking problems and manipulating society are actually pathetic. Metaphorically speaking, it's a dog's tail whacking a sleeping elephant. Without this tactic of stealth operation, they could not have achieved their agenda for planetary domination.

Thus, for many centuries, this evil cabal has shrewdly managed to keep itself secret and evade public exposure or scrutiny. Most people who work to push its agendas know virtually nothing about its existence. Even today, in the midst of the massive worldwide awakening, scores of the globe's inhabitants remain oblivious of this occult society and its overarching control system. The full spectrum of its reach and impact over the planet is still, quite unknown by most, for it has always operated in total mystery. Unfortunately, this obsession with secrecy is not simply to keep a low profile, but rather an essential part of the sinister and diabolical plan it is prosecuting at all time.

The Global Control System & Its Ultimate Aims

As we see the earth from our vantage, there is indeed an established authoritarian global control system that artificially manipulates the collective perceptions of humanity. A variety of modern techniques are employed to do this successfully, but some are more common than others. For examples, mass transmissions of misleading information, subliminal messages, fear propaganda, social conditionings, organized religion, racism, politics, nationality, classification, culture, pseudo sciences, illicit behavior and violent entertainments, etceteras. Just to name a few of those that are more or less known. But this ongoing global manipulation program has an even more sinister purpose behind it.

The real motive is to weaken the moral fiber and suppress the spiritual nature of mankind in order to ascertain your eternal allegiance and servitude to them and their celestial masters.

Excessive amounts of resources are used to pursue four main objectives rigorously to achieve this:

- [1] Mislead the human psyche by distorting and falsifying all accessible informations—notably history as well as current actualities.

- [2] Disconnect man from the infinite source of his being by concealing and twisting the true nature of reality, the universe, and the fundamental unity of all that exist.

- [3] Promote narcissism and vainglorious pride as laudable expressions of great successes and achievements in order to exalt egotism, and thereby constrain humanity to the divisive realm of duality. This generates conflicts, which maintain a persistent climate of fear and insecurity among the populaces of the planet.

- [4] Control the global narratives of history and current issues, living habits, and socioeconomic activities of all mankind through deceptive information, dogmas, programming, mass hypnosis, conditionings and indoctrinations.

For centuries, moving according to a scripted plan, which was specifically designed by Caligastia, this dark cabal of extreme personages has secretly manipulated and directed human affairs to accumulate vast resources and wealth, consolidate and centralize all global authorities in order to create what they notoriously hail as a "New World Order"— which is a plutocratic planetary government that is answerable to no one but itself. And they are now vigorously trying to finalize that long-cherished goal.

As we've said before, most of the current problems that affect particularly the biosphere, the eco-system, the economics, the political and social structures of the planet are anything but normal or accidental events. They are deliberately orchestrated, and are intended to do one thing: *provoke global chaos.*

But why do they want chaos? Because it can quickly destabilize and break up society, which is exactly what they need in order to execute their plan, by proposing new solutions to reorganize the world after their own choosing. In fact, according to their doctrine, political turmoil and social disruption are the most effective means to bring about drastic and comprehensive legal reforms rapidly. So, disorder is the critical keystroke in their nefarious machination to finalize their conquest for full-spectrum global domination and officially impose their new order. This is the forerunner, which prepares the terrain for them to implement and enforce radical changes; such as abolishing existing laws that guarantee civil liberties and passing new ones that revoke them, and so forth.

Sociologically, the conflict creates a clean platform for them to continue to enfold and prosecute their nefarious agenda with impunity and no opposition. Politically, it not only offers novel opportunities to do what they could not do before without force, but it also provokes a massive trust and authority vacuum, which they can easily fill up with little to no resistance under the circumstances.

At this crucial moment of tremendous political, social and economic upheavals, the greatest danger mankind has ever faced in history is the possibility of this dark cabal getting its way in provoking a *Third World War.* This is the last violent scenario they are hoping for to bring in the "New World Order." It is the final drama on their script that must transpire before they completely disenfranchise and enslave humanity, or rather, whatever that will be left of it.

As we've said before, an infernal conspiracy to cause this unthinkable situation and attain their ultimate goal, which is to decimate over 90% of the global population, has been unfolding for many centuries now.

Since they reached the final phase of their plan a few decades ago, much was done to provoke and escalate social unrests, economic hardships, corruption, famine, pandemics, crimes, terror, and political instability throughout the world.

They silenced, suppressed, and concealed the works of all genuine scientists. They censored and counterfeited real science by replacing it with a politically bias and subservient pseudo-scientific community.

They infiltrated all the leading established religious institutions in the world. These organized cults were never genuine, but some of their leaders have been issued new orders.

With a handful of exceptions, the dark ones dominate the political, monetary, and legal systems of virtually all nations. No mainstream movements or organizations exist without their permission. They have covertly placed all global communication networks under censorship and compelled them to diffuse only the version of events that suit their agenda.

Overall, there is hardly any philosophical idea, religious thought, or scientific invention conceived in the last three centuries that has not been tested for its usefulness, as a control device or employed, in one way or another, to manipulate the global population, with the endgame of planetary hegemony and human destruction in mind. These acts and many more, we have observed and documented since the start of our mission here.

The Three Pillars of the Cabal's Power Structure
Government, Science & Religion

The overarching matrix of the dark cabal is quite a complex and sophisticated global control system, which is established and supported by the three most predominant institutions in the world:

- [1] *Government*—the sole legitimate entity with the "legal authority" to enforce the cabal's wishes on society.

- [2] *Religion*—the traditional belief systems.

- [3] *Science*—the technological inventions and applications of modern life.

Together, these three institutions constitute the foundation upon which stands the cabal's edifice of authority and control over your planet.

Every culture on earth is fundamentally influenced or dominated by one, two or all three of these pillars of power. To the majority of the inhabitants on your sphere, government is never an option, but a necessity. Religion is also an indispensable factor in the lives of most Urantians. And science is firmly integrated in the social fabrics of all the progressing civilizations. Therefore, it is obvious why the dark ones chose these three main components of civilization to wield their influence and control the world.

The Global Domination of Secularism
The Complicity of Mainstream Science & Religion

The pervasive influence of secularism is an obvious phenomenon on your planet today. However, unknowingly or by willful ignorance, many people do not realize this is seriously retarding the moral and spiritual evolution of humanity. In fact, it is dangerously threatening to destroy some of the finest and most valuable qualities to be found in your species – primarily your sense of compassion, altruism, and faith.

Since the rise of capitalism and its consequential component—materialism—secularism has been highly hoisted and embraced as the principal model of civilized thinking throughout your planet, especially in the Western hemisphere. With this event, the ever cunning and opportunistic cabal discovered new grounds in these misleading ideologies to support their abominable cause. By associating and promoting them together, they managed to create the most formidable anti-spiritual movement in modern history. Consequently, the dynamics of the combined influences of these dubious principles provoked an uncontrollable revolution of human independence and estrangement from God.

"God has no place in modern society because men are sufficiently endowed and able to conduct, regulate and manage their own planetary affairs without any assistance or support from the celestial realms," so reason many professed experts of the 'free world.' From their narrow and localized perspective, that may seem to be true, for men do possess the capacity to conceptualize, organize, and administer their representative institutions. However, since their inception thousands of years ago, these artificial establishments have not accomplished the fundamental aspirations of humanity; such as world peace, justice, equality and prosperity. To the contrary, most of them have done the total opposite.

They miserably failed to respect the very principles and aims for which they were allegedly designed, which is to support and provide effective services to the communities they represent. For example, most of your governments do not serve or protect their common people. Your schools are not about education. Your medical systems are not concerned with human health and wellness. Your correction facilities neither improve nor rehabilitate. Your religions are not preoccupied with your spiritual edification and enlightenment. Your militaries are no longer used to maintain territorial integrity. Your "news networks" do not inform, etcetera.

The fact is most of these institutions are corrupt and do not do what they were created to do because they are performing at the behest of an illusive cabal of detached and apathetic individuals who are profoundly inimical to humanity.

You live in a serfdom civilization where the agents of an exclusive elite minority are employed to deceive, oppress, and subdue the majority. The "legal system of authority" is designed purposely to work against you.

True, the remarkable scientific and technological achievements of the last few decades particularly do clearly demonstrate men's formidable creative abilities to do certain impressive things right. However, these physical talents and accomplishments do not necessarily prove that you are perfect or infallible. Mankind is certainly gifted with the power to plan and design his civilization after his own choosing. Humans do have a relative free will and a resourceful imagination to foster ideas and produce mechanisms to improve the quality of their temporal existence on earth. Nevertheless, you are utterly incapable of realizing a peaceful, tolerant, harmonious, truth abiding, and loving social order without spiritual insights, cosmic wisdom, and divine guidance.

The masterminds of secularism deliberately sought to dethrone God in the hearts of men. They arrogantly claimed the supremacy of human ingenuity above all spiritual values. As a result, the blind embracement of this fallacious mentality by much of the global community has negatively affected almost everything in contemporary society, from the basic ethical values such as mannerism and respect, to social justice and moral dignity. Consequently, this brutal campaign of suppression has severely hindered mankind's spiritual development. It caused too many naïve souls to deny the sublime truth of their profound affiliation to God.

Most of today's secular societies, particularly in the Western hemisphere, regard faith as an archaic affair that is no longer necessary to help mankind lead a good existence. Those among their populaces who still claim to be religious basically observe a religion simply as a nominal social ritual, not a genuine personal relationship with Deity.

Since the 16th century, the peak era of the secular revolution to this day, scores of agnostic ideologues have reasoned out dozens of theories that categorically excluded God as an essential factor in the human experience.

Modern people are mostly taught to look up to and place their confidence in their representative leaders and experts for answers and solutions to all life-problems. The 21st century educated materialistic, secular, social automaton sees the universe as a mechanistic and law-dominated creation, but utterly fails to acknowledge the Personality of its majestic Creator and Law Giver. Today's youths are strongly encouraged by their educators to seek the counsels of their superiors for guidance rather than to work out their problems with God, their real teacher and guide. The Godless doctrine of secularism is included in the pedagogies of all the most prevalent and influential educational institutions in the world. In the Western hemisphere particularly, many categorically believe that man does not need God, that divine direction or assistance is unnecessary to lead a positive, moral, and meaningful life. Human ingenuity and conventional wisdom are praised and honored as the sole powers able to fix and resolve all planetary issues.

With this foolish and pretentious attitude of complete independence from God, secularism has most certainly thrust modern men into an abyss of decadence, deception, spiritual poverty, and irreverence. The results are rampant escalation of greed, infidelity, violence, arrogance, vicious pride, selfishness, bigotry, diseases, delinquency, superstitions, social unrests, crimes, warfare, and terrorism, to name a few. But these are only the early harvests of this most ungodly of all social philosophies ever conceived by men. More unpleasant circumstances and difficult times are looming for those who remain subservient to it.

The terrible travesty and frankly, pathetic issue with

secularism is that most of its champions not only literally regard it as a redeemer from religion, but also as a mean to ignore and escape all moral and spiritual obligations. While this is technically accurate, but their wish is impossible, for there is no escapism from God as all exists and moves by virtue of His Infinite Being. Nevertheless, this reveals two serious shortcomings; 1] their abject ignorance about the universality and infinity of God; 2] their desperation to be as defiant and sinful as the celestial rebels who inspired this deceptive ideology.

This irreverent attitude is remarkably identical to Lucifer's blasphemous doctrine of *unbridled liberty without recognition of any universe sovereignty.* His erroneous assertion of creature infallibility and license to act with impunity cast a striking resemblance with the current established secular mentality on Urantia. It is not altogether improper to regard secularism as a planetary repercussion of the primary claim in the Luciferian Manifesto, which denied the existence of God. It is quite clear to us that it was inspired by that miscreant to ascertain the propagation, continuation, and perpetuation of his rebellious mindset on earth.

Secularism, Capitalism & Materialism
Their Negative Effects on Society

Although the current high-speed international trading system greatly stimulates industrial growth and competitions between the nations of your planet, nonetheless, it has also severely damaged the moral and spiritual fabrics of civilization. The worldwide splurge of greed, egoism, and irreverence that was unleashed following this revolution is now literally threatening to destroy even the fundamental values upon which civilized societies are founded; such as justice, morality, and fairness.

Apart from encouraging avarice, excesses and debauchery, global capitalism has also vigorously fostered and strengthened secularism–the father of the modern totalitarian state with all its corruptions. Although they may carry different connotations, and may be conceived as having separate meanings or objectives, but in reality, *there is actually no significant distinction between secularism, capitalism, and materialism.* They are, in fact, very similar and complement each other. They fit perfectly together, and they constitute the three dominant forces that drive the "free world."

Since the appearance of these spurious socio-economic philosophies with the relatively recent creation of 'globalization,' there has surfaced in society an aggressive tendency to suppress and belittle the moral values that sustain human dignity, and thus further alienate men from God. Using the supporters of these misguided ideologies, the dark cabal has built and maintained their global hegemony with relative ease and impunity. Now they want to continue to sway over the world through their forged institutions without oversight or accountability. They are desperately attempting to reenergize their ailing system to ascertain their domination for at least another millennium, if not forever. However, at this point, their efforts will be unavailing, for the era of their reign has come to term, and their removal has been ordered by divine decree. As we observe this from our vantage, in the opportune time, their imperial dynasty will certainly collapse.

Conversely, we do also acknowledge that this threefold philosophy, which dominates the current world order on Urantia, has unquestionably freed its peoples from the bondage of religious traditions. The 16th century's Protestant *"Reformation Movement"* may have loosened the grip of the ecclesiastic hierarchy over Western societies, but it was the industrial revolution of the 20th century that certainly delivered them from the universal influence of the medieval church.

However, unfortunately, a profoundly serious error was committed following the so-called "Renaissance" of the mid-16th century. The initial activism that culminated into the revolt against the Roman Catholic establishment was later wrongly directed against God Himself. Many people erringly perceived the church's dishonor as an opportunity to forsake a religious life generally once and for all. Scores of believers construed their emancipation from its convention as a total liberation from all moral responsibilities and spiritual obligations. Some saw and interpreted its troubles as an affront to the God of Christianity, and thus started to search for secular alternatives.

Since these erroneous perceptions and impious sentiments were so quickly spread throughout the Western World, their influences were well nigh universal in less than two decades following the conversion. This mistaken and falsely so-called 'spiritual renaissance' had so thoroughly impacted the thinking of the hemisphere that the atheistic scientific revolution of the 19th and 20th centuries found a bitter, self-seeking, and materialistic society upon which it could, almost effortlessly, exert tremendous powers. The resulted dynamics of skeptical and lukewarm religionists with arrogant and irreverent scientists promptly led to the categorical sanction of secularism and the reinforcement of the Godless totalitarian state in the modern world.

Following this adverse historical blunder, a radically assertive, carefree, and anti-spiritual mindset has virtually permeated and enveloped the world.

Inflated with pride from a prolonged and complex learning system, now almost all 'cultured minds' in the secular world are practically agnostic – and thus, indifferent to divine values such as love, truth, mercy and goodness.

Secularism gained its greatest influence over the modern world mainly from the two most prevalent forces of human society, i.e. religion and science. Initially, from the failure of Christianity to remain a unified religion, and subsequently from the vainglorious scientific revolution of the last three centuries. Since its emergence, secularism has succeeded due to the overwhelming supports it always receives from these two highly influential institutions.

From our vantage, the rather quick and sudden evolution of science and technology from the last two centuries has had two dynamic but opposite effects on your global society, which technically, could be classified as positive and negative. Positively, it greatly increased the industrial output and improved the productive capacity of many of your most affluent countries. Negatively, it created a setting which favored cupidity, narcissism, and selfishness, and that, consequently, strengthened the power of secularism the world over.

Of course, the vigorous scientific ingenuity and innovation that followed the ascendancy of secularism in the world should never be overlooked or despised under any circumstances. Undoubtedly, the physical aspects of civilization, the quality of life, and human productivity have been tremendously improved by the secular revolution, though these ameliorations are not global. However, it freed men from the yoke of the ecclesiastic church only to betray and place him under the ruthless control and authority of the totalitarian state. The positive results of secularism must be acknowledged and respected as the negative ones must equally be recognized and condemned.

✦ ✦ ✦ ✦ ✦ ✦ ✦

Today, as we observe the progress humanity has made in receiving the light of the Correcting Time, we are deeply humbled and moved by your devotion and sacrifices. And you should take full credit for participating in raising the spiritual vibration of your world, which, consequently, redirected her from her former path of chaos and destruction. Yes, the awakened souls did it together. You averted catastrophe and prevented the demise of your species.

Now, bear in mind that the lifeline of the cabal's global secular hegemony is primarily their control over all significant monetary transactions on the planet. However, as we've seen, apart from being the money masters, they have always enjoyed the backing of two powerful forces of civil society—namely religion and science. From religion, they have secured the confidence that the people will remain obedient to the totalitarian state. As for science, scores of scientists have and continue to develop ever more efficient and sophisticated technological devices to ensure the continuing influence of their control system over humanity.

But today, as your planet slowly moves into the higher frequencies of dimensional reality following the recent end of the solar cycle, which will soon definitely dispose them from power, it is very unlikely that those institutions will remain blindly submissive. Like all living organisms, some institutions possess survival instincts because they derive from some integral features of the human mind, such as reasoning, ethics and spirituality. Like these indestructible constituents of the mortal psyche, these institutions may survive the demise of the dark cabal because they are essentially cosmic. They may be corrupted, but they will always survive the turmoil and the crash of any civilization.

As it stands currently, even if the dark ones should manage to keep their scrounging economic system running for a while longer than we anticipate, that will only serve to ensure a bigger and more humiliating collapse at the end. In fact, as we observe the situation, this already severely damaged tyrannical order is now facing its toughest and most convoluted challenges yet. One of which is the emerging truth-hungry generation with increasing social awareness and spiritual zeal to strive for the ultimate triumph of righteousness and peaceful co-existence among all the peoples of the earth. Actually, the mental faculties and creative capacities of this upcoming age group are presently being upgraded. In due time, mankind will take on new heights. Society will appear to be of a higher order of refined, intelligent, and peace-loving individuals. The opportunities for goodwill and harmony among the nations will supersede all evil machinations to provoke chaos and wars. And eventually, when enough people are firmly grounded into this novel mindset, then, the two major backers of secularism—namely mechanistic science and organized religion—will definitely have to reconsider their positions if they wish to move forward with this thoughtful, progressive, and spirit-conscious generation. That is all we are permitted to say about this unfolding development at this time. But we can already visualize the emergence of this gracious, lenient, insightful and peace-loving generation on your planet.

Historically, several unscrupulous leaders have frequently utilized religion and science as propaganda tools for political support, or to implement their socio-economic programs. Since time immemorial, many of your most infamous monarchs and dictators have used the influences of these social institutions to sustain their domestic policies and justify their military aggressions against other countries. And, arguably, this practice has remained a grim reality in the current world. Many of your present-day scientists and religionists are still deeply involved in this trade of furnishing the rationales and the blessings for the agendas of despotic officials. Together, these two presumably dissimilar constituents of society have equally supported and bolstered the authority of secularism, and have indirectly cooperated in maintaining its power for the past three and a half centuries.

The Military-Industrial-Media-Political-Money Complex
An Unsustainable Alliance Doomed to Fail

Unsurprisingly, we recently observed that the dark ones took a novel and radical step to strengthen and secure their global hegemony by forming an unholy alliance with the most powerful organizations ever devised by men. However, beware! This fraternity is ill fated. As it has already, this will continue to foster worldwide social, economic, and political instability with serious transnational hostilities. The current trends of events will persist, and they will ultimately bring about the fatal collapse of the global economy. *This time it will not be possible to define such a scenario with fancy terms such as recession or depression, for the crash will be total and definitive*. A completely new international trade and monetary system will have to replace the present order. This crisis will not be a temporary event, as it will utterly destroy the structure of the established paradigm of the dark cabal permanently. The system will be insolvent.

As we understand this from our perspective, the current predominant international exchange system widely known as "globalization" on your planet is, in reality, a gross crime against humanity. For it mainly serves the interests of a super-rich minority that openly intend to destroy the livelihood of the world poorest and most vulnerable communities. This is clearly reflected in the underhanded rules and regulations, which grandly favor a few special parties to the detriment of the rest of the global community. The real motives behind that which you call 'globalization' are essentially indifferent, even hostile to the values of justice, honor, and decency. It was never designed to benefit mankind necessarily, but to manipulate, control and enslave him. The deceitful plotters of this grand scheme deliberately ignored and rejected the most profound aspirations of humanity, which are peace, liberty, equality, and prosperity.

The overall potential and ultimate consequences of this ill-motivated enterprise are yet to be completely identified, even from our viewpoint, for they are extensive, and they are increasing and compounding globally everyday. Nevertheless, we do foresee that this rather desperate association is inevitably doomed to fail in time. In effect, the horrible costs of its actions are amounting worldwide. They are now unmistakable to most of the planet's inhabitants. As we observe this development from our vantage point, recently, the spreading of information regarding the evil nature of this order has been drastically intensified. It is reaching a critical point of no return.

There is now such a massive rising global momentum for freedom and justice that the cabal's control system has been overwhelmed and rendered ineffective to find any solution to quell the tensions other than starting a third world conflict. And that, we assure you they will not be allowed to do!

Apart from other activities of the Correcting Time, the present emerging worldwide social renaissance alone, which is highly charged with powerful cosmic energy for peace and justice among all nations, will soon bring the cabal's machine to a halt. By this, we are not referring only to those who protest for change, for the number of those who are awakened but who do not participate in the public demos is actually greater than those who do.

Now humanity is increasingly realizing that globalization—this complex and sophisticated model of transnational commerce—

was cunningly designed to benefit merely the interests of a small cartel of larger-than-life sociopathic tycoons–what we call a "sinister elite minority." People view it as a colossal fraud created to enrich an already affluent exclusive oligarchy while maintaining the average person in constant financial difficulties, poverty, and slavery. Hence, besides growing geopolitical tensions, your world is also beset by social violence due to this bureaucratic "*moon-opolized*" economic system by a wealthy minority over an oppressed, deprived, and battered majority. Most of you now see this international system for what it really is–a neo-colonial, exploitative, and enslaving enterprise.

Observe from the narrow viewpoints of its deluded champions and beneficiaries, the system is entirely safe and sound. They do not believe that the current growing awareness and resentment of society due to this incredibly unjust distribution of wealth and the control of the world's natural resources by a vicious "superclass" is significant enough to harm and destabilize the existing international order. But it has already done that, and this movement will continue to "shock and awe" these doubters until the system completely fall apart. Even if the dark ones should manage to prevent an imminent collapse that will not necessarily avert the inevitable demise, for the foundation of their organization has been crumbling for a long time, and the edifice of power will not stand much longer. *If we may, let us be clear by emphasizing that the relatively new wave of international awakening is certainly a serious challenge of severe consequences to the global control system, and it will continue to unfold throughout this century until this Luciferian establishment is totally disintegrated.*

Facing the prospect of an approaching collapse, lately the dark ones have mobilized all their resources to augment the effectiveness of their oldest and most pervasive control techniques— notably terror, deception, warfare, but especially the widely anticipated religious prophecy of a "Doomsday" or "Armageddon." These methods are being reinforced as their last desperate attempt to arrest the momentum of a potential massive global awakening. But again, they will not succeed! These frantic efforts are in vain;

they will only exacerbate an already dismal situation, and they will cause the acceleration of the cabal's eventual demise.

We urge those who regularly interact with us to continue to abide in the Creator's peace and feel his embrace in your meditations. Be firm and steadfast in your resolution to go through the final days of this age, for you are now closer to the end of this polarized dualistic paradigm than your ancestors could ever imagine. It is your generation that will close this fourth tragic dispensational chapter of the human experience. The dark cabal is virtually finished as we see it from our vantage, for they've lost the information war, the scheme is losing steam, and their organization is in disarray. They are unable to achieve their long-cherished satanic objectives against humanity. Their engineered socio-politico-economic crises around the world may still affect you, but they are neither capable of destroying your spirit nor control the progress of civilization here anymore. Hence, we encourage you to carry on patiently and keep the sacred flame of Truth shining ever brighter for all to see. I will now withdraw for a season of rest and worship of the Father – good afternoon.

The Deceptive 'Doomsday Prophecy'

FOSTERED BY RELIGION AND SCIENCE

The Cabal's Last Desperate Act to "Impose the New World Order"

Celestial Teacher: Anomaly ~ Channel: Joseph Elie 9-26-2012

EVER SINCE THE TRAGIC EVENTS of the Lucifer rebellion in Satania, followed by the Caligastic revolt on Urantia, we've observed that all subsequent generations have lived in fear of a pending 'Doomsday' – expecting the total destruction of this world. The anticipation of some extraordinary catastrophic events that would permanently terminate the human drama has been well nigh universal in the mentality of your global society for ages. But this is not necessarily co-incidental with the outbreak of these wicked acts of spiritual disloyalty. The rebels had invented a plan to achieve this effect.

Subsequent to their cosmic betrayal, using their planetary minions, the archenemies of creation forcefully implanted a distorted mindset of fear and doubt in your species. This was done to suppress consciousness and conceal the Truth of the higher nature of man, which is *love and trust*. Through the main institutions of human devotion and creativity–such as religion and science–they meticulously designed and developed a hypnotic program for every epoch and generation to maintain this illusive and depressing gloom and doom perception in your collective mind. This vicious trend has continued to this day even though the celestial rebels live no more.

Lucifer and his unrepentant accomplices may have been adjudicated and executed recently, but many of his hybrid mortal representatives are alive and are still attempting to fulfill his nefarious plan. Until those miscreants and their control system are totally removed from the surface of the earth, they remain a serious force to be reckoned with, especially for the people who are not well grounded in truth and spirit. Fortunately, lately their influences have been diminishing quite significantly. More of you are now receiving and radiating the divine light as the programs of the Correcting Time unfold and resound throughout the world, beckoning all hearts to seek for Truths, stand for justice, and embrace peace.

Taken from the Bible in the book of revelation by Apostle John, the concept "Armageddon" as a 'prophesied' event has been, and still is, one of the dark cabal's favorite weapons to control the global population. This 'prophecy' is the most insidious device intended to be used to achieve their infernal objectives. One of them privately said, *"We may have many useful mechanisms to suppress the masses' ability to see and know the Truth, but none is more efficient and fail-safe than their belief in a coming apocalypse – the End of Time projection fits perfectly with our plans for the world – it is inexorable."*

The bizarre and deplorable thing about this statement is its accuracy. From our observations on this side, out of the numerous methods of mass control used by the dark ones against humanity, none has been as effective, universal, and enduring than this religiously charged and fear-motivated "prophecy." Many other tactics of manipulation and submission such as social division, terrorism, warfare, blackmail, threats, co-opting, silencing, etcetera, work successfully. But sometimes they may fail or become obsolete. This one, however, has remained potent, pervasive, and persistent, generation after generation. It is apparently "foolproof."

Even today, in the midst of the unfolding massive global

awakening, unfortunately most of you are yet to emancipate yourselves from this grim conspiracy under the guise of so-called religious prophecies that must transpire, which categorically anticipate the destruction of the world. Scores of gullible souls remain strongly dominated by this apprehensive idea of a pending planetary fatality. Too many of you who yet ignore the grace of God and tarry on the road of darkness are still expecting a "doomsday scenario" even though the possibility of such an ominous event is spiritually baseless.

However, to our delight, hopefully to yours as well, we also observe that those who embrace this false understanding of religious narratives are gradually decreasing numerically day-by-day. Lately, more of you have begun to open your minds to wiser interpretations of creedal philosophies and prophecies. Consequently, this has provoked a tremendous truth-seeking movement with a drive to avert the bleak and terrifying future that the evil cabal projected for you. This growing awareness has confirmed more obviously to us that the Correcting Time Plan will definitely succeed on your earth. We duly rejoice seeing the luminosity of spirit shining brighter in a lot more souls than we have ever seen before on this planet.

Knowing the power of thought and the ability of the human mind to create reality imaginatively, especially when it is inspired, the celestial rebels in collusion with their earthly agents, implanted an overarching planetary broadcasting grid, which is ever diffusing an egocentric, fear-motivated mentality to manipulate and gradually lead men to madness and self-destruction. Most of you should know by now that *fear, division, and hatred are always destructive – they kill.*

The methods used in this diabolical scheme to dominate man by terror and ignorance, even to compel him to self-destruct, were fully tested against all known features and dimensions of the human species, save the spiritual because of its perfection. It is impervious to evil. Hence, they could not access or influence it, for that would require genuine spiritual transformation, meaning renouncing fear and espousing love. But of course, they would not do such a thing. Accordingly, a specific plan was designed by the three chief celestial rebels to compensate for this limitation and ensure the success of their terrestrial cronies. This program was tailored precisely for your planet, and it was jointly implemented by their supernatural as well as mortal agents. As far as we may comment on this any further, we would say that it was quite a sophisticated plot that slightly exceeds the range of the average human imagination. Succinctly, it was like this: while the demons – the mischief-makers of the infernal hierarchy of Caligastia tormented mankind mentally; their mortal counterparts were ordered to do the same physically and emotionally. Thus, leaving man no opportunity to rest and contemplate the Truth of his Higher Self – the Mighty God Presence that indwells his mind.

Being cut off and isolated from the spiritual circuitries of the universe, your world was vulnerable to this clever and well-organized assault. It was decreed that all planetary sources of information be seized upon and manipulated to support this occult agenda. Consequently, even your religions, which were supposed to relieve you from fear were infiltrated and utilized to instill and sustain it.

The loving nature of the Prime Creator was severely distorted and grossly misrepresented in most of your ancient religious records. The infinitely kind and merciful Father-Mother of all spirits was portrayed as a wrathful, jealous and vengeful deity who smites and destroys His so-called enemies. You were depicted as a cursed and degenerated species, cast out by your Maker to suffer the burden of life because of an alleged "original sin." Like a spell, this legend has kept so many of you in abject spiritual servitude and hopelessness.

Up until recently, most of you accepted this twisted theology on the nature of God and the quality of your relationship with Him. Society's blind embracement of this fabricated spiritual notion is the most rewarding accomplishment of the dark cabal. They really flatter themselves about this one because it fits precisely with their ultimate goal of full-spectrum global domination. The cunning strategies used to conceal the truth of your Sonship with God are always being filtered through virtually all accessible sources of information on the planet. Hiding the facts of your infinite nature and cosmic identity is the key element the dark ones have used to suppress mind and keep you oblivious of your creative powers. The main objective is to keep you in a profound spiritual slumber, ignoring who and what you truly are during the entire human experience.

We on this side feel a lot of sympathy for your kind. Not just because you are our fellow spirits on a transient physical life here, but also because of your intense and extraordinary experience. Observing and learning about your history, we cannot help pondering how deep you were taken into the abyss of darkness, as you were made to fear everything-even the very Source and Originator of your personalities.

I, Abomaly, if I may speak in my name as this is a joint, co-creative assignment. I've been in existence for a long time. But I never knew the depth of illusion and the degree to which misguided egos can fall into the chasm of unspiritual thinking until I was assigned to minister on this planet. This is why I am delighted and grateful to have this opportunity to draw near and work so closely with you. I feel great joy and satisfaction knowing that humanity's deliverance from the dark ones has finally arrived for good with the execution of Michael's Correcting Time Plan. My profound gratitude and happiness for this development are unspeakable. I am ecstatic!

A Dangerous Transitioning Period
Not the "End of the World"

As we often mentioned throughout our communications, today your world is undergoing many drastic changes that will lead into a new era of peace and harmony. But presently, as it reaches the peak of this transitional period, the possibilities for greater dangers increase. It is now crossing the threshold of a decisive moment that could possibly lead to one of the most tumultuous time humanity has ever experienced. Yes, you are indeed facing a dangerous time of enormous challenges, some of which are unprecedented in your recorded history. Problems such as militarism, nuclear proliferation, poverty, pandemics, famine, warfare, religious discords, dwindling natural resources, democratic representative crisis, racism, patriotism, injustice, immorality, institutional corruption and family disintegrations, to name a few, together constitute such formidable menaces to your civilizations that it will necessitate the collective efforts and cooperation of virtually all nations to confront and solve them.

In effect, many studies on global emergencies conducted by some of your experts have demonstrated that it is becoming increasingly difficult even for the most developed countries to deal effectively with these critical issues. Moreover, because the existing authorities somewhat favor and aggravate them, they are growing evermore rapidly and severely – spreading virtually out of control. In fact, some of your leading social analysts have estimated and concurred that containing or solving these problems will become not only more challenging in time, but also perhaps nearly impossible if serious actions are not taken "immediately" to restrain their impacts. But of course, do not expect the dark ones to address these concerns honestly, for this is not in their interest, and that would totally contradict their plan for world domination. Remember, they mastermind most of these ills to prosecute their iniquitous agenda— which is to ultimately bring about Armageddon as expected by society, and forcefully install their New World Order.

Nevertheless, since the problems are compounding and worsening without any feasible solutions in sight, the logical question is: what can humanity do to avert a catastrophe? There are various opinions among some of your 'learned' authorities concerning the proper approaches and actions that should be taken to resolve these ominous issues. But regrettably, most of them differ and disagree regarding the correct methods or even the appropriate manner their ideas can be implemented. Consequently, as their differences continue to delay a collective effort to address and fix these crucial problems, they continue to increase exponentially. Eventually, they will become too difficult for the current global powers to solve successfully, and much less to face their possible future escalations.

We do sincerely believe that if serious and adequate measures are not taken to resolve these grave international predicaments soon, especially the ever-present menace of nuclear warfare, they may suddenly sparrow out of control. We do not ignore the facts or belittle the potential threats your world faces as they actually exist. Yes, a combination of the most precarious situations is now simultaneously threatening the survival of civilization on your planet. However, it is highly unlikely that they will cause the destruction of your species, for it has been authorized on high by divine decree to prevent such an unthinkable event.

Let us make this clear. The widespread teaching in a coming "Holy Judgment Day" is rather a fictitious idea rooted in a satanic mindset. This erroneous notion has no spiritual foundation. As we said at the onset of this Paper, it originated from the archenemies of the universe. It was then imparted unto those who have had dominion upon your planet for eons of time. It was quite easily embedded in your collective mind through your creedal philosophies, using your most influential religious leaders. The plan was for mankind to be completely subservient to the traditional records of institutional religions, and that has been successfully achieved. Being thoroughly conditioned to the dead letters of scriptures accepted as the word of God, successively, generations of indoctrinated religionists utterly failed to identify the true nature of the Creator's relationship with his children on earth. Thus, they continue to sell and spread their misleading ideas in His name to this day. But irrespective of their claims on any spiritual affair, be it Armageddon or the return of Jesus Christ, thinking people should categorically reject the conception that a loving Creator would purposely, secretly schedule the destruction of his own creation and keep his offspring in suspenseful fear regarding their bleak future. Such a callous attitude is grotesque and despicable. This is unbecoming of mortal man, let alone the divine Ancestor and Father of all personalities. True, by their various misguided empirical activities, men may accidentally or purposefully harm and render the natural world unsustainable, or even temporarily uninhabitable. Nevertheless, bear in mind that once human evolution has started on a planet, it is never the intention of the universe rulers for such a realm to be disturbed, let alone destroyed.

Christianity and the 'Doomsday Prophecy'
The Misinterpretations of Apostle John's Revelation

In his apocalyptic revelation, the Apostle John figuratively described the final drama of a decisive war between the forces of good and evil. Among his many depictions and pronouncements, he said, "Then I saw the heavens opened, and there was a white horse; its rider was called Faithful and True. He judges and wages war in righteousness. Then I saw the beast and the kings of the earth, and their armies gathered to fight against the one riding the horse and against his army."

Although many of John's peculiar descriptions may be symbolically associated to some modern days' global events and situations, but it would be unwise and foolish to interpret his entire revelation as the last prophetic drama of the human experience. It would equally be a grave error to read and define the Apostle's book according to the perspectives of any religious sect. Since its inception around 90 A.C., different denominations—especially in Christendom—have a long history of interpreting this document for various "questionable reasons." An obvious one is to twist, stretch, and modify its meanings as much as possible to reflect their own circumscribed interpretations and beliefs about the prophecies. The idea is to render it suitable to their worship style.

Today, we deem it critical to shed a new light on this revelation as this is urgently needed to discredit the deceptive voices that have misrepresented the great and noble work of the Apostle. For centuries, theologians have provoked much confusion among believers by their erroneous interpretations of these and many other biblical records. And that persistent disingenuous attitude has consequently inhibited the spiritual evolution of numerous honest and faithful souls.

According to several modern denominations of Christianity, the entire book of revelation is supposed to be a symbolic portrayal of fated events, an allegorical depiction of things that must occur prior to the return of Jesus Christ to adjudicate the world and inaugurate a new dispensation. Yet, many past cosmic events with no obvious possible connection with any future time on earth are mentioned in the text. For example, John described a war in heaven between Satan with his accomplices and Michael with His loyal angels. There was indeed a spiritual feud in the universe of Nebadon during the Lucifer rebellion in the Local System of Satania. But that incident occurred more than two hundred and forty-eight thousand years before the Apostle was given the revelation, a little over nineteen centuries now. Additionally, he visualized a unique corps of twenty-four elders gathered in circle on a sea of glass before the throne of a majestic personality whom he referred to as God. After Jesus ascended to the heavenly Father, upon resuming his full authority as the Sovereign of Nebadon, he had immediately appointed this special council of mortal origin personalities to oversee the spiritual affairs of Urantia, and the other quarantined worlds in Satania. It is probable that this transaction took place several years before the revelation of John was written. Furthermore, the Apostle described a majestic assembly of one hundred and forty four thousand mortal pilgrims who were victorious over the beast. This was neither a futuristic vision nor a scene of earthly significance. John was offered a unique opportunity to visualize the graduation ceremony of a group of mortal ascenders from the seventh morantia world to their arrival on Jerusem – the Capital of Satania. Such ceremonial events actually happen quite often in the System as the morantial ascenders from the material worlds of space are prepared and mobilized periodically for citizenships on Jerusem after traversing the seven previous mansonia worlds of preparatory education. Victory over the beast is a figurative speech indicating the complete divestment of those ascending mortals from their former animal natures. For once they arrive at the shores of Jerusem, they practically become first-class spirit ascenders.

Regardless of the reason why they are mentioned in the book, one thing is certain; these cosmic events seriously question the veracity of the meanings assigned to John's revelation in the Christian world. We have no doubt that the Apostle at least, relatively understood the importance of the symbolisms and perhaps even the spiritual imports of his cryptic writings. But we cannot, in good faith, admit the same degree of reliability on those who later committed to the interpretations of his revelation.

Most of the meanings assigned to these symbolic writings today are done with spurious motivations and questionable intentions. Many self-proclaimed Bible scholars incline to unravel John's symbolisms as to concur with their traditions and doctrines. They cleverly twist the connotations of his narratives to reflect their own preconceived definitions of the prophecies. Consequently, there are in circulation scores of controversial explanations for the book of revelation throughout Christendom.

However, though most Christians tend to regard the book of revelation as a prophetic document that predicts the events which must occur before their anticipated return of Jesus Christ to adjudicate the world, this view is not universal. There are significant differences among them concerning John's Apocalypse. As we've said, several denominations have shrewdly interpreted the Apostle's work to coincide perfectly with their own conceptual beliefs. This is deliberately done to serve the fundamental interests of their own congregations, which essentially demonstrates that the Christian world is utterly confused about the true significations and values of the apocalyptic symbols.

But if their interpretations are basically flawed as we say, naturally one may ask: What is the proper reading? How can we discern the true import and accurately define the symbolisms of this mysterious document? Well, honestly, there can never be a perfect intellectual definition to any cosmic revelation. Revelation is not a product of human intelligence. Hence, it cannot be correctly decoded using the concepts of a mortal language for illustrations and explanation purposes. As a spiritual phenomenon, the symbols of revelation are mysterious. They are decodable and comprehensible only by direct interventions and assistance of celestial entities, such as your Mystery Monitors, the Spirit of Truth, or some angelic helpers.

Spirit is the sole avenue by which man may *truly decipher* and comprehend the in-depth meanings and importance of cosmic revelations. Absent of spiritual guidance and inspiration, mortals are unable to interpret or understand the profound significations of transmitted transcendental informations. In effect, without the ministry of their indwelling spirits, men's highest religious ideals are merely the reflections of their finite imaginations. This is extremely important for the truth-seeker who sincerely aspires to know and grasp the real viewpoints of God in revelational documents. Theology is the psychology of institutional religion. To be legitimate, it must evolve continually by virtue of new inspired revelations. Otherwise, it is hardly authentic, much less spiritual.

By embracing their own forged interpretations of John's revelation, the concept "Armageddon" has instilled superstitious fear in men. But such erroneous conclusions of the Apostle's cryptic symbolisms certainly do not have anything whatsoever to do with the divine procedures of adjudication in the universe. The early disciples and even the Apostles of Jesus, including John himself, confounded the Master's prophecy on the destruction of Jerusalem with his promise to return on earth. Thus, Christianity was founded upon the belief of an imminent return of Jesus-Christ to usher the final judgment of mankind. Christ Michael did promise to return on Urantia. But he never associated that future visit with any specific world event. He at no time indicated that some special occurrences would necessarily announce or precede his second coming. As the

Sovereign Chief and Master Creator of this local universe, Michael of Nebadon may reappear on earth at any given moment. But alas, like in the first century post his departure from this world, modern Christians are zealously anticipating his imminent return to fulfill this promise according to existing and unfolding world actualities. Many erringly continue to look upon global events as signs of the impending manifestation of the Master.

Honestly, it is painful for us to observe this phenomenon age after age. Most of Urantia's inhabitants are fervently expecting the termination of life and the sphere itself by first-time catastrophic incidents. The notion that the world is fated to end is virtually universal. Every culture possesses a story that underscores this "prophesied" apocalypse.

According to their analyses of supposed sacred writings, many profess religious scholars have claimed that "the events which must precede the end of days are upon men." Some dogmatically believe that humanity is now living the final moments of time. Generally, the global population is either consciously or intuitively expecting its own demise. By viewing and interpreting the future from the narrow prism of organized religions, the majority of your planet's inhabitants firmly believe this erroneous idea. They are anticipating imminent annihilation as if this is a fait-accompli. Some think of the apocalypse as the last grand and decisive conflict to be had between Satan and God. What a terrible travesty this misleading belief has created! Such an enormous misconception of the Creator's manner of dealing with His bewildered and disobedient creatures must be categorized as the wildest of man's attempts to interpret the divine-will vis-à-vis himself. It is perhaps the most absurd interpretations of mankind has ever imagined.

It is alarming to behold the sheer number of people throughout this globe who are dominated by this fallacious thought. We truly pray for the enlightenment of those who continue to live under this wrong and fearful impression of the Creator because of these ludicrous interpretations of alleged inspired scriptures.

Although the theological and philosophical assessments of the concept Armageddon significantly vary in many respects in different cultures, nonetheless, they are all practically driven by the same apprehensive spirit of a grim and perilous future.

To avert the danger of falling victim to these fictitious interpretations of so-called sacred visions, one must be open-minded, spiritually receptive, and independent of all the opinionated viewpoints of modern theologians. It is imperative for all truth seekers to understand that though the so-called holy predictions of a coming apocalypse are overwhelmingly supported by most religionists; while their sophistries may sound convincing, supposed ominous prophecies do not in any wise way necessarily reflect the intention of the eternal living God.

The Creator is not a static force or an automatic power that is subservient to the laws of the universe. Indeed, materially speaking, God can be envisaged as energy, force and power, but he is also will and personality. Moreover, primarily, God is a loving Creator. He does not personally judge or punish the unruly intelligences of His creation.

Most of men's sufferings are predominantly the ensuing consequences of their deliberate evil attitudes toward divine realities, not judgment from an almighty Deity. God is indeed an impartial Creator – a righteous personality, but love and mercy are the dominant qualities of His divine nature. His reactions to the universe intelligences are always motivated by a fatherly affection, for He is truly the Universal Father of all.

Furthermore, essentially, man is a sentient, will-endowed personal being. He is not called to experience life passively according to a fixated spectrum of immutable or inescapable circumstances predetermined for him. Within the limits of his ability to exercise his creative faculty, he can even provoke the emergence of new, never-before experienced realities of temporal or spiritual significances. However, he must use his creative intention wisely in full accordance with divine values in order for it to be truly beneficial to his overall personal development. Total absence of wisdom and ignorance of Truth can only lead man to devastating situations and embarrassing predicaments.

To perform adequately during this life, the human mind must be attuned to the facts of time, but the temporal meanings of material things do not necessarily reflect the values of the celestial realms.

The idea of the end of the world as conceived by men is a pure abstraction that derived from their distorted finite perceptions of universal reality. This notion is in no wise way a divine policy.

In principle, the opening of a new dispensation always marks the beginning or the end of a planetary epoch. However, the upheavals that may chance to accompany such a transition are always consequential to human activities, not the benevolent rulers of the universe.

Always bear in mind that God dwells in you as a super guiding spirit, his influence is a transcendental ministry to your inner evolving souls. He does not interfere with your thought processes or determines the outcomes and the consequences of your misguided choices, decisions, and actions. Hence, the material difficulties and problems of your existence are not consequential to the Father's divine will and universal ministration.

The Pseudo Scientific Notion of a 'Doomsday'
Futuristic Discoveries

As for the potential cosmic threats Urantia faces according to some of your astrophysicists, they are really nonexistent. Like their presuming theory, which suggests that earth's current spatial trajectory will eventually lead it into a fatal collision with some massive extraterrestrial bodies such as an asteroid or a comet. Such fear-driven 'scientific' conclusions are merely the products of their inflated minds and limited understanding about the nature of the laws that govern the universal order of the starry realms. Scientists may speculate on the probability of future events based on their general analyses of observable physical facts, but the idea that humanity will be exterminated by cosmological accidents and disruptions illustrates their profound ignorance of the Creator's plan for His evolving will-creatures on the whirling planets of space. Such intelligent but flawed theories will invariably remain just what they are—science fictions.

Empirical observations, examinations and studies of the universe's material phenomenons may allow scientists to gain some knowledge of their natures and behaviors. But such localized informations are not necessarily cosmically sound and authentic. Mechanistic science deals solely with the domain of physical realities. Thus, it can never be a viable tool for spiritual discovery. It cannot explain the purpose of intelligent, moral, and personal living organisms such as man. Physics have nothing whatsoever to do with the ethical values and the spiritual aspirations of the spirit-endowed human being.

The cosmic plan behind intelligent life or the destiny of the human personality is not discoverable scientifically. Above all, man is a spirit-endowed creature; the transcendental ideals and the religious values of his evolving moral character are beyond the localized concepts of empirical judgments, and therefore, transcend all finite understandings. After all, it should be remembered that although the scientific findings about the physical laws, behaviors and other processes of creation may be true and reliable on earth, but they do not necessarily explain the mysteries of life in an ever growing and expanding universe.

Future scientific discoveries will disclose that unpredictable events or unforeseen accidents never occur in the cosmos. At some point in this or the next century, science will make some of its most surprising modern discoveries. For example, your scientists will discover that there is always an underlying force that sustains, controls and balances all material phenomena, even amidst visible chaos. They will learn that though matter-energy normally behaves according to established, immutable cosmic laws, the universe is not essentially a mechanistic handiwork, but rather a conscious, mind-dominated, spirit-motivated, and personality-managed creation.

They will find that though they are apparently intertwined, absolute and endless to the restricted perception of men, time and space are, in reality, two limited and illusive manifestations that allow the finite to co-exist with the infinite in the universe. They will also realize that all evolutionary creations are cosmically purposeful; that they are the expressions of an intelligent design with an unfolding plan of infinite possibilities. Your scientific community will be thunderstruck when they discover that the apparent hellish commotion astronomers observe among space bodies are actually intelligently structured, monitored, supervised, and directed by what some will dub as the "*Supreme Mind.*" Involuntarily, the new findings will induce them to assume an original theory about the universe that none could have ever anticipated since Einstein's concept of general relativity, $E=mc^2$.

We are not permitted to disclose the details of these futuristic discoveries of science on your planet. But we may say this much: when they come out, the scientific society will unanimously consent that above all previously accepted theories and conventional understandings, there has to be an actual "*Intelligence*" throughout space that is monitoring and controlling the activities of the universe's material and mindal phenomena. After exhaustive discussions and deliberations, for the first time ever it will be established that the universe could not be intelligible or accurately explained without the recognition of a "*Higher Mind*" of superior creative imagination and powers beyond mortal comprehension. However, they will cautiously abstain from acknowledging the personality of such a postulated being. Those who will make this startling discovery and pioneer this new hypothesis will be tempted to believe they have finally discovered God. Yet, within a few months following the memorable event, they will be disappointed.

Although this finding will radically change many of their previously held theories about the universe, it will not be the discovery of God. Bear in mind that the works of an artist do not necessarily reveal his personality. Naturally, logic supposes a great mind is behind the material creations, but examinations of the cosmos cannot disclose the true character, nature and personality of the Creator. God as a person is discoverable only spiritually, through communion with His Fragmented Presence that indwells the human mind.

Limitations of Science and Technology
Spirit Is Essential to Transcend the Limits of Time

Unaided by spirit, man's perception of time-events is basically linear and finite, therefore, greatly limited. For example, though science is significantly advanced on your world today, but the degree and magnitude of the catastrophes facing the nations if the dark cabal succeeds in starting another world war cannot be accurately estimated using any of the technical devices yet made for such purpose. The current rising suspicions and tensions between the most potent rival States within the Security Council—the body of nations that are entrusted with preserving global stability – are indeed real signs indicating the proximity of possible great clashes of civilizations on your earth. However, no scientific examination of the situation can truly predict or provide an accurate figure of the scale and enormity of the destructions that will ensue if this tragedy should transpire. For instance, can any existing science positively secure and guarantee the survival of your civilization if the MAD doctrine [Mutually Assured Destruction] of your two most powerful nuclear-armed nations is ever implemented? We can certainly assure you, as exist today none of them could!

Science and technology alone cannot protect or ensure the lasting existence of civilization. They are hopelessly restricted to physicality, conditioned by mortal perception and limited to theoretical mathematics. Thus, they cannot supply the wisdom and character essential to preserve and ascertain the continuity of a civilize society. Basically, they treat and deal only with the unstable and ever-changing realities of the material world. But the meanings and values of culture; the foundational concepts of any evolving social order; spring from the creative intelligence and imagination of man—his inner life. Largely, civilization cannot survive long without continuing intellectual, sociological and spiritual progress.

Any nation faces a great risk of disintegration when most of its youths devote their lives in pursuing merely technical and self-gratifying materialistic ambitions. The quality of a society's value system will certainly decline when more than eighty percent of its constituents manifest no interest in higher pursuits such as Truth, anthropology, astronomy, cosmology, the fine arts, poetry, nature, ethics, philosophy, religion, and spirituality.

In the great responsibility to sustain and guarantee the long-term material progress of civilization and improve the quality of life, ongoing positive scientific, industrial and technological advances are crucial. However, if we may reiterate, both science and technology have limitations. They are utterly restricted to the finite realms of physical reality. For example, though your scientists have invented methods and mechanisms to evaluate the potential or would-be devastations of likely natural disasters, nonetheless, their calculations are only reliable in comparison with previous types of environmental cataclysms. Therefore, it is utterly unwise to trust and rely on such limited synthetic apparatuses when facing new and unknown ecological dangers. As far as we know, there is yet no hi-tech climate-evaluating device on your planet that can accurately estimate the gravity of unprecedented natural or even human-generated catastrophes.

Your world's sciences have made some great leaps forward since their inceptions, and they will continue to progress indefinitely. However, being limited to physicality, they can neither protect nor secure the survival of civilization from utter destructions. And…like all major establishments, the dark ones fully control the scientific community and its operations. Far from being independent, this discipline is purposely utilized as the sole authority on all knowledge to manipulate human perception and manufacture ignorance. This enables the cabal to rule the world with impunity fostering the fictional "doomsday prophecy."

Regardless of the level of their intellectual and technical developments, Urantians seem to remain trap and limited by olden superstitions and backward traditions. We on this side yearn to see man living up to his full potentials. Today, as the current paradigm of global authority vanishes into the dustbin of history, there is an urgent need for you to wake up and seek for your own Truths and path to destiny. At this late hour approaching the apex of the planetary shift, we wish for all of you to stop tarrying on the shores of spiritual darkness, and step towards the light for a renewal of yourselves and your planet.

You have indeed come a long way since the Lucifer rebellion, but now you must continue to move forward. And as you advance in this journey, it should be borne in mind that you are neither a victim of *fatalism* nor a slave of an imposed *determinism*. But instead, you are a will-endowed personality who is mentally indwelt by a divine spirit—the very Presence of God. Sure, there are a number of problems and vicissitudes to grapple with as the present world order continues to yield and crumble. But your biggest challenge today is personal, for every one is called to transcend the fear-motivated and offensive mentality that the dark ones have encoded in your collective reality. We advise you to be sagacious and patient while you continue to find your center by developing a relationship with your Inner Guides. This will not necessarily change your lives into a bed of roses, but it will most certainly transform you into more than you could ever imagine. Our challenges to you at this time are to rise above your shortcomings, lose your fears, seek your own Truths and create your reality. Have good intention towards your felllow kind, including the evildoers. Then you shall experience the Creator, for He is indeed *Infinite Love* and the Father-Mother of all. Remember, only a spirit-illuminated soul can withstand injuries without rancor.

We have covered quite a bit of information in this Paper as I anticipated. Again, as always, you have shown your willingness to continue cooperating with us in this peculiar endeavor. Our zeal and commitment to perform and conclude it in conjunction with you is tremendous. We appreciate your patience, gratitude, enthusiasm, courage, and faith for participating so willingly with us in this co-creative project, even though you cannot yet visualize its real ultimate purpose.

I will now bid you farewell for a short season until we rejoin our energies again for another session. Good evening.

Paper 5

Dominant World Problems

USED AS 'PROPHETIC SIGNS' LEADING TO THE ARMAGEDDON

Exposing the Most Challenging Global Issues

Celestial Teacher: Abanaly ~ Channel: Joseph Elie 09-29-2012

TODAY, EVERYWHERE WE LOOK AROUND your planet, there is a panoply of serious problems that continue to affect humanity with virtually no feasible solutions in sights. From ongoing wars and famine to poverty and corruption, the list is quite extensive. Although most of these grave issues have existed for eons of time here, but their impacts have been reinforced lately by the dark cabal as prophetic signs to support the "doomsday prophecy." As we saw in the previous Paper, religion and science are rigorously used to promote the imminence of this apocalyptic event, while these predicaments are now being deliberately intensified to bolster and confirm their predictions in the public mind. The success of this strategy is crucial to finalize their nefarious plan for the world. For several centuries, your societies have been tacitly rehearsed, indoctrinated and conditioned to expect the inevitable end of the world scenario by a last dramatic clash between civilizations. In fact, the concept of this final war, which is to be the mother of all mortal conflicts because of the unprecedented scope of its devastations, was quoted directly from one of the most popular religious scriptures in the world. The coming of this madness is deliberately promoted and widely anticipated as the *"Armageddon."*

In the last century, all the traditional channels of mass control have been activated to fulfill this long-cherished goal.

From our point of observation, the dark cabal has now arrived at the final stage of its nefarious plan, which is, as we've said, the decimation of undesirable populations and global domination. As indicated in Paper 3, we are cognizant of the varied suppressive methods they employed to reach their current position as well as those they intend to use to achieve these evil objectives. Nevertheless, there are three key motives behind their scheme that must be identified first in order to see and understand the full picture of their diabolical design:

[1] *suppressing humanity's spiritual nature by instilling fear into the global mind and by controlling your perception;* [2] *orchestrating and fostering of transnational conflicts with severe socioeconomic predicaments to provoke worldwide chaos;* [3] *executing the apocalypse by engaging the most potent and nuclear-armed nations on the planet in a third bloody world war.*

Number 1 and 3 were exposed in the previous Papers. In this one, we will focus our attention on the second aspect of their control strategy. We will outline an array of many of the world's foremost actual problems along with some of their dismal consequences. As most of these issues are predominantly social, we will also endeavor to provide some counsel to reduce their influences, especially pertaining to marriage and family relationship.

Global Issues
Facts & Statistics

Imminent World Crises: An article that occurs in an American magazine [U.S. News & Reports of 1998] stated the gravity of the world crisis at that time and the future. This investigation commission exposed the problems with these remarks: If new and effective measures are not taken immediately, in the next 20 years, [our world] will be an unsure planet with detestable impurity over which millions upon millions dispute the rare resources at extremely exaggerated cost. Furthermore, according to this mission, in the year 2020, the world population will attain 8.2 billion humans. The price of necessary goods will triple; the deserts will spread; an estimate of 72% of the forests will be destroyed, and more than half of the world reserves of petroleum will be consumed.

Poverty: Extreme poverty now seems to be a permanent fixture in the world. Even the richest countries are bounding knees under the overwhelming weight of poverty. For instance, in Canada, according to the global mail of Toronto, it is estimated that one-third of all Canadians will experience some tough financial problems over the course of their working lives. The Newspaper also said: "family breakdown is one of the main reasons for poverty, and the trend has accelerated during recent years."

Drugs Addictions: Drug abuse is another sign of the deterioration of modern society. What can government do about it? Evidently, very little overall. Physical, mental and moral degradations are often the direct results of their abuse, and the problem is spreading like a wildfire.

Disease Epidemics: Scientists seem to be losing the war against diseases these days. Apparently, modern medicine has won many battles against pandemics. Yet, some scientific procedures in themselves have contributed to the emergence of new drug-resistant strains of dangerous microbes.

Family under Assault: Family is the oldest human institution. In many ways, it is the most important. It is a society's most basic unit. Entire civilizations have survived or disappeared, depending on rather family life was strong or weak. However, viewed from today's prism, those words take an unpromising, almost sinister tone. The last two decades of the 20th century witnessed what, to us, amounted to a frontal assault on family life. There's a huge and growing crisis within the family these days. The high divorce rate, teenage disorder and domestic violence are some of the evidence. Particularly alarming is the environment existing in many homes in recent times. In the United States alone, it is estimated that tens of millions of children are being raised by alcoholic and abusive parents or guardians. Indeed, evidence that something is radically wrong with this invaluable institution today can be found all over the world.

For instance, in Europe, from 1965 to 2012, the number of divorces among married couples with children has increased almost threefold. For the past four decades or so, single-parent families have sharply increased throughout the continent.

Many developing countries, likewise, are seeing a steep rising in family distress. For those living in societies that have known a relatively regular, predictable, and unchanging way of life for years, today is certainly a time of tumult.

There is little disagreement among leading experts that family violence has sharply increased around the world in the past five decades. Today, it is more likely to be physically assaulted, beaten, and killed in your own home in the hands of loved ones than any other place, or by anyone else in society. If civilization survival really depends on the strength of the family, then there is a good reason to fear for civilization.

Money and Work: Economic pressure is one of the most damaging weapons of assault against the home currently. These are critical times hard to deal with. Many families today are facing serious obstacles in dealing with the common hurdles of daily life. In emergent and poor countries, problems such as unemployment, low wages and shortages of basic necessities cause families much hardship. But even in the affluent countries such as the United States, economic pressures take their toll on its poor citizens and too often destroy the home. A number of U.S. surveys conducted recently revealed that money was one of the main causes for the family conflict. The time, attention, and energy devoted to meeting the demands of work certainly are a subtle enemy that erodes marital commitment.

Circumstances have forced a record number of women in the job market. Presently, in America, tens of millions of American infants and toddlers under age three have mothers who down some sort of an outside occupation. Caring for the almost insatiable needs of small children and maintain an employment can be a grueling, exhausting endeavor with negative effects upon both parent and children. Naturally, this has provoked a serious shortage of adequate child-care provisions. Quite a few million American children today are short charged on good care during their early years.

Weakened Marital Ties and Family Distress: The matrimonial institution itself has also come under assault. In the past, the expectation was that a couple would stay married unless one of the spouses committed some gross offense against the marriage, like adultery, cruelty, or extreme neglect. Nowadays, most people see the purpose of marriage as a mean for personal fulfillments. Yes, marriage is treated as an antidote for unhappiness, boredom, or loneliness, and not as a lifelong commitment to another person. The focus now is on what you get out of marriage, and not what you put into it. This major change in the values surrounding marriage has greatly weakened marital ties. When personal fulfillment eludes their grasp, couples often seize upon divorce as a quick solution.

Today, many people see family distress as a sign that the traditional rules of marriage and parenting are obsolete. Others believe it is the product of political, economic and social transformations while some regard it as just one more casualty of modern technology. But in reality, if we look deeper into the problem, family grapples today point to something of far greater significance and implication. Note the Bible's words in Timothy 3: 1-4 – "know this, that in the last days, critical times hard to deal with will be here. For men will be lovers of themselves, lovers of money, self-assuming, haughty, blasphemers, disobedient to their parents, unthankful, disloyal, having no natural affection, slanders, without self-control, fierce, without love for goodness, betrayers, headstrong, puffed up with pride, lovers of pleasures rather than lovers of God." Do not these words get to the very root of today's social problems? Is there any doubt that this excessive exaltation of egoism has provoked serious and costly global consequences? Would any moral and balance individual deny that such irreverent attitudes are direct violations of divine principles that do nothing but isolate men from God?

The Marriage Institution
Its Human Origin

Abomaly: As an institution, marriage is merely an evolutionary by-product of culture and civilization, not necessarily a divine injunction from God. If marriage was foreordained and sanction by the Creator, then, once married, couples would not have been able to separate or divorce.

The marital rules of modern civilizations originated from the mores and taboos of primitive men. They started long ago at the onset of social evolution on earth. In fact, many clans had already developed their own matrimonial codes way before the Adamic Dispensation. And those were sometimes very dissimilar depending on how far apart the tribes were situated. For instance, in some African tribes, young couples were often [but not always] constrained to remain under their parents' authority so long those were alive, while in others, the parents were compelled to disown their offspring completely once given into marriage.

Not much has changed in this regard even today. In other continents, however, things have evolved significantly since those anterior times of emergent civilization. The matrimonial standards of humanity have developed from those early periods to the recent marital statutes and norms of the 21st century.

It was sex and hunger that attracted the average primitive man to a woman, not necessarily love and the desire for a life companion. Naturally, procreation can be a strong bond between couples, but it is not powerful enough to sustain and secure a marriage, which is supposed to be a lifetime commitment of unconditional loyalty to another person. Marriage is not a natural desire of the human species. The home institution is purely an evolutionary circumstance. In fact, because the traditional concepts and criterions of marriage derived from diverse ancient ethnic stocks, they remain quite different in every culture to this day, and they are subjected to periodic amendments.

Marriage and Family in a Progressive Society

In a truly progressive society, the established norms of marriage should steadily evolve proportionately with the population's intellectual, ethical and spiritual development. As the arts of civilization continue to advance and humanity becomes more pacific and proficient at abiding to the values of divinity, the existing matrimonial rules and standards must be redefined or changed consequently. The principles and meanings of marriage must be – should we say, recurrently upgraded until this union is generally viewed and understood spiritually, in its sacred form as it should be. Every passing generation has the responsibility to set new goals, to renew the values, and to improve the dynamics of this most intimate of all human relationships, which is invaluable to the family institution and thus indispensable to the preservation of civilization on your planet.

If this evolving process is respected, conjugal ties would increasingly strengthen as the very nature and quality of the family relationship would greatly improve and perfected worldwide in a few generations. However, it is not necessary to wait for some revolutionary change in marital conventions in order to understand the spiritual purpose of marriage and the family, even now.

There is a definite originality of goodness that is strikingly discernable in the relationships of truly God-knowing individuals and forward-looking couples. In reality, two human beings simply cannot experience true love without a certain degree of moral and spiritual affinity. Love is indeed a selfless expression of personal devotion to another being, but it is really experiencible only between two mutually affectionate personalities. Divine love is always accompanied with a profound consciousness of affiliation to a caring Deity.

Men could barely tame or control their own egos and animal propensities absent from the influences of their indwelling spirits. Two egocentric persons may be reciprocally friendly and even amorous, but their relation can last only to the extent it suits their mutual interests. Selfishness is absolutely inimical to love and goodness. A self-centered individual can never experience or appreciate unconditional affection sincerely. The egoist is primarily motivated by his-own invested interest in all relationships with others. He simply doesn't relish the idea of giving or doing something for nothing. Such barren souls really cannot love another unconditionally, for they are totally dominated by their own selfish motivations.

Overall, the marriage and family institution has been, is, and will remain always significant and positive for the moral development of humanity. But without spiritual guidance, men lack the wisdom and virtues to ensure its success and ascertain its permanence.

As we mentioned earlier, family is the most natural and fundamental constituent of any civilization. It is paramount to the existence and continuation of a moral social order. Yet, for centuries now, there has been a systematic erosion of this essential fabric in your global culture. This is a dangerously harmful and detrimental situation for humanity at this moment, to say the least.

Civilization is now suffering greatly from the continuous worldwide decline of family values and the steep attrition of the marital institution. There is little question among your social experts, that in the past fifty years particularly, filial bond has been drastically depleting throughout the world. And this trend is seriously threatening the very existence of the home globally. This is the wish of the dark cabal, which is anti-union and anti-family. In the past five decades or so, divorce rate and single parent families have exponentially soared, especially in America and Europe.

There is currently an ongoing massive breakdown of the family institution throughout these continents. And this alarming development seems to become a permanent fixture in your global society, for despite many efforts to curtail the trend nothing has been able to diminish or stop it.

Today, as marriage is typically viewed, defined, treated, and understood throughout your world, there is little doubt that family life is dangerously approaching the shores of an unpleasant future. It is now incumbent upon society to take all necessary actions to prevent the home institution from complete destruction. The world's current "legal establishments," dominated by the dark cabal, are clearly more inclined to push it down that path.

Nearly all your respectable sociologists on this issue have unanimously concurred that the marriage institution is in a global crisis. They seem to agree more or less that the home, which constitutes the foundation of civilization, is currently undergoing a very difficult period, and is under enormous pressures worldwide. Generally speaking, there is little doubt that natural love has been slowly eroding and the principles of family life have been disappearing around the globe for a long time.

Family is the most basic unit of a civilize society. It is absolutely critical that its values are protected in order to preserve civilization itself. The continuing survival of any nation as a viable, stable and progressive society largely depends upon the strength and unity of its homes. This rule is equally important and applicable to the entire global community. Today, there is an urgent need to revitalize the values within the home globally, and that is achievable only by supporting and strengthen all genuine families throughout your world.

First, it is imperative for couples and parents to learn about the transcendent significance of marriage and family. They should know while marriage and procreation are completely natural and optional to man, parenting is essentially a transformational experience, a divine obligation that must be fulfilled either on earth or beyond. The tender and highly stimulating experience of rearing children carries a profound meaning critical to the spiritual growth and universal ascension of men. True, it is your personal prerogative to marry or have children, but parenthood is a celestial requirement essential to attain your Paradise destiny. Such an intimate and unique form of human relationship [parent and child] is neither an evolutionary accident nor a purely mundane affair.

Although He is not the sponsor of the marriage tradition, however, God ordained the natural union of mankind in order to produce the family association. And this, He did according to His eternal plan and perfection mandate to elevate man from the lowly state of a mere mortal to the exalted status of a divine personality. Love predominantly requires some degree of self-sacrifice.

The parenting experience offers every morally sound individual the opportunity to exercise such a degree of selflessness toward other human beings—whether direct offspring or adoptions. Parents and children alike must be willing to engage earnestly in a real search for the authentic universe meaning and purpose of the family association.

Procreation is natural to mankind, but parenthood is not. Simply put, parenting is essentially a spiritual experience. It's a humble but divinely fulfilling responsibility when it is willfully executed with love, patience and wisdom. It is invaluable to humanity's ascension career in the universe because of its relevance to the perfection mandate of God to man; *"Be you perfect even as I AM perfect."*

There are certainly great satisfactions in human reproduction, but parents can barely enjoy them if they do not truly commit themselves to the care and guidance of their offspring. Although parenthood is potential in all morally sound personalities, it is, however, appreciated for what it really is only by those who are able to discern its spiritual and cosmic imports.

Your higher knowledge of the purpose of parenting, marriage and the family may or may not help you transcend all their traditions on earth. But it will definitely enlarge your perception and understanding of these most intimate human relationships. As you mature in this awareness, you will be able to discern their intrinsic universal meanings and values.

The established principles of family life prior to the eras of Light and Life on an evolutionary world are never ideal or perfect. But if you are faithful enough to follow the directions and teachings of the spirit, which dwells in you, you may even now foretaste the true significance of the family beyond the horizon of this realm. You can preview the sublime purpose of this most tender and rewarding life experience on high. Your mind can be quickened and empowered to accomplish this task successfully, which is necessary to your spiritual ascension.

The Youths under Assault: Children are traumatized and reeling from today's pressures. Shocking numbers of children are being violently battered and verbally or sexually assaulted and abused by their own parents or guardians. Through divorces, millions more are deprived of having the loving influence of two parents, which provokes chagrin that often last a lifetime.

Youths are bombarded by powerful negative social influences nowadays. For instance, according to a statistic, by the time an American youth is 14 years old, she or he will have witnessed 18,000 killings and countless other forms of violence, illicit sex, and sadistic crimes simply by watching television. Much of today's popular music also greatly exerts and influences the youths harmfully. A lot of it is shockingly suggestive, exalting delinquency, irreverence, and sexually explicit. Basically, the music sometimes teaches youths that they don't have to listen to any adult or obey their parents, and that they should live life the way they want without principles, integrity or self-respect.

The magazine U.S. news and world report stated: In 2010, three U.S. networks displayed more than 22,000 sexual incidents during prime time. And for every single scene depicting sexual intercourse between married partners, the networks showed 19 scenes of sex outside marriage. By showing over 22,000 incidents of illicit sex during prime time in one year, would it not be just to concede that television is a negative teacher?

We would say if an adolescent observes many years of TV where people freely engage in flirtatious or explicit behaviors, these thousands of images over the years will teach them that sex is only a pleasure without any consequences. There are little to no judicious arguments against this, in our opinion. It is clear to us that most of the entertainment industries—be they music or movies—teach youngsters there are no rules; that fornication is cool and acceptable, and they are no consequences for leading a lifestyle that praises immorality and glorifies disloyalty to God.

Additionally, schools expose youths to theories such as the **Big Bang** and *materialism*, which tend to undermine faith in God. Peer pressure prompts many to engage in premarital sex and alcohol or drug abuse.

Teenagers face enormous risks of HIV because they like to experiment with sex, drugs, take risks, live for the moment, and defy authority. Sexually active teenage girls are emerging as the next leading edge of the AIDS epidemic, a United Nations study in Europe, Africa, and South-East Asia has found recently.

What are the causes? Well, virtually any observant and thoughtful person would admit that disobedience to parents is rampant nowadays, and the trend is growing throughout the globe. Many parents complain that young people seem unthankful for all that is done for them. Many youths protest that their parents are not really loyal to them [or to the family in general], but are wrapped up in their jobs, pleasures and themselves. Rather to figure out who is at fault, look at the results.

Estrangements between adults and youths frequently lead teenagers to form their own code of conduct and ethics, and usually;

manners, self-respect and values are disregarded. The consequences are a soaring rate of delinquency, teenage pregnancies, gang violence, and sexually transmitted diseases. All too often, lack of parental surveillance and care at home leads teenagers to adopt a life of violence. You can probably relate examples from your own neighborhoods, proof that natural affection is quickly disappearing.

The assault on the family unit is therefore, broad in scope, and can be devastating. A legitimate question is: Can the family survive? The parenting rules of the Western World notably have not been seriously updated in 190 years. My opinion is that the old rules no longer work. However, more man-made regulations are not the solution. God—the author of the family institution knows far better than anyone else how important it plays in our personal joy and what it takes to make a family happy and strong. Should it surprise us that he provides the solutions to our domestic issues?

Corruption: The 20th century witnessed the emergence of a gross mentality particularly in the Western world that promoted a new breed of corruption in modern civilization. Although this novel strain of immorality and social decadence was partially alive in the 50s and 60s, but it was actually intensified in the 70s—the birth age of the *"anything goes, manner-free, libertine lifestyle"* of the so-called free world.

For those who've known a simple and invariable social life in the past, that period definitely unleashed a spirit of irreverence, debauchery, excesses, and tumult in society. Generally, the last four centuries have witnessed what amount to a vicious global assault against morality and spirituality in society.

There are many verifiable traits of those infected by this terrible disease of madness. Among them, we have compiled a short list outlining some of their most recognizable characteristics:

- [1] They have no form of respect for conjugal relationship. They are reckless, insensitive and violent. Though they might have received some form of education, but they remain repulsive and unmanageable. They are inimical to intellectual and moral development. Most of them believe that violence is a normal and effective self-expression, and stupidity is cool.

- [2] They have no regard for law, order, or life itself. They get into a car and think they are speed demons and invincible; they drive like maniacs, just so they can attract the public's attention. They suffer from such a lack of self-esteem, which leads them to think that by being unruly, by disrespecting others, by being vicious and acting stupid they may eventually escape their deep sense of inferiority.

- [3] They have no consideration for natural beauty and the finer things in life. They reject anything that does not support their corrupt behaviors and immoral acts. They love to create destructible devices. To them, it's ingenious to manufacture weapons of death. They are attracted to things that can hurt and destroy others.

- [4] It is precisely from this group the great mass of criminals who are roaming and ravaging society comes from. They make it unsafe to go out on your own street at night. However, when they are arrested, billions of dollars are spent for their care and maintenance. Their budget program is higher than the amount voted for important issues, like childcare.

- [5] They are thoughtless and puffed up with ego. To them, peace and decency are dirty words.

- [6] God is often rejected or ignored by the majority in this circle. It is almost useless to try approaching them with the Gospels of good deeds and common values. For, to them these moral teachings are rather old, inappropriate, weak and wimpy.

But, what are exactly the roots and causes of this lower element in society today? Publishers, writers, experts, and even political leaders have many thousands of different answers for this question. However, few of them dare to point out clearly the reasons. Why? Because the magazines, newspapers, television networks, book publishers, and even political parties dare not offend their sponsors, advertisers, or the people with strong financial influences.

We alone dare to put the spotlight on the truth. And, we can do this because we are beholden to no one, except you, who are above the average in intelligence, otherwise you wouldn't be reading this book. We serve no master, but those who are seeking for Truth and aspire to know God and develop a relationship with Him. We serve you individually, with a special consideration, for this text is intended to assist you personally in the quest for Truth and enlightenment.

Television: Although there are many causes for this problem, but a few are most influential, and therefore have a stronger effect on society. An objective observation of this highly negative social attitude would emphatically reveal that its roots lie in the lust and immorality that pervades much of the Hollywood movies, television programs, and many of the books, videos that are being published today. These powerful influences do not compel the mind to think, but to dream and inflame the sex passions of the susceptible youth, particularly.

Television has had such strong and powerful influence in recent time that most people now are slaves of its programs and the movies. The impact of this invention is almost total and irreversible in the Western World. Television is like an attractive demon under the disguise of an angel. It's a box created by man, which has played a major role in destroying him intellectually, morally, sociologically and spiritually.

For instance, today, much of the television shows appeal to the lowest instincts in man; such as violence, crime, corruption, promiscuity, selfishness, greed, ignorance, and rejection of values.

So, after years of filling the brain with this trash, one practically has no room left to assimilate things that are truly meaningful and valuable to their personal development and maturity.

As long as people keep buying the dirt that is coming out of Hollywood, the TV box, and many books and magazines, society will continue to experience growing problems with crimes; such as burglary, rape and murder. Anyone who wants to get ahead in a chosen discipline, or make a success of his life, will simply have to cut out this dreadful waste of time. This will take strong willpower because everywhere one goes, there is this "idiot box" blaring away at you.

The resourceful person does not waste his time watching these junks. He is too busy increasing his efficiency by study of good books, or by expanding his field of work.

Television and Hollywood have found their formula in that most people want to find happiness and flee from boredom and frustration in escapism, living within a dream world of fantasy. This is a form of emotional immaturity, fulfilling dreams and hopes with illusions. This is not helping people solving their problems. Advertising on television is one of the biggest psychological influences in modern life. However, it retards society's mental maturing because it makes people want too many things for the wrong reasons. One of those reasons is appealing to their lust for prestige and attention to keep up with group conformity. This is an immature feeling. The advertisers want the consumers to indulge their egos constantly.

Television is doing more to restrain human development than maturing society. Most of the programs are mediocre and immature. The formula is to entertain the people, rouse their emotions, and not to tax their minds. However, TV makes for great frustrations in the daily lives of most of its regular viewers, because the dreams of a continual honeymoon and romance in marriage and success in business are constantly being denied in actual living.

Crimes: Serious crime is a grave social problem for most countries today. Primarily, domestic offenses have escalated to alarming proportions, with particularly severe consequences of physical violence, intimidations and corruptions of public officials. Terrorism has claimed tens of thousands of innocent victims. Predatory trafficking and addictive narcotics have become a worldwide tragedy. Criminally reckless environmental destruction has taken such shocking forms and dimensions that it has become recognized as a crime against the world itself.

Assault: An increase from just over 150 for 100,000 individuals in 1970 to nearly 600 for 100,000 in 2012.

Thefts: An increase from just over 1,000 for 100,000 people in 1970 to 5,000 for 100,000 in 2012.

Homicides: An increase from 2.5 to 4 for 100,000 individuals between 1985 and 2012 in developing countries.

Drug Related Crimes: Major trafficking cartels combined can literally outspend and outgun the governments of small nations, and so far have been able to stymie the interdiction and low enforcement efforts of the industrialized countries.

Felonies: Expected to triple from 4,000 for 100,000 individuals in 1985 to close to 12,000 in the year 2020.

Most Violent Nation: Universally, it is considered that America is the world's most violent nation. If we consider these facts, in 1990 handguns murdered 10 people in Australia, 22 in Great Britain, 68 in Canada and 10,567 in the United States. It is also the most heavily armed nation. It is estimated today that its civilians possess over 310 million firearms—more than one per person in a country of 307 million inhabitants.

Schools are not immune from the violence. In America, nearly 20 percent of all high-school students carry a weapon of some sort. Almost three million crimes occur every year on the near school campuses. Each day, 40 teachers are physically attacked, and about 900 are threatened with bodily harm.

According to the national education association, more than 100,000 students carry guns to school each day, and a typical day will see 40 children killed or injured by firearms. Society's tolerance for violence is extraordinary, and schools are merely a reflection of that. An English teacher, who previously had only a 10 percent rate on getting his 12th grade students to write an essay, had 100 percent success when assigned the topic "my favorite weapon."

Slavery Today: Although the universal declaration of human rights states that no one should be held in slavery or servitude, but hundreds of millions of people are suffering as slaves around the world. The number of people subject to slavery today, pointed out a UN Chronicle magazine, is greater than the number of slaves during the 16th to the 18th centuries, the peak slave-trade era.

One alarming aspect of today's slavery is that many victims are children. Young adolescent from seven to ten years old, are recruited as slaves to toil in factories for 12 to 14 hours a day while others are enrolled as household servants, prostitutes, or soldiers. Child labor is in great demand, reported the UN center for human rights, because it is cheap and because children are too frightened to complain. Slavery, notes the UN, remains a grim modern reality.

The Global Warming Hoax: The 80s were a hot decade. Perspectives, a magazine published by the International Institute for environment and development, reports that six of the seven warmest years over the 140-year period that temperature records were kept have all occurred since 1980. And according to data released by the British meteorological office, 1990 was the hottest year on record. This information, claimed perspectives, confirms that the average surface air temperature is rising and provides new evidence that the globe is set on a general warming trend.

Increasing Depression: Twelve independent studies involving interviews with 43,000 people in nine countries have corroborated earlier American research by suggesting that during the 20th century human society became more depress than any other time in modern history. After grouping the subjects into cohorts determined by decades of birth, beginning before 1905 and ending after 1955, almost every study showed that people born later were more likely to have been seriously depressed at some periods during their lives. Most studies also showed a steady increase in major depression throughout the world.

Children Health: More than 230 million preschool children in the developing world or 43 percent are stunted because of malnutrition due to the lack of food and to diseases, said a UN press release. In 1993, an estimated four million children died because of malnutrition, either directly, or because it worsened the impact of infections and diseases. The world health organization W.H.O recommended that all infants be fed exclusively on breast milk for at least a year, and thereafter they should continue to be breast-fed, while receiving appropriate and adequate complementary food for up to two years of age or older. Mothers and health care providers are urged not to miss-interpret the growth of breast-fed infants as growth faltering and prematurely introduce other foods. This can contribute to malnutrition and diseases because it is nutritionally inadequate.

Blood Transfusion Scandal: Germany, which consumes more blood products per person than any other country, has been rocked by scandals that have turned one of the world's most dependable branches of medicine into a target of criticism. The scandal involves a blood processing company that, for some years has sold huge amounts of improperly tested blood products to hospitals. Hence, thousands of hospital patients who have used these products have been exposed to the risk of HIV infection.

The health department had to advise strongly that anyone who wishes to make certain that he has not contracted HIV through infected blood of Phoma products during an operation should undergo a test. It is estimated that 50 percent of the populations are now afraid of getting AIDS from a transfusion bag.

Pollution: In 1971, the astronaut Edgar Mitchell had from space a vision that triggered his attention and enthusiasm while he was flying to the moon onboard of Apollo 14. He saw the earth globe like a joyful brilliant blue and white. However, today, if he was to return in space, equip this time with special glasses that would allow him to see the invisible gas of the terrestrial atmosphere; he would discover a totally different spectacle. He would see enormous holes in the ozone masses above Artantica and North America. But in reality, to be aware of this problem it is not necessary to fly 36,000 kilometers in space.

Today, we drink, breath, feel and see pollution everywhere. The fuels of our refrigerators and our air-conditioners destroy the ozone mass, which exposes us to skin cancer and alternate the genetic structures of small animals. The destruction to the environment has become one of the principal threats facing humanity.

Declining Trust in Government: Nowadays, vast numbers of individuals from all walks of life the world over are increasingly being disillusioned from the existing ideological and political paradigms of the current world order. There is a growing global movement of all kinds of people who are determined to break free from the control of the dark cabal once and for all. Even those who are normally complacent and loyal to their countries' establishments are searching for alternative leaderships. They no longer want to rely blindly on traditional authorities. And this trend will persist as society awakens and trusts in these authoritative institutions continue to decline dramatically around the world.

A strong and imposing sense of betrayal by their rulers and governments is now dominating the mentality of most societies. And nowhere is that more real and vivid than in the so-called democracies, which supposedly have governments by, of and for the people. More and more, the nations are becoming intuitively conscious that there is a great need for radical reforms in the present international order if future generations will inherit a world where hope and dreams are still possible. The current domineering transnational monetary system is totally discredited as a safe and reliable insurer and preserver of the global economy.

In reality, faith and confidence in government to solve society's problems have dangerously sunken to new lows globally. The average citizens of most countries now normally do not trust their political systems. They regard their leaders as usurpers and tyrants; as agents of a superclass, not honest public servants. They view them as deceivers and opportunists who are in collusion with this oligarchy to plunder the world and enslave society. Even an ex-president declared: *"we are witnessing a democratic representative crisis."*

Today, many people around the world are angry for having corrupt leaders with such lack of integrity and originality as representatives. In countries like Italy and Japan, it's not only the elite that deprave the public, but it's the political system in general that is held responsible. If the government becomes unpopular during a difficult economic period, the situation is exceptional because the anger is displayed not only against the incumbent officials, but also against the opposition parties. To go further, we even say that economic amelioration will not be enough to reestablish trust in system, because it is important to have a broader vision for the future.

In a number of surveys taken recently from Canada to Japan, the majority of those enquired said they don't believe in the governments of their countries. Most agreed that their countries' economies are at their bottom phases, and the situation far from recovering is degenerating. In France, for example, an estimated 60% of the people interrogated are expecting the condition to worsen in the future.

In Italy, about 75% of the people asked estimated that their governmental system no longer worked like it used to. In Canada, more than half anticipated the following generations will face much more oppressing economic conditions than the present one.

World Health: In 1985, the World Health Organization [WHO] made the remark that the tropical diseases are spreading like a wildfire. About 20% of the world population, around a billion and half people suffered from grave health problems. In fact, the cholera virus reached America for the first time during the 20th Century. The yellow fever epidemics affected more people, and tuberculosis has gained more lanes. Today, nearly 7 million new cases of cancer are registered every year in the world. The sexually transmitted diseases like AIDS, tuberculosis and polio are affecting more people the world over. The most affected regions are Africa and Asia, where more than 180 million Africans carry the H.I.V virus, and about 40% of the Asian populations are affected by malnutrition, an estimate of approximately 500 million people.

The Erosion of Manners: At the turn of the 20th century, etiquette seriously got off the wrong foot. In the late 19th and 20th centuries, those in the upper strata of society regarded observance of the most trivial demands of etiquette as a diversion and, for the women, an occupation. More and more elaborate rituals were designed to create a sense of exclusiveness for the initiates and to keep the unworthy, ignorant of them, at a distance. That is a far cry from what good manners should be.

The finest rules for behavior are to be found in chapter 13 of first Corinthians—the beautiful dissertation on charity by Paul. In 1 Corinthians 13:4 -18, it says, *"love is long-suffering and kind. Love is not jealous; it does not brag, does not get puffed up, does not behave indecently, does not look for its own interest, and does not become provoked. It does not keep accounts of the injuries. It does not rejoice over unrighteousness, but rejoices in the Truth. It bears all things, hopes all things, endures all things, love never fails."*

What a marvelous transformation it would be to see love like this practiced today! Everywhere, all manners would be impeccable. The starting point in teaching and learning such manners is the family. A family is a delicate machine whose parts are in close contact with one another. Only expert lubrication can keep it in smooth running order. Knowing how to be helpful, courteous, pleasant and polite will go a long way toward making a home happy.

Learning how to voice the accepted everyday expressions of courtesy and consideration such as *thank you, please, forgive me, I'm sorry,* will do much to dominate destructive friction in our social associations. These are little words with big meanings. Everyone can say them properly. They cost us nothing. But with them, we make friends, for if we practice good manners daily in our homes, they will not leave us when we go outside the family circle and mingle with the public.

Good manners involve showing consideration for others' feelings and treating them with respect as you would like for them to treat you. Unfortunately, these basic moral principles have undergone a breakdown in modern times. Today, most societies are seriously wanting in courtesy, and if ethics should survive the threats of the 21st century, a dramatic revival of these values is desperately needed now. Selfishness is such a horrible thing that we invented politeness to conceal it.

These days many people think polite means weak, and that putting others before yourself is wimpy. Was it not the free rude decade of the 70s that plunged most of the western world into the present "*me*" first mentality? One big city newspaper said: "The problem as related to this issue has reached the point where common modesty and decency can no longer be described as common."

Nowadays, children as young as five years old are increasingly aggressive and rude. Most teachers surveyed feel that parents are spoiling their children, and believe that this is the main cause for the increase in unsocial behavior among kids. In many surveys we observed, those who were interviewed blamed lack of clear standards and expectations at home as the principal reason for the erosion of manners among young students. Eighty percent pointed to the absence of parental example as the culprit. Broken homes, divorce living-in relationships, too-much televisions, no disciplines, no sanctions; it all boils down to the eventual destruction of the family.

Today, we are seeing more than just plain unkindness among children. On the playground, kids do not seem to play like they used to. They rave around in gangs. They are quick to identify the weak ones, kids on the fringe, kids who don't wear the right sneakers or jeans. They go after them and haunt them down. There is a vicious edge to it. Some measures have been taking to stop the trend, but they have not been very successful.

Society and Street: It is almost a battleground on the highways. A monthly letter of the royal bank of Canada speaks of the relentless carnage on the roads and concludes that the core of the problem is uncivil behavior. The courtesy, consideration, forbearance, tolerance and respect for human rights that go to make up civilizations are disgracefully lacking. The New York Times characterizes the street of New York this way: "It's motorists vs. ambulances." More motorists in that city are refusing to yield to emergency vehicles, such as ambulances and fire trucks. Increasing the danger that someone who is critically ill or injured will die because he or she cannot be reached or transported to a hospital quickly. An emergency medical service reported on a man driving on Pelham Parkway in the Bronx who refused to clear the way for an ambulance responding to a cardiac-arrest call. He tried to be a tough guy and not move over, but when he arrived at his house, he realized just how stupid he was. His mother had a heart attack and the ambulance was trying to get to her. The New York Times international told about an English Organization called "the polite society" that was founded because people have become absolutely beastly to one another, and something must be done. A Scottish insurance company concluded that more than forty percent of all road accidents can be traced back to an act of discourtesy.

Another big factor causing this increasing lack of courtesy in society is television. Television has contributed heavily to the erosion of manners, especially with children and teenagers. How people dress, talk, cope in relationships, and repeatedly solve problems with violence. The world finds satisfaction in speaking with loud, authoritative bluster, interrupting, proud of being domineering, boisterous, cynical, condescending, provocative and challenging. It used to be that rude behaviors were frowned upon by community at large, and the perpetrators were chastised. But today, an uncivil act can be committed publicly without concerned or stigma to the offender. And if anyone objects, he or she may come under verbal or physical assault.

In the youth category, some of them travel in noisy groups. They fill the air with foul language and obscene gestures while offending observers with their crude conduct. All these scatological scenes are deliberately designed to attract attention to their defiance, and to shock adults by their blatant display of rudeness.

The laws that men have compiled to manage the conduct of society would fill a big library, yet they have not resulted in the guidance humanity needs. Do we still need more, or maybe fewer? How about just one law? This one, for example, taking from the Bible: "All things, therefore, that you want men to do unto you, you also must, likewise, do unto them"—Mathew 7: 12. No generation has ever even partially observed this principle since Christ Michael gave it to his followers. Modern men practically reject this notion of spiritual equality and universal goodwill. Their new morality is an open way that gives room for any lifestyle individuals may choose. Similar to the broad pathway that Jesus identified as the road leading to destruction, and many are those going into it—Matthew 7: 13, 14.

The New Morality & Its Consequences on Manners: Manners have been rejected by the new morality. The 20th century saw a sweeping change in social behaviors and morals. In the decades that followed the two world wars, the old value systems gradually came to be viewed as outmoded. Changing conditions and modern theories in the fields of human behavior and science convinced many that the old values were no longer valid. Spiritual guidelines, once respected were rejected as passé. Old values and inconvenient moral restraints were brushed aside to clear the way for the splurge. A new 'morality' of indulgence and selfish pursuits was informally installed—basically a *"care-free, anything-goes approach."* Consequently, the fresh 'ethical' code inevitably carries with it broad changes in manners.

However, the substantial values that give richness and meaning to life were never found in that new paradigm. They were not sought for after the exciting "me-first jovial lifestyle" of the roaring seventies freed people of moral constraints, which suited them just fine.

This steep decline in manners created many problems for the political institutions, and caused severe turbulences to the social fabrics of most contemporary civilizations. The main problem is that modern society has steadily moved away from the principles and values of self-respect and self-control to unbridle self-expression and unmitigated self-exaltation, without adequate wisdom and spiritual maturity. And…if this trend is not wisely redirected, it will continue to degenerate and may eventually collapse.

The way we think and act, even if forced at first, influences internal feelings and changes the heart. To overcome juvenile delinquency, for example, it is necessary to educate a youth's emotions rather than his or her intellect. By his feelings, he becomes what he is encouraged and inspired to love, admire, worship and sacrifice for. And in all this, manner plays an important role because good manners are nothing more or less than showing sympathy and consideration to others.

Abomaly: the dark cabal have manipulated and oppressed you for a long time, but they could not have done this without your participation and complacency. Bear in mind, no one can control you absent from the consent to relinquish your creative powers.

Many of you often claim lack of intelligence as an excuse to accept this treatment as a fait-accompli. However, make no mistake, knowledge may be power, but your will and determination to live free constitute such an awesome spiritual force that it is more powerful than the sum of all the data they can process. Your firm and steadfast choice not to be subservient to the infernal game of the dark ones is an unfailing strategy to transcend and opt-out of their global matrix. Your cause is just and noble. Always remember that as children of the Almighty God, it is your divine birthright to exist and choose your experiences without interference, hindrance or pressure from other creatures—be they mortals or celestials. What we are saying is that you do have the power to change this paradigm. And it is your inalienable right to do so, starting by reaching from within to your Higher Selves; by taking responsibility to grow spiritually and improve the quality of your collective relationships as a global family; and by conceptualizing and developing the ideal government of, by and for the people.

We shall address the subject of government thoroughly in our next session, for it is central to the quality of life as it is lived on your planet. Thank you for your kind and devoted attention. Good evening.

Paper 6

The Condition Of Government On Urantia

ALL RIGHTS TO RULE ARE INHERENT IN THE PEOPLE

A Single Soul Is More Important to God than the Sum of all Human Institutions

Celestial Teacher: Abonady - Channel: Joseph Elie 10-12-2012

SINCE ITS EMERGENCE AND TRANSFORMATION from the tribe to the state, human government has made but a single significant technical progress: the standard three branches of administrative function and co-ordination—the executive, the legislative, and the judiciary. For untold ages, the quality of governmental systems on your planet has slowly evolved systematically in accordance with every generation's intellectual and sociological maturity. It will continue to develop until it attains the full potential of its true ideals and purpose.

The human races can never co-exist peacefully and prosper under the control of militaristic, oppressive and merciless political establishments. Physical and social achievements are the results of progressive civilization. But excessive greed and vainglorious pride are as life-threatening viruses that beset a morally deficient and spiritually bankrupt nation. They indicate that a society is blinded by materialism, disconnected from God, thus has sunken into an abyss of depravity and iniquity.

Most modern Urantians display a rather naive tendency to accept complete dependence on the institutions of a technologically controlled, socially polarized and militarily dominated world, without really weighing the cost. The reliance on science and government to resolve global issues is practically general in today's society. The pursuits of wealth and vanity have long exceeded any effort for ethical improvement, social justice, and spiritual salvation —especially in the most affluent countries. This is a very precarious situation, for it is unbalanced and unsustainable, and thus, detrimental to the preservation of global civilization. Beware; this trend will continue to thrust the so-called free world into intense troubles and unrests with even greater planetary upheavals.

The common tradition of global society to blindly rely on these institutional mechanisms for direction will soon prove to be a reckless and irresponsible attitude. No world afflicted by division, hatred and violence can be cured and salvaged by scientific inventions and governmental legislations. The nations will never find durable and peaceful solutions to their problems through such physical agencies. The most ingenious technological devices coupled with the smartest political strategies or policies cannot possibly resolve the moral issues of a strife-torn and divided multiracial planet—especially of dissimilar cultural and national identities, much less protect the values or guarantee the continuity of civilization.

Urantia's current diverse governing systems are, of course, temporary in its long, very long evolutionary journey toward the Ages of Light and Life—the far-flung future era when [It] will be administered by the ideal government. However, because of the Correcting Time's transformational effects in global society today, we do foresee greater and better forms of public representations in the horizon. Indeed, we anticipate that the quality of your "legal authorities" will be drastically improved not too long henceforth. Your children and grandchildren will definitely enjoy a superior planetary order with better administrative institutions than the existing ones, which are presently passing away into the dustbin of history—where they rightfully belong.

Nature of the Ideal Government
Of, By, & For the People

Essentially, the ideal form of government on a normal inhabited life-planet is usually global—a single, worldwide politico-socio-economic order. It is always intended to be invested with supreme authority in all matters pertaining to the security, wellbeing, and social development of the evolving realm. However, to be legitimate and to function adequately, it must acquire this power by the *unanimous consent* of the world's inhabitants. On a sin-free world, notwithstanding its preponderance, such a government never abuses its authority or claim sovereignty through arbitrary acts of coercion and violence. Time, patience, and wisdom are always necessary to win the voluntary approval and allegiances of the global community.

The divine authority to rule and administer society can never be secured or guaranteed by force, oppression, and brutality. *There is no such thing as legal authority of government without the people's consent. All rights and powers to rule a world are always inherent in its inhabitants.*

No leader can successfully defend a country's sovereignty and preserve his or her throne without the support and cooperation of the citizenry. Tyranny may traumatize and paralyze the will of a society to resist injustice for a time, but it only allows a government to delay its demise, not avoid it. In fact, it is interesting to remark that repression is the leading cause for the collapse of mortal governments throughout the inhabited planets of space.

In principle, most inhabitants on a world administered by a consensus government generally recognize [it] as the highest planetary authority. However, the unanimous treaty of all nations concerned to coexist under the spiritual tutelage of a unique God is always necessary before this administration can be empowered and universally accepted as the legitimate and incontestable *world sovereignty*. And, when an evolving realm has reached this level of political, social and religious unity, it is ready to inaugurate the *Golden Age* of peace, liberty, equality and fraternity among all men. Such a God-conscious community of fraternal mortals is then fully endowed and empowered to create magnificent intellectual and spiritual wonders, far beyond your current level of knowledge and understanding.

The well-nigh total hegemony of secular and imperialistic powers on your earth today resulted mainly from humanity's abject moral and spiritual deficiency. But today, as the activities of the Correcting Time enfold, these oppressive states are facing new formidable challenges. Their reign can no longer be secured by force and deception. They have virtually lost all credibility among the peoples of the planet. Like many previous parasitic and autocratic dynasties, they are increasingly passing away into the oblivion of history. After the year [2012], which marked the end of the solar cycle and the precursor of the new dispensation of enlightenment, world events began to move rather quickly to accelerate their demise. The global awakening movement will take on higher dimensions from now on. Eventually, fewer to no law enforcements will be necessary to ensure order, peace and goodwill among the common people. As they evolve in the knowledge of the Truth of who they are, and become self-realized in God consciousness, men will gradually transcend all their evil tendencies.

Moral thinking and virtuous motivations are the antidotes to the ailments of egoism and animalism. During the future times of true intellectual liberation and spiritual blossoming, the current oppressive global authority exercise by the dark cabal with their subordinates will be forgotten. Many syndicates of sincere spirit-born men and women will voluntarily elect to assume great planetary responsibilities for the common good and welfare of all mankind.

The numerous laws and policies of governments to manage society are, in fact, a clear evidence of their flaws and inefficiency. It is a tangible proof of their lack of creativity and leadership failure. None of the existing governing models on your planet can provide effective solutions to its manifold problems.

Modern Urantians would be wiser and thoughtful in their perception of government by considering [it] as an evolutionary institution to maintain peace, social order, and territorial integrity, but certainly not as a 'reliable' agent to protect and solve their problems.

Society & the Quality of Government

Essentially, the quality of a government usually reflects the collective intellectual, moral and spiritual maturity of the people it represents. The rule is simple. The more thoughtful, imaginative, and ethical a nation is, the more peaceful, tolerant, and honorable she compels her representative leaders to be.

For example, if the incumbent executives of a powerful country should find it easy to invade and militarily occupy a weaker state under false premises of security concerns, that is simply because many of its most influential citizens are in collusion with them, and they fully support the agenda.

The most endowed rulers cannot solve the least significant social problems without the full cooperation of their citizenries. Irrespective of its material resources and the aptitudes of its executives, a government is virtually powerless to efficiently and permanently resolve daunting public issues without the support and participation of society.

The real authority and legitimacy of any representative government mainly derive from the people it represents, not the so-called legal agencies it supposedly controls.

The Impediments of the Secular Empire
Its Future Demise

Secularism—the materialistic, anti-spirituality ideology that encourages separation from God, will duly continue to belittle the higher values of life and impedes humanity's moral progress even during these days of awakening. As long as most humans persist on chasing self-gratifying ambitions, there will be no end to greed, injustice and warfare on earth. A peaceful and equitable social order is simply impossible if men continue to ignore the supreme purpose of their temporary existence, which is to learn and grow in greater consciousness of their connection to all that exist. Irrespective of their current positions on this planet, men should bear in mind that the greatest successes and achievements in worldly endeavors are temporal, and they cannot substitute or replace the transcendent values of a pious life centered in the ideals of spirit, grounded in Truth, and motivated by love and service.

Presently, if the champions of the secular Empire do not improve their policies and seriously change their conduct vis-à-vis humanity, their leadership credibility, which has never been lower, will practically be guttered in the foreseeable future. If there are no signs of concession for real transparency and positive reforms in their system soon, we are afraid that the world will no longer wait idle for things to change.

The global population will eventually take drastic actions themselves. If the despotic rulers remain stubborn and try to stay beyond the dead line of the divine decree for their removal from power, then they shall witness the fury of the greatest worldwide revolution that will ever occur in the history of civilization on this planet.

We understand that from the mortal perspective, often it may appear that these so-called established authorities are irremovable. However, we can assure you that none has ever been allowed to remain another day pass its relevance. Simply put, when the ordained time for any political order has expired as this is recognized on high, absolutely nothing can avert its removal. And it is with pleasure that we declare to you now…if the dark cabal continues to support the use of brute force and fear as control mechanisms to pursuit its diabolical plan for world hegemony, the downfall and the end of the Empire will come even sooner than expected. In fact, the trends of current global events are increasingly indicating such a possibility. Like all previous tyrannies, the final days of this one is certain, and it is approaching more rapidly than was previously thought. As we view this from our vantage, the curtain of deception is closing before the termination of their time mandate.

The Systematic Cynicism of the Cabal
Global Control By Wars & Deception

Throughout the last two centuries, most of the wars fought by the most powerful states on Urantia, either among themselves or against the developing world, were directly at the behest of the secret cabal in complicity with corrupt public officials pursuing their own transnational interests and agendas. None of these brutal military conflicts and illegal occupations was ever truly for a just or noble cause, such as to protect society from some imminent danger or to defend their borders and territories. In fact, they were never about safeguarding anything valuable to society, but to preserve the economic interest and power of the dark cabal.

As we observe this situation from our vantage, the sinister motive of the dark ones in taking control of global society is driven mainly by pride, greed and bigotry, not principle and ideology as such.

How they are able to do this for so long with impunity is a question we believe all Urantians should ask themselves. Quite frankly, the tremendous success of this exclusive cabal in seizing the political and economic systems of virtually all countries on the planet is absolutely astonishing, even from our perspective. This is utterly an unprecedented phenomenon in the history of civilization here. By buying-off, or by co-opting or blackmailing the incumbent leaders of a state, this cartel of vicious overlords has been able to put them totally at odds with the views and needs of their citizenries. The strategic programs and applications to infiltrate and control the destiny of any nation, rich or poor, are shrewd, deceitful and malignant. This is why they are so deeply enshrouded in secrecy and regarded as "classified information." They are exceptional in many respects to any earlier methods of imperialism employed by ancient empires.

The lethality and sophistications of their controlling techniques are incomparable to any previous generation of usurpers and colonizers. Although they usually employ many different strategies to manipulate and galvanize the society that is about to be overtaken, but the key policy to their hegemony is actually quite simple. The principal rule to seize any country's political establishments, economy and natural resources is always to co-opt and transform its leaders into double agents, loyal to some secret fraternity deeply implicated in the evil conspiracy. Corrupting and winning them over to their cause by any possible mean, especially bribery and threats, are the main priority of the dark ones. And those who refuse to comply or object are usually demonized or simply assassinated.

Like many awakened souls among you, we are deeply concerned about this recurring theme here. It is disheartening to witness that in the 21st century war remains the prime mean of alleged "civilized nations" to resolve their differences and sustain their economies. Such a travesty to observe that brute force is still the favorite method of action often used by your rulers to solve transnational problems.

At this crucial moment of growing social awakening and change, it is imperative for these warmongers to reconsider their irrational actions, and stop their evil crusade of death and destruction. They need to cease this global orgy of slaughter and chaos before it is too late to reverse their stride into an abyss of hell.

The Distortion of History
A Necessity to the Cabal's Global Hegemony

Undoubtedly, the falsifications of historical events have played a major role in the ascendancy and current domination of the cabal's global Empire. If it were not for the concealment and distortions of antiquated facts and the effective impacts of misinformation on the human mind, this secular dynasty would not have been possible. Creedal philosophies are always fundamental to the human species. The diverse empirical philosophies of life and disciplines, such as materialism and physics, spring from the consequences of your altered evolution and history.

Basically, except for the family, most of your authoritative institutions, such as government, religion, and the military, emerged from fear and falsified historical accounts. To this day, they are practically, still functioning according to the narrow and distorted visions of ancient ideologues. Though many have been somewhat modified since their inceptions, they were, however, founded upon the erroneous beliefs and traditions of backward generations, and, for the most part, they have never been properly revised or improved.

Clinging to history superficially only impede the evolution of the human spirit, especially if it is adopted as a "guide" to assess and solve current international problems, shape modern institutions, and determine how new generations experience the present world.

May we exhort all stanch conservatives to consider that while you may stabilize society and learn from the failures of your ancestors through history and tradition, they will never improve your moral characters. Bear in mind ladies and gentlemen that "time—i.e., your linear perception of time, is illusory. *Only the Eternal NOW truly exists.* Past and future are but abstractions that your finite mind conceptualizes—they are not *"real"* as such, or in the actual sense of the term.

Technically, past events wield no influence over the future. In some cases, they may contain information and lessons that could be useful and serviceable for the present, but they are utterly irrelevant to impending developments. Conceptually, the future is infinite. We can aim at it forever without ever revisiting or considering the past. In reality, *the present is invariably eternal*; it is where we normally exist. Neither the past nor the future can affect or change it.

Under the domination of a sternly conservative government, no society can experience true democratic values such as freedom and self-determination. The common inclination of some world leaders to take history as guidance in their efforts to solve current problems is a dangerous mistake. The former episodes of political affairs are but mere reflections of obsolete times. Historical events may be similar to recent actualities, but they are never the same. True, past and present situations can be similar, but no two events or circumstances in time are ever identical.

Naturally, it is occasionally profitable to examine history in order to identify and learn from the mistakes as well as the leadership quality of previous executives. But current leaders should not attempt to copy or repeat their performances when addressing existing issues. Their politics and administrative policies must not be taken as guidelines to govern the modern world. Their ruling styles and ideologies represent the cultural values and customs of earlier generations, and thus, are useless to resolve recent dilemmas.

History is certainly valuable and must be preserved for social reminiscence and educational purposes in any progressive society. It should be studied to discover and explore the cultural characteristics of ancient civilizations, to learn the customs and behaviors of past generations. But it is utterly irresponsible to use it in search of solutions for contemporary problems. Essentially, it is certainly polite to show consideration and respect for world leaders who distinguished themselves in some noble and proficient manner—especially those who displayed impressive skills and abilities in the art of leadership during certain decisive moments in history. However, it is utterly unwise to continue to use their philosophies as guidelines for modern governmental policies.

In a progressive society, peace, justice, and the future of the people are always among the primary concerns of a responsible and dutiful government. The continuing existence and growth of any nation strongly depend upon the careful plannings, wise decisions, and thoughtful preparations of its existing leaders for tomorrow's generations. Essentially, the laws of a state are redundant if they are not looking-forward, if they are not designed to improve and facilitate social cooperation between all classes of its citizenry, and if they are not in the interests of its youths.

Humanity, Politics & Government
Their Co-dependence

Because of its close identification with most cultures, politic is, figuratively speaking, a *'dynamic living force'* in practically all countries on your planet—especially in the industrialized and affluent ones. But it is neither indigenous to the human race nor necessarily indispensable to manage and safeguard a successful social order. Though politic is deeply rooted in the diversities of civilization – it is not essentially inherent in man.

Primitive men had no real political culture. Their tribal regulations were totally natural and arbitrary. Though at the earliest stages of cultural evolution, many semi-civilized tribes had already developed several crude forms of authority to govern themselves, the notion of politics, statehood, and representative government were yet unborn in humanity.

Politics, the legal state, and administrative authority are all derivatives of men's ongoing intellectual and sociological evolution. These concepts emerged in the mortal mind during the early days of the second planetary dispensation. But according to our records, and by universe standards, they were really actualized in your 'modern time.' To survive into the future, they must continue to evolve in pace and in accordance with humanity's ongoing developments.

Political dogmatism is quite dangerous to the progress of a country as this can severely reduce its influence, impedes the growth of its institutions, paralyzes its leadership, and perhaps, eventually destroy it as an effective society. Again, every moment is unique in time. No two instances or situations are ever identical. And...labeling does not connote similarities between events either. In your calendars, the days normally carry the same names every week, but they are always different.

Controlled by the dark cabal, the wealthiest and most powerful governments on your planet are practically paralyzed to act for the collective good and welfare of humankind. Many an effort could be made to solve the numerous dangerous situations facing humanity. Problems such as the spread of terrorism, famine, unrests, war, and poverty could be resolved. Yet, little has ever been done earnestly to properly address these urgent issues, much less to solve them. To the contrary, these powers are escalating and exacerbating them. They show no genuine interest in sharing some responsibility to repair the damages. In fact, the reckless and cynical conducts of their conceited rulers only aggravate the impacts of these ills. Considering this irresponsible attitude from the world supposed foremost authorities, it is logical to be concerned about the future of civilization here.

We say honestly, with no intention to frighten you, were not for the Correcting Time programs, which are intended to restore the Creator's will on your sphere, we would probably need to start devising a contingency plan to evacuate your species from the planet in the foreseeable future.

As we perceive the global situation, the two big questions at this moment are: [1] Will humanity ever escape from the domination of the existing totalitarian world order represented by the 'state?' [2] When will you finally free your perceptions from the dark cabal's overarching control system? Most of you cannot readily answer these important questions. However, we on this side can clearly see that you will overcome the challenges and eventually triumph over those few miscreants. Based on our analysis, the one great obstacle that prevents this anticipated event from occurring is the ferocious systematic suppression of society's perception, which must be ultimately set free. You certainly embody the creative powers to emancipate yourselves from the yoke of this corrupt order, but they remain dormant and only as potentials so long they are not willfully activated. This is why the main objective of the dark ones is always to suppress and conceal from you the transcendental knowledge of your true multidimensional Higher Selves.

Political struggle is inherent and persistent in all ideologically divided and morally depraved societies. However, modern men are called to be idealists, tolerant, ethical, and even altruistic. Too often, politicians deliberately misguide and deceive their constituencies with impunity, because they have always been shrewd enough to claim immunity for their services to society while maintaining that politic is utterly an impersonal affair. Even in the so-called law-abiding democracies, the notion that incumbent or ex-officials should be charged and prosecuted if found to have abused their powers or committed crimes during their tenures is vehemently opposed. And worse, although evidently this is a cunning approach to hoist themselves above the law, yet, strangely enough, this pretentious assertion has never been adequately contested or challenged publicly.

While politics and society are indissolubly connected, traditionally, your political executives have rigorously strived to absolve themselves of all blames and responsibilities for their criminal actions. Throughout history, they have always sought to define politics as entirely a collective matter of society. Thus, arguing that politicians and leaders must be protected from the legalities of the law and exempted from prosecution by virtue of the state.

Like nature, politic is a flexible and renewable resource. It is subjected to periodic alterations as a result of ongoing geopolitical shift of episodes in the fabric of global society. Likewise, the agendas and policies of a state may change or vary occasionally depending on the visions and characters of its rulers.

True moralists may be good leaders, but they can hardly be real politicians because their conscience and integrity will always prevent them from applying the ploys and cynicisms of politic. As it exists on this planet today, politic is naturally a bias, precarious and cynical game. Its nature can be improved to serve society earnestly only if those who practice it would surrender their self-seeking ambitions to a comprehensive effort for positive global change and progress.

Presently, the ongoing tensions in geopolitics – primarily the excessive militaristic approach adopted by the potent nations are doing more harm to transnational peace, goodwill, and stability than any other force on your planet.

As we see this, too often, using so-called 'legal institutions,' unscrupulous and self-serving rulers are inclined to manipulate, tyrannize, and subjugate their peoples. One of their most abhorrent misdeeds is the constant brutal effort to undercut dissent and crush all oppositions to their authority.

It is indeed appalling to observe how so many allegedly 'public servants' have never hesitated to employ abusive methods to subdue and silent their would-be rivals - sometimes including their own partisans. When patriotism and militarism are too passionately joined and inflated with political pride, they practically become a menace to the very existence of the society they are supposedly protecting. Always remember, the laws of a government are positive and progressive *only* when they are purposely created in the interests of, and implemented for the common good.

Time or evolution greatly influences the world's political trends. Although humanity continues to evolve slowly, increasingly aspiring to higher and greater achievements, the future however remains absolutely dependent upon the choices, which are made *now* in the ongoing processes of planetary developments. It is indeed very difficult to assess a generation's potential capacity for political, social, economic, and spiritual growth without factoring the abstract element of time.

Being a partisan affair, politic must be viewed and interpreted as an ideological mechanism to preserve some degree of equilibrium between the comprising factions of a given nation. It may also be seen as an active legal mean to ensure dialogues, diplomacy, and concessions between those different groups. Thus, it is not altogether wrong to consider [it] as an impersonal, collective matter. However, remember that politic and human beings are interdependent; the effect of their dynamics is basically mutual. As people strive to direct and influence geopolitics, equally, politics simultaneously affect them and shape the quality of their lives. It even impacts their perceptions, mentalities and behaviors. Indeed, men and politics are profoundly linked in a reciprocal association.

Typical to all species of life, the survival instinct is innate in humankind. But administrative law and order are the technical results of intellectual, social and cultural developments. Society invariably requires some legal regulations to exist and function orderly and effectively. Class-conscious and egoistic mortals simply cannot coexist peacefully or interact harmoniously without appropriate managements under effective law-abiding leaderships.

Nevertheless, none of the existing governmental systems on your planet should be permitted to assume world sovereignty if it does not actually represent all mankind. As an evolving institution, government must recurrently transcend itself if it is to survive indefinitely in the world. There is certainly an ideal type of government for the peoples of Urantia, but such a utopian order cannot be revealed. It must evolve through trials and errors.

However, if we may say this much: throughout the next dispensation, your world will eventually have a supreme ruling administration basing on universal Truth, liberty, equity, and service. Inasmuch as we are conversant with the future, we are pleased by the fact that this excellent council of authority will be established on earth prior to the Ages of Light and Life – way before the will of the Creator completely prevails on your planet. While we are not permitted to reveal the political, social, and economic characteristics of this impending time, but when it occurs, peace and goodwill will permeate all hearts here as the oceans cover the surface of the world.

Usually on this strife-torn planet, people are often betrayed and deceived by their own appointed or elected representative leaders. Political minded Urantians constantly face the harsh reality of duplicity by those invested with authority over them. But this trend shall end in the foreseeable time, for the existing geopolitical order will collapse, and society will undergo drastic changes.

Subsequent to this coming liberation, humanity will be reborn in truth and spirit, and thus, will practically be immune from such deceptions. Though people will continue to live communally and fulfill their social obligations, they will transcend the prejudices of politics. Actually, most of that emancipated generation will know the truth of man's affiliation to the Prime Creator. Yes, your great grandchildren will be certain and profoundly conscious of their relationship to God. They will strive to abide in his eternal Truths while constantly experiencing his loving embrace.

Bear in mind that like God man is also a spirit. If he was not, he would not have been able to invent and experience science, ethics, religion or even politics; nor could he understand their meanings and appreciate their values. Therefore, he could not have evolved or developed a civilization. Secular, materialistic, narrow-minded and atheistic individuals may reject the concept of man's spiritual nature and a universal Creator. But that very incredulous attitude demonstrates the fact of the supermaterial quality and capacity of their minds. Thinking, judging, postulating or negating, etc.. are all psychological exercises that are clearly indicative of spirit and personality presences—two mysterious immortal endowments, which are bestowed upon mankind directly by the Father-Creator Himself.

That mortal man is actually a son of God is a profound cosmic reality which every genuine personality will certainly discover sometime in this life or the next. No finite examination is necessary to prove or confirm such a transcendental Truth. In fact, realizing the truth of your "Sonship with God" is absolutely a spiritual experience. It is possible only through revelation.

Doubting is too often the result of intellectual resistance to spiritual realities. Its antidote is to seek for more and higher Truths. Man should never allow skepticism to rob him of his inalienable cosmic right to know and commune with his universal Maker.

This will end our various commentaries on the principal ideals and purposes of government as a universal institution. We hope that we have shed a new light on this broad and intricate subject for your edification as well as for those who shall peruse these lines in the future. I will now take my leave temporarily for a few days of rest and energetic rejuvenation. Farewell.

Paper 7

Current World Order In Peril

The Destructive Nature of this System of Things

Values of the Three Principal Mind Faculties to Civilization

Celestial Teacher: Abonady ~ Channel: Joseph Elie 10-16-2012

JUST AS THE STRENGTH OF the human body to fight any illness depends upon the condition of its immune system prior to health issues, so does the survival of a civilized social order depends on the state and quality of its institutions to continue to function effectively during hard and challenging times. As the body must be nourished regularly in order to operate and remain alive, a civilization must be infused with new ideals, higher goals, and better functional mechanisms periodically, to maintain its vitality and preserve itself during difficult periods. Civilization is, figuratively speaking, the collective body of the expressions of humanity's endless creative imaginations. It is a manifestation of men's greatest inspirations and aspirations; a vivid demonstration of the results of your intelligent efforts, creativities, passions, and sacrifices. It encompasses all ranges of human ingenuity, pursuits, and ambitions. It is the matrix wherein humanity's diverse potentials for intellectual, social and spiritual growth are exhibited and actualized.

Today, the body of your current 'civilized' global order is badly suffering from numerous life-threatening diseases and infections. From rampant institutional corruptions and militarism to societal conditionings and imperialism, many grave and terrible situations are dangerously menacing to destroy the international fabrics of law and erode the civil liberties that many of your contemporary societies have so recently gained in the last two centuries. Nevertheless, even the most critical problems affecting the ability of this system of things to sustain itself and function adequately are yet to be addressed. In some cases, they are ignored or still unknown. For instance, little to no attention is paid to the fact of the massive erosion of love. The gradual disappearance of rationality and morality civilization has been experiencing for the last several decades, which is a symptom of serious internal afflictions. Your decision makers totally ignore that the rejection of God, the willful ignorance of transcendental Truths coupled with an abject lack of appreciation for life and creation, are actually the main causes behind the ongoing global ills that beset humanity.

The Importance of Unity In Preserving Social Order

As a system that relies on order and stability to function properly, a civilization needs some degree of social unity to survive; and to remain viable and effective, especially during vulnerable times of crises. And, this is absolutely contingent upon the intelligence, wisdom and spiritual maturity of its citizenry. Oppression is the surest mean to the demise of any form, or quality of public representative authority; be it a Republic, a Democracy, a Federation, a Kingdom, or an Empire. No civilization can survive long without the social harmony and union of its constituents— especially its families and communities.

The importance of a people's unity in protecting and preserving the values of civilization is second to nothing. The foundation, strength, efficiency, and integrity of a country are mainly dependent upon the good organization, cooperation, and harmony of its citizens. Mechanistic inventions alone cannot guarantee the continuity of civilization. The lasting existence of a society predominantly depends upon its ability to coordinate its resources to meet any challenge and renew itself according to the changing episodes of time. And, it is incumbent upon each of its members to take responsibility in order to ensure that readiness when necessary. This is absolutely crucial for the preservation of any nation. It's imperative for an organize society to remain active as an integrated and united community in the midst of depressing and challenging circumstances.

The Assault Against Spirituality
Secular Religionists

Since the emergence of the three atheistic philosophies, i.e. materialism, capitalism and secularism as mainstream thinking throughout Urantia—particularly in the Western hemisphere—the dark cabal has increased their assault to corrupt and suppress humanity's spiritual nature. The aim is to further fuel antagonism and social divisions among the races of your world.

They have been deliberately raging a covert but fierce war against God Himself, by purposely imposing an egocentric model of life throughout the world that is fundamentally hostile to His plan for humanity's spiritual development and ascension. The ideals and values of divinity, which add higher meaning and richness to human life were categorically refuted and replaced with a so-called humanistic approach that basically separated modern men from the Creator.

Although many contemporary societies do believe in and worship some deity, nonetheless, as religion is generally viewed and defined on your planet today, nearly all professed religionists hardly ever derive any real spiritual benefit from the experience. Notwithstanding all the confessions and claims about keeping the commandments of their respective creeds, in reality, most modern individuals practice a religion merely to conform to the norms of their cultures. Many ostensibly do it simply to pay tribute to tradition.

To the highly cultured but narrow-minded, self-seeking modern aristocrat, the notion of personal faith in God is a rather ambiguous and unrealistic ideal. It really bears very little to no importance to him. For such a conceited and incredulous soul, religion is primarily a social, not a spiritual affair. Thus, it must be systematically defined, structured, and organized like society itself, in order for it to be practical, sensible, and controllable. Those pessimists who think like that, are seldom sincerely moved by any transcendent influences, which are in and around them. They are not receptive to divinity. Even as they pray and apparently worship a deity, they rarely have genuine personal spiritual experiences.

Generally, the fact is most of the self-proclaimed religious societies on your planet are actually secular, or, at best, purely humanistic. Ever since the unprecedented rise of the misguided scientific revolution in the Western Hemisphere, the newly emerged *system of agnostic thinking* has persistently endeavored to replace the spiritual values that sanctify the human race and add divine meaning to life with speculative abstractions that completely reduce man to a subservient incredulous social automaton. Although this secular movement had already overthrown the ecclesiastic monopoly of the church in the Western world during the Protestant activism more than three centuries ago, its recent absolute domination was firmly established at the dawn of the industrial revolution.

As we've said many times over, the current so-called "free world order," control by the dark cabal, is facing enormous formidable challenges that dangerously threaten its survival. Most are the result of many decades of inept governance, and merciless exploitations of the globe's natural resources to the detriment of the majority of its population.

This system is now reaping the consequences of its own persistent abuses of the earth and its inhabitants under the pretension of a deceitful philosophy of freedom and democracy. But the worse is yet to come, for it shall thoroughly harvest the results of its immoral deeds tenfold. At this moment, its abject lack of humanity and low regards for the peoples of your planet are being clearly exhibited in the excessive use of force and imposition of economic sanctions to subdue them to its demands.

The vainglorious attitudes of its champions coupled with the willful ignorance of its population are primarily causing the degradation and downfall of this imperialistic order. In fact, for many of its headstrong leaders and proud people alike, dialogue and diplomacy are no longer relevant or appropriate methods to press for world cooperation and peace. These bilateral methods of rapprochement between rival nations are refuted as wimpy, ineffective and unnecessary. Military might and technological supremacy are viewed as the main resources to project power and maintain the global hegemony. They have adopted the infamous motto of the Roman Empire, *"We need no friends so long they fear us."* This delusional and narcissistic attitude is extremely dangerous, and it should be of the gravest concern to the whole international community.

Now recent international situations strongly suggest there are serious geopolitical tensions that are steadily brewing among the most powerful states of your world, which could, at any given moment, ignite into World War III. While it would be presumptuous to anticipate such a terrible event definitively, those diplomatic tussles should not be surprising at all. Essentially, world powers simply cannot rub shoulders peacefully unless they are compelled to show allegiance and answer to a unique and greater sovereignty.

Nevertheless, as we've mentioned in previous interactions, the current trends of global events are clear indications that the shameful breakdown of this *ill system of things* is dangerously near. The cabal's days of terror and arbitrary domination are approaching an end. We are convinced that their artificial and depraved organization is now seeing its last days before collapsing. Their political and financial infrastructures are deeply fractured, and they are rapidly approaching their final stage of total disintegration.

Modern men have steadily gravitated to this precarious position by your continuing arrogance, egocentricity, and blind patriotism. Your steadfast refusal to co-exist peacefully and relentless efforts to replace *divinity* with *humanism* and *democracy* are largely responsible for the current dreadful situations you are experiencing. These foolish attitudes have severely retarded and undermined your intellectual, social, and spiritual development.

As for the opposition to God, the evil ones have done all they possibly could to eradicate faith in the collective mentality of your global society. Largely, they have scorned at the concept and belittled the principles by which the diverse cultures of the planet could achieve lasting peaceful and equitable co-existence. In other words, they have categorically refuted the notion of the universal brotherhood of men, and stood against the very plan of the Paradise Father to unite his children on earth.

They have systematically abused the four primary virtues that constitute the foundation upon which stands the edifice of human civilization; which are power, prudence, temperance, and justice. They misused power as a violent and destructive device to inflict pain and sufferings on society.

They show no mercy and exercise no prudence as they treat the vulnerable peoples of the world by defiling their cultures and desecrating their religions.

Their temperance is a ruse; it is totally unreliable. The partiality of their supposed judiciary system has been so often blatantly and disgracefully exposed that it is absurd to call it by that name. But today, at last, the box of their malediction is replete. Woe upon them as the time of their reckoning has arrived, and they must now reap the consequences of their iniquities tenfold.

Today, the most powerful nations on your planet are dangerously embroiled in many petty and serious geo-political predicaments, both among themselves as well as with less-fortunate countries. Most of these troubles are self-inflicted, not necessarily intentionally, but by the ignorance, bigotry, pride and arrogance of their decision makers. Another reason for this is that in the last several decades following the industrial revolution, the sprawling economic growth, scientific and technological progresses of these affluent powers have created such an illusion of invincibility that most of their peoples became complacent and totally indifferent towards other civilizations. Consequently, rather than helping the weaker nations pull themselves up, instead, the dark cabal, using these potent and wealthy states, seized upon the opportunity to extend their reach and ascertain their full-spectrum domination over the world. But they could not have successfully done this without; [a] society's consentment; [b] if these impressive powers were subjected to international regulations.

But currently they are at a loss, being unable to start-off the last necessary scenario that would serve as the ultimate ruse to finalize their nefarious plan for an absolute global government. They are bereft of idea and are growing increasingly desperate, for they erringly, but truly believe it is their God-given right and destiny to rule the world and dispose of humanity as they please. What they essentially desire is unmitigated power without any political accountability or social responsibility. A system of governance, which is so powerful that it surpasses the rank and authority of all other legal representative institutions on the planet. In brief, a power that is answerable to no one but itself, meaning those who are secretly in charge.

If we may reiterate, although this small illegitimate and obscure group of globalists has been in existence for many centuries, but most of the world's inhabitants are yet, unaware of it. Using all kinds of cunning techniques to suppress knowledge, to falsify and manipulate information and cover its tracks, it has been carefully hidden since its inception. But it is now self-evident that the world is at a turning point, and that more must be done immediately to strengthen and maintain their dominance over the international community. Clearly, they realized they must act swiftly to ensure the longevity of their global hegemony.

As we've said before, most of the problematic events and situations that beset your world are deliberately planned or authorized by this little-known cartel of detached globalists. The majority of the earth's inhabitants are manipulated and controlled by this exclusive occult organization through a vast network of force, conditioning and programming – what we infamously call the 'Control System.' With this worldwide power-grid in place, to a great extent, they have hoisted and established themselves as the overlords of your societies, as they have shrewdly infiltrated the government of every country and systematically influenced every culture on the surface of your planet.

Unconcerned, the dark cabal always fully supports any form of government so long it is willing to oppress its people at their request. There is no such thing as international laws, ethics or regulations when it comes to securing their interests and maintain their hegemony over the peoples of your planet.

However, these few notorious individuals may be a group of delusional and callous villains, but they fully understand the relationship between control and power. They know that it would be impossible to achieve their global ambition if they allow any form of social-political movement in the world to unfold freely without their oversights.

Naturally, they view any organized activity that is not under their control, and that empowers people to think and express themselves unconditionally as a significant threat to their agenda. So they strongly support any type of ruling dynasty; be it, a despotic or a democracy, provided it is committed to restraining and subduing its constituencies at their behest, and for their interest. The rationale is: as long as we control its incumbent officials, the nature and quality of a country's political system are irrelevant.

In fact, this exclusive cartel of elitists only supports a government if it can effectively manipulate, tyrannize, and censor its citizens. Because it is exactly by these coercive methods of suppression, backed by the legitimacy of government, they are able to maintain their influences over the world. To them, force and fear are the two underlying pillars upon which stands the edifice of global power. Yes, the possession of sheer might is still regarded as a justification to rule and dominate your species with impunity.

Of all the dire consequences, the machination of their nefarious agenda may cause; the dark ones are the least concerned with collateral damages. This striking apathy to human sufferings is the top-secret that motivates them; it makes it possible for them to destroy millions without any emotional repercussion. It allows them to pursuit their planetary agenda easily and unaffected. Their ability to inflict pain upon humanity through wars, financial tyranny, sanctions, pandemics, etcetera, is extraordinary.

Their illicit behaviors are utterly unbecoming of right-minded human beings. Absence of conscience and with total immunity, they have been able to deliberately engineered world conflicts, wrecked havoc on the environment, plundered the economies of nations, pillaged the natural resources and true wealth of the planet, promoted genocides, controlled the perceptions of the world's population, and much more.

After every major and decisive international event, such as the two previous world wars, the global population was simply told that the political restructuring that followed were done for the common good of all concerned. And that the new order was actually established in the interest of peace for a safer, better and more prosperous world.

No serious investigation was ever conducted to determine the facts, which led to the crisis because they were part of the cabal's agenda to centralize and consolidate power globally. For many decades, this small group of elitists has secretly manipulated world affairs designedly to fulfill their nefarious ambitions of planetary dominance. Through practically all the popular social institutions of the civilize world, they've established a vast network of loyal and committed agencies to unfold their evil agenda.

However, they are themselves virtually invisible on the international scene as they exert influence in the shadow through their institutional proxies such as governments, science, education, religion, entertainment, and so forth. They wield great power over humanity, and yet their names, societal statuses, let alone their activities have never been disclosed or discussed publicly. They perform unilaterally above all laws of civilization.

Their influences over the political, social, and economic spheres of the world are virtually universal and absolute. They have shrewdly managed to evade international justice thus far, and there exist today no lawful court in the world that would even consider prosecuting these extraordinary criminals. In fact, they are the sponsors of many of these so-called international courts and humanitarian organizations. Essentially, this highly secretive cartel of arrogant, larger-than-life opportunists is an enigma to most of the global community. And this is for a good reason. Secret is the lifeline of their hegemony. The effort to remain anonymous on the world stage is not only an integral part, but arguably, the most important aspect of the whole scheme. Otherwise, it would not have been possible to conquer the world and tyrannize its peoples as they've done without an effective program of mass disinformation enshrouded in secrecy.

But today, they are at a serious juncture where the very existence of their control system is severely threatened. As we've mentioned many times before throughout our communications, the cabal's global dynasty is going through a pivotal moment at this time; all indicates that it is gradually fading into history. The sudden shifts that are occurring in the world's political, social and economic structures are causing a lot of unexpected tensions that are extremely harmful to their agenda. Presently, they are bereft of ideas as to how to regain and keep their power; and all of their efforts are absolutely in vain at this point.

In their calculations, many geopolitical developments in the past two decades or so are now greatly threatening to thwart their plan for the world. In effect, the rapid modernizations of some Asiatic countries, especially in the scientific, educational, and military spheres, were not exactly anticipated. These events are viewed as serious challenges that must be dealt with. Much of the progresses made by these troubling and stubborn nations have been detrimental to their strategy. The elitists have realized that unless they apply their most horrible technique of suppression, which is global warfare, sooner or later, they will not be able to maintain their global hegemony. Consequently, out of desperation, preparations are being made at this moment in anticipation of an unprecedented dramatic eventuality, which will serve as a pretext to restructure the global mechanisms of power by formulating new international regulations, and set fresh legal standards for what they've already labeled as a "New World Order."

The classified agenda of the vicious elite to lord it over humanity using force, duplicity, and terror should not be surprising to any objective and pensive thinker. Naturally, when all the official, social, and financial institutions of a nation are secretly controlled and dominated by private, unelected individuals immune from its laws, inevitably the public will be marginalized, and so-called "legal authority" will rapidly become a tool of suppression and tyranny. The privatization of the government, military, financial, and industrial organizations of a state is the perfect formula to strip its people of all political rights and sovereignty. It is the most efficient mean by which to effectively disenfranchise a republic and destroy its constitution.

The Survival of Civilization
Its Dependence on the Three Key Mental Faculties

Urantia's current civilizations are the results of several millennia of man's intellectual, technical, social, and spiritual development. Generally, during the early stages of evolution on any mortal inhabited world in this universe, civilization is usually a finite experiment. However, a realm must attain global peace and sustainability first, before it can be ready to enter the Ages of Light and Life. No matter their level of achievements, all mortal societies remain vulnerable to the fluctuations of time, and thus, susceptible to its laws of causes and effects. Essentially, the survival and continuity of any sòcial order predominantly rest upon the steady coordination and the harmonious function of the *three fundamental cosmic endowments of the human mind*, i.e.:

- *Causality:* knowledge – the intellectual quest for the First Cause of creation; of universal facts and material realities.

- *Morality:* conscience – the intrinsic sense of right and wrong.

- *Spirituality*: faith—loyalty and devotion to God; love and service to humanity.

Civilizations are always unstable, mainly because they are not cosmic realizations, but these three faculties of the mortal mind are. Man is endowed with the creative ability to invent science, appreciates ethics and seeks Truth, which together, constitute the fundamental values of a civilize society. But humans can hardly hope to create the ideal civilization yet, until you have fully mastered the art of associating, coordinating and harmonizing these inherent gifts of your physical intellects.

Civilizations may collapse, but those deep-seated mental faculties will always survive their crash. Although they form the basis of human psychology, to actually and effectively coordinate them is usually an arduous evolutionary process.

As a civilization advance, to safeguard and preserve its integrity, its leadership must make certain that these three different faculties are fully balanced and coordinated. If a social order is founded upon their harmony, be it in a given country, continent or internationally, then it is secured, stabilized and its citizenries will definitely prosper. But, if in the contrary, they are not paralleled or are set in oppositions, troubles, tyrannies, wars and despairs will ensue.

Humans are essentially gregarious creatures. Most of you profoundly crave social association. You are endowed with a relative intelligence, which enables you to create your representative institutions for public services; to pursuit education, to guarantee security, liberty and civil cooperation. One of the prime moral duties of the state is to provide the means by which its citizens can easily cooperate to improve their associations in the three major and leading fields of human culture: i.e., science, ethics and religion.

By virtue of these basic cerebral endowments, mortal men are fully capable of producing a complex and sophisticated social order, but its survival and continuing existence is conditional upon their wisdom to harmonize and maintain them in equilibrium. Consequently, the sustainability of civilization is something you must unfortunately learn progressively through trials, errors and, sometimes, tribulations. Civilization is not a planetary coincidence, nor is it the product of a technical universe. It is instead an evolutionary realization of man using the three constitutive faculties of his mind— which are causality, morality and spirituality.

The future of the current world order is obviously bleak. But this is not necessarily because of the ever-present threats of warfare between disputing superpowers, persistent global unrests, or economic upheavals. Rather, this gloomy prospect is due to modern men's abject failure to harmonize these essential mind gifts. That is, in reality, the gravest danger to this global structure of authority; and this will eventually cause its demise. Believe it or not, all other pressing geopolitical problems are secondary in their impacts to the decline of this system of thing.

Presently, Urantia is facing several dangerous challenges that are potentially capable of destabilizing or even destroying its current international order. Men's intellectual genius, wisdom, and creative imagination to successfully govern themselves and co-exist peacefully are rapidly exhausting because of excessive misuse of force and irresponsible managements of headstrong and arrogant politicians. The foolish, uncompromising hierarchical leadership of secularism has plunged the world into chaos and desolation.

Warfare is almost unavoidable on the inhabited worlds during their early stages of evolution, including the normal ones. However, on a spiritually isolated planet like your earth, these primitive conflicts among the human races are much more frequent and lethal. Hence, they pose a greater menace to civilization.

One of the most damaging sociological errors of the Western World, particularly from the mid 16th century, was the total embracement of the Godless philosophy of secularism that ushered society into a vain, apathetic, trendy, and immoral paradigm. Consequently, a novel mindset of irreverence, violence, cupidity, corruption, and atheism materialized from that misguided social revolution, and has ever since totally dominated the hemisphere. True, Western societies were not necessarily free of those shortcomings prior to that revolution, but the unruliness of secularism coupled with the atheistic science of Darwinism—which were strengthen in the 50s and culminated in the 70s—were exceedingly intensified by the new materialistic rationale that was established at the dawn of the industrial revolution. This fresh mindset not only rejected but *ignored* the relevance of God or spirituality in all human affairs.

Nowadays, most American and European societies are more or less entirely secular, while many Asian nations are rapidly embracing this egoistic and pessimistic attitude of independence from the Creator. This view evidently support and exalts the idea that man doesn't need spiritual guidance. Beware! This attitude is silly; it is actually the very cause of Urantia's many overbearing troubles, and if it is allowed to flourish outlandishly, it will provoke enormous problems beyond human capacity and understanding to resolve. In effect, this thoughtless position of isolation from divinity is the most critical spiritual issue of your time. It has plunged your world into extreme confusions and chaos. Nevertheless, the negative trends this outlook has created could be easily stopped if men simply muster their moral courage and submit themselves to the leading of their indwelling Mighty I' AM Presence. This is why we honestly believe that the programs of the Correcting Time must be rigorously propagated by all real *Jesusonians* for the spiritual rebirth of Christ Michael's genuine teachings as they are focalized in his spirit that permeates the hearts of all his children on earth.

Throughout history, men have committed many faux-pas that seriously affected and hindered your planetary development. However, today's highly conceited materialistic view of total separation from God and complete reliance on secularism is the worse of them all. For it is the most detrimental to your spiritual progress. By all previous accounts, this is the greatest distortion of Truth the human spirit has ever encountered since the dawn of civilization here.

After all, it is clear to us that the lavishness, the exorbitant lifestyle and excesses of modern society, promote by this self-exalted philosophy, while apparently suggest great prosperity, are in essence keeping man from tapping into the reality of his Higher Self – his legitimate cosmic identity—his indwelt God Fragment.

We have conveyed quite enough information on our topics this evening. I'm delighted once again for your diligence and steadfast cooperation. As we continue to move forward with this co-creative endeavor, much remain to be done to successfully usher the world into the next approaching era. We anticipate for our transmissions to take new heights and dimensions in the few weeks and months ahead. There are an array of different issues that need to be addressed and are yet to be discussed, which are absolutely relevant to the present development of the Correcting Time upon your sphere. Nonetheless, since you've asked to continue with the subject of government, we will gladly accommodate your request and provide more information on that subject in our next session. I will now take my leave until we fuse our energies again for another transmission. Please be patient! Gradually, we are conceiving and assembling the bulk of information needed to complete this joint assignment. Keep anchoring the light dear one, good afternoon.

Paper 8

The Universality Of Government

ITS EVOLUTIONARY NATURE, FLAWS, AND LIMITATIONS

The Obstacles to World Peace & the Futility of Warfare

Celestial Teacher: Abonaly ~ Channel: Joseph Elie 10-21-2012

GENERALLY, GOVERNMENT—WHETHER ON THE mortal or celestial realms—is a reality in all the seven finite superuniverses, which constitute the aggregate of all the existing evolutionary creations of time and space. It is literally true that the universe of Nebadon, like all others, is wisely administered by spirit-personalities, quite similarly to how such arrangements are made on your planet. But it is needless to say that the quality of the universe's administration infinitely surpasses the crude governing institutions of a spiritually backward and politically maladjusted world such as Urantia. In fact, the divine laws and wisdom by which the affairs of a universe are governed are virtually absolute, and well nigh perfect. They are essentially above all mortal criticisms, for they transcend even the ideal administrative orders of the enlightened worlds.

Normally, representative government—be it autocratic, theocratic, or democratic—is usually the institution that rules and regulates the affairs of an evolutionary world after its inhabitants have evolved from tribalism to statehood. In principle, as we mentioned in Paper 6, the type and quality of any government always reflect the intelligence, the ethical and the spiritual maturity of the *people* it represents. Therefore, the characteristics and performances of government are dissimilar on every life-supporting sphere. On some very ancient and exceptionally advance planets, it borders near perfection. Thus, in comparison to these enlightened realms, its overall quality as exists on your earth today, resembles the primitive governing orders on a normal inhabited world.

Statehood is an evolutionary realization, but representative government is a consequence of progressive civilization. The need for some form of social order is inherent in the human species, but authoritarian leadership is not.

Just as the mortal mind cannot function without thoughts and awareness, true government is organically founded on the *rule of law and justice*. To be equitable, it must operate in accordance with the highest values of society. Remember, human laws are not divine decrees. Thus, a state should never be dogmatically fixated on its supposed legal ideological conventions if the intellectual and social progresses of its people are to continue. The legalities and values of any nation must be revised periodically, or when necessary, sometimes abolished and replace with new ones to foster and accommodate the continuing progress of successive generations. Arbitrary authority should never be imposed on thinking people under the yoke of tradition or the law. All truth seekers must be allowed to pursuit knowledge and wisdom unhindered, for they should always endeavor to transcend the past and outshine its political, socioeconomic and religious conditions. Government is a creative achievement of the human mind; it should never be utilized as a tool to oppress and subdue man's spirit under any circumstances. Though it must protect the vital interests of society, nonetheless, to be legitimate and to remain true to its trust, government must never challenge or become an obstacle to the development and progress of the people.

Naturally, the policies and deeds of any country vis-à-vis the rest of the world always reflect the level of intelligence and wisdom of its leaders. Fundamentally, the degree of influence of a state over others is determined by the quality of its administrators and citizenry.

To some extent, like any perceptive individual, sometimes imaginative and sagacious leaders can visualize or even reliably predict the future. One may develop this special faculty by keen observations, analyses, and assessments of current global trends. But irrespective of their mental aptitudes, dubious politicians can never anticipate forthcoming events precisely, nor can they really control the course of geopolitical developments. Empirical examinations of history and recent actualities do not necessarily yield factual insights on potential probabilities.

Unfortunately, in its present manifested form on earth, government is an arbitrary system of authority, which is utilized by a detached elite minority as a tool to subjugate and dominate the global population. From the tribe to the state, the institution of government has gradually evolved throughout Urantia's history. It attained the continental level recently, and presently it is going through even more drastic transformations. Although your planet's inhabitants are yet to establish an official world government, but, for several decades now, the dark ones have taken vital actions and significant steps in that direction. And, despite enormous challenges confronting this 'Big Idea,' considerable strides have been made in that respect; such as the creation of the United Nations, [UN] which is basically tantamount to a centralized planetary administration. Although this organization, the second of its kind, which is a precursor to global governance, is yet to be structured fairly, or fully legitimized and empowered by humanity, but already, the diverse nations of Urantia are learning to solve their differences through a mechanism that encourages peaceful cooperation, solidarity, and shared sovereignty. The main obstacles preventing their success in this extraordinary enterprise are: 1] *lack of political will; 2] absence of mutual trust; 3] abject moral and spiritual poverty.*

Essentially, government, may or may not control all the public and private establishments of a state, but it usually exerts the greatest authority over it. It systematically determines the pace and degree of a country's development and achievements, for it creates and enforces its laws, oversees and regulates the operations of its military forces and civil associations.

On your world today, a government is considered to be good and positive, if it is democratic, progressive, and respect its social obligations, such as protecting, educating, and defending the interests of its citizenry. However, even with such impressive track record, the best administrations here are not yet the ideal human government. The nature of government is of little importance so long it responds to its basic duties, and creates opportunities for ongoing progress. A nation's overall development practically depends on four major things, which an ideal government must provide: liberty, security, education and the peaceful cooperation between all of its public and private institutions.

Unfortunately, the legacies of the Lucifer rebellion have so badly affected condition on your sphere, that achieving world peace under the auspices of an ideal government has never been possible throughout the long and unpleasant history of your kind. But today, rest assured, sooner than later, the finest type of representative authority shall ultimately emerge here. Yes, looking into the possible future of Urantia from our side, a highly tolerant and transparent planetary administration that will permanently guarantee peace, justice, cooperation, and sovereignty to all mankind will definitely replace the present corrupt and disappearing ruling system. As we've said, there does exist an ideal form of social representative order for the evolving worlds of space. But it cannot be enforced upon a race; it must evolve progressively in time.

When you think about world peace, you should also consider the many obstacles that are preventing the nations from realizing this utopia. Your planet is a vast network of different countries with diverse value systems, languages, cultures, and histories. Each has deep-seated national pride and objectives, and, among the most powerful ones, international agendas. Reconciling their differences through peaceful means is obviously not an easy task. Hence, steadfast multilateral dialogues, cultural exchanges, and fair socioeconomic transactions between them are critical to direct such a variety of dissimilar peoples toward lasting peace and mutual trust. It is very imprudent and irresponsible for a state, regardless of its preeminence, to believe that it can unilaterally contain and dominate the rest of the world indefinitely for its own profits and interests. Irrespective of its preponderance and might, no country can single-handedly protect itself and guarantees the security of its people from all foreign threats without the cooperation of others. Alone, no nation will ever be immune from all international hazards unless all nations unanimously consent to ratify a global resolution for peaceful and harmonious co-existence.

But alas, men have been endeared to the narrow concept of nationalism for so long, that most are profoundly inclined to support the fallacious, self-exalting ideology of unilateralism — autonomous and isolated sovereignty. As we view this situation from our vintage, before an international consensus is reached through open and sincere dialogues among all the nations; global peace will remain an unfeasible idea in the consciousness of your species. In a progressive social order, it is utterly immature to rely solely on military forces for security, just as it is equally immoral for a powerful minority to utilize its political and economic influences to buy-off government and sway over the majority with impunity.

The true representative government is a dutiful public service institution. Its edicts do not have to be enforced upon the people for them to recognize its legitimacy and voluntarily cooperate with it. A noble leadership unfailingly guides a country peacefully through intelligent actions and wise management. When the principles of government are grounded in Truth and justice, it effectively reign by virtue of its ability to unite its citizenries for harmonious and mutually beneficial associations. Although they can be physically harnessed and utilized for different purposes, but essentially, power and law, are not necessarily human derivatives. They spring from God—their absolute cause and origin. Irrespective of their myriad forms of expression, fundamentally, they are, and they will always remain–energy. *Everything is energy.* Simply put, this is why no men-made social order can long survive the test of time if its ideologies and laws are not in keeping with the values of divinity, such as Truth, justice, peace, equality and fraternity.

Unchecked and unrestrained governmental power over a society is extremely dangerous to peace and detrimental to the progress of civilization. Viewed from our perspective, as it is exercised by most of your world leaders today, authority is virtually always a politically charged phenomenon of selfish imaginations; a mundane exaltation of localized intellects; a crude attempt to devise a viable social order by apathetic and conceited mortals. The sources of such mediocre and self-serving leaderships are neither divine nor cosmic; and thus, they are transient, unreliable, and worst, fundamentally destructive.

Since the emergence of culture and civilization, all the governing systems that were ever designed upon your world have been registered and catalogued in the archives of Satania, but only those that depict the courage, sagacity, devotion, loyalty, and the bravery of man's spirit are meaningful and valuable, and are thus, recognized on the higher dimensions of the universe. Too often, what is described as government authority on your planet is a rough exhibition of arbitrary force, which is ordinarily exercised by questionable characters with inflated and pride-intoxicated egos. This crude model of leadership is absolutely inimical to the spirit of freedom and liberty; it can only be utilized to oppress, subdue, and dominate society, for it is entirely Luciferian - ungodly. This is why it has caused so much pain and sufferings to humanity for generations.

Nevertheless, as we've said, during the advance eras of spiritual enlightenment, the ideal government of mankind shall emerge. Yes, there is indeed a *Golden Age* of universal peace and goodwill for every evolving world, even those that were quarantined because of rebellion, including earth.

Representative government does not necessarily disappear during the advance epochs on an inhabited world. Instead, normally, it expends from state and regional, to continental and international sovereignty. On the more progressive planets, it eventually becomes universal, ruling by the unanimous consent of the inhabitants with supreme authority over all global affairs. On these highly-developed life-kingdoms of unique sovereignty, there are no military institutions. In the future, when Urantia's legitimate government finally appears, it will be accepted unanimously by all its peoples, and it will function under the guidance of the most qualified administrators. Lawyers and economists will be obsolete. The leaders in the fields of science, philosophy, and spirituality, who are distinguished for their remarkable intellectual achievements and selfless services to humanity, will rule the earth.

Besides revealing God to the inhabitants of an evolving world, Truth always enhances mortal culture by refining ethics, expanding philosophy, elucidating science, and enlightening religion. Under the guidance of a leadership founded on truthful values, much of the energy and resources allocate to solve your world's problems now will be utilized to uplift and enrich its peoples. Politics may generate new ideas and even advocate progressive changes, but it cannot improve man's moral character. Genuine ethical progress is always the result of man's personal efforts together with the inner influences of his Higher Self. Thus, it is foolish of your decision-makers to continue to spend so many resources trying to safeguard a material system of authority while completely ignoring the spiritual powers of humanity. It is not surprising that this attitude has provoked so much conflicts, disappointments, evil and failures.

Throughout this century, the governments on your planet will gradually be divested of their current negative characteristics;

such as militarism, impunity, and nationalism. They will slowly but surely advance toward a more positive and idealistic age of global peace and cooperation, which will precede the opening of the wonderful dispensation of love and fellowship. Government will never completely disappear in your world, even during the remote ages of Light and Life. But its quality will consistently change to accommodate the progressive developments of every consecutive generation. As men continue to evolve morally and spiritually, society will become more and more pacific, intelligent and wise. Consequently, militarism will become obsolete as nationalism will no longer constitute a barrier to peace and global associations. Intolerance, hostility, and violence are animalistic behaviors, and thus, have no place in a Truth enlightened society of God-conscious personalities. Therefore, during these times ahead, warfare will be abolished as a technique to resolve transnational disagreements. Already, some of your decision makers are realizing that *"war is always the ultimate result of the problem, but never a part of its solution."*

As we mentioned at the onset of this Paper, in the universes of time, irrespective of the general condition on a life-planet, subsequent to the emergence of statehood, government is usually the legal institution that regulates and administers the affairs of its inhabitants. Traditionally, upon the arrival of such an age on a normal and sin-free world, the "rule of law" invariably prevails in virtually all societal relationships. However, on the worlds isolated because of sin, such as Urantia, this is not always the case. In contrast to the realms that were never touched by rebellion, for ages, these strife-torn and evil-stricken planets are often ruled by brutal monarchs, dictators, unscrupulous politicians, military strongmen, bankers, industrialists, or worst.

However, although governments on the normal worlds may be superior to their less advance counterparts, but they are by no mean, idyllic or perfect. Prior to the era of *global peace and unity*, thus far, no inhabited evolving planet in the universe of Nebadon, has ever been able to develop the ideal representative government as it is portrayed in the autonomous and superlative administration of the Melkisedeks. In fact, even the highest types of mortal governments on the advance worlds have never successfully demonstrated to be effectively capable of securing and assuring the continuing survival, security, and stability of planetary civilization.

On the inhabited planets of time, hierarchical authority is usually necessary to regulate the affairs of early and segregated mortal societies. However, this model of order is always a transient experience in the evolutionary histories of global leadership and sovereignty. Truly modern and progressive worlds are ruled by a single planetary administration - the supreme council of authority in which resigns all final jurisdictions concerning the welfare and security of the entire world. Though government is always essential for peace and security in the early stages of cultural evolution on any given life-planet, it is not however indispensable to preserve civilization during the advance ages of spiritual enlightenment. Thoughtful and wise statesmen may contribute to the ongoing efforts of idealists to upgrade and refine the fabrics of society, but no political genius can improve the moral character of humanity.

Like government, race and nation are also universal realities. They exist on all mortal inhabited worlds, especially during the early epochs of planetary evolution. Race is always biologically blended and unified, but the demographics of nation vary extensively on each evolving planet. Nation is usually, but not always, a group of mortals of similar racial, cultural, political, and often religious identities. It is a collective of different types of human beings who, due to mutual circumstances, are gradually learning to appease their differences through group activities and shared achievements.

Technically, a country's representative government is connected and beholden to its people mainly by the *established foundational law* of the land. On your planet, this is commonly referred to as a *"Constitution."* The legal canons of a state essentially determine the quality of its policies, and define the nature of its public relationships. Consequently, if its constitutional directives are not supportive of an egalitarian society, then, inevitably, except for their enforcers, those who swear allegiances to them are bound to suffer.

This is blatantly demonstrated in the current transnational socioeconomic structure widely known as 'globalization', a term which is understood quite differently among the exclusive members of the cabal. Obviously, vast numbers of people around the world are suffering severely because of the unfair regulations and shady actions of this order. The so-called 'international laws of commerce' [Maritime admiralty laws] decided by the champions of this system have certainly facilitated a few to reap fortunes rather quickly to the detriment of the rest of humanity.

The small minority that has accumulated vast assets quite naturally praise this global system as a noble power that promotes peace and prosperity. But for the rest of humanity, it has been rather a nightmare. In fact, most Urantians now regard this feudal dynasty of extortion and exploitation, which egg on greed, cruelty, and slavery, for what it truly is. There are major concerns that it has all but devastated the natural environment, even among those who profit from its existence. Presently, there is little doubt in most societies that this is a parasitic system that was designed to allow a few to plunder the resources of your planet and left the vast majority of its inhabitants destitute.

The miscreants who designed this system acts supremely above all international laws. They conduct their activities fully secluded from any public scrutiny or supervision. They don't play by the rules as they require the rest of you to do. They are well protected and immune from any legal prosecution. Their political agents–namely the 'leaders' of the world's biggest economies— always claim that everything is sound, equitable, independent, and transparent. But in reality, no government can function without violating the most basic liberties of an egalitarian society under this parasitical and demonic order. Its criterions—which were mainly designed to serve the interests of the owners—profoundly and flagrantly violate the *Golden Rules* of humanity, which are the moral foundation for a just, fair, tolerant, and equitable world.

Theoretically, it is believed that the more civilize and ethical a nation is the more transparent and democratic it compels its representative government to be. But in reality, that is not always the case. The social and scientific progresses of a country do not necessarily expand the spiritual consciousness of its citizenry. Regardless of the level of a society's morality and ingenuity, nothing guarantees the survival of freedom and democracy unless the people remain in perpetual vigilance to safeguard their sovereignty. And…understandably, this is not an easy task on this realm, for the dark ones have instilled too much fear in the collective mind of your world. Thus, it requires a lot of courage to investigate their satanic activities, let alone bringing them to justice.

Public opinions may and do sometimes play a significant role in determining the governmental policies of a country. But the people's voice has been mainly treated as a tool to grab power since time immemorial here; it is desirable by politicians only when it is politically convenient, or when it favors the interests and suits the agendas of their overlords.

The citizens of your world's 'modern democracies' are instructed and conditioned to believe in the electoral processes. They are taught that they choose their leaders through 'free, fair, and popular elections.' To convince them and secure their trust in the system, 'monitoring organizations' are appointed to verify the results and report frauds. But in fact, truly free and fair election is a very rare case in the history of any nation on your planet. Traditionally, the art of governing has always been regarded and treated as the exclusive privilege of a few bloodlines that are ordinarily classified as the 'ruling class,' such as your self-appointed royal dynasties. Those supposedly 'anointed ones' are usually from affluent and powerful families that are practically disconnected from the public they rule over. Only occasionally some nations have elected conscientious individuals of humble ancestries who indeed advocated and represented the common peoples' aspirations. However, despite the rarity of this, the dark cabal has never allowed those sincere leaders to succeed.

Irrespective of their claims and pledges, the main goal of the governments under the control of the dark cabal is always to gain more power, not lasting peace, or international cooperation. Their principal objectives are to safeguard their authority and expand their sphere of influence. As the coalition that constitutes the central nerve of the control system, these states act indiscriminately, with absolute impunity, in total disregard of all consequences to humanity. Regardless of the severity of the crises society must face because of their reckless decisions and failures, everything is always fine and normal; so long they are in command.

Government is indeed a universal actuality, but if it is not created by, answerable to, and functions to fulfill the aspirations of the people it represents, it can be a dangerous tool of tyranny in the hands of a criminal oligarchy. Most souls on this planet know too well the accuracy of this statement, for that has been the case since time immemorial here. But today, you are called to split with the past, to develop a greater consciousness and expand the meaning of your existence. The immediate task at hand is to correct your global order by changing the quality of your current planetary leadership. It should not be a surprise to anyone that there is so much cry-out for social justice and equality in virtually all 'states' on the planet now. To us, this is a long-overdue phenomenon. We praise your courage and echo your desire to be finally free from the evil ones. This is actually the main goal of Christ Michael's Correcting Time Plan for this world, and we are honored and delighted to be of service here, working closely in collaboration with our devoted human allies to bring about the ideal condition for the formation of your novel planetary socioeconomic structure, and eventually, your new earth.

When we observe it from our vintage, Urantia's overall circumstances—be they political, social, or economic, are largely determined by the character and actions of human leadership. Thus, we deem it essential to cover this topic as the final Paper to conclude the first part of this manuscript with your assistance as our channel.

Accordingly, I shall prompt you in due time to commence our next session for the ninth and last transmission that will complete this phase of the book. Until then, be of good sheer, and keep the flare of truth lit and shining. Thank you for your kind attention. Good afternoon.

Paper 9

The Future Of Human Leadership

THE PERILOUS FATE OF THIS SYSTEM OF THINGS

A Confused World of 'Modernism' Mixed with Barbarism

Celestial Teacher: Abbonaldy – Channel: Joseph Eke 10-25-2012

FOR THOUSANDS OF YEARS SINCE the emergence of culture on Urantia, humankind has been experimenting with various systems of government and models of institutions in search for solutions to the world's many complex and diverse problems. But have men found the solutions, or are the problems getting more serious and difficult to solve every day?

Since the dawn of the industrial revolution in the mid 19th century, those who presided over the industries and finances of the imperial states have systematically exploited the world's natural resources to the detriment and ruination of the vulnerable ones. They plundered their economies, destroyed their livelihood, seized their lands, divided their peoples, and worst, more than often, enslaved them. They shrewdly established a complex international network combining political, social, financial and military forces that allow them to interfere in the internal affairs of any nation and control its government. They have committed countless gross atrocities against humanity, and purposely damaged the global environment with impunity, for there is practically no truly independent and credible judiciary court system in the world to prosecute such notorious and powerful criminals. They have brutally accumulated and generated enormous fortunes for themselves while their insatiable greed and ferocity continue to impoverish and ruin the globe.

Throughout the 20th century, economic covetousness, wars, and industrial recklessness were responsible for great disasters that not only claimed millions of victims but also degraded the natural environment, often to incalculable limits. Disguised under the name of development and modernization, the dark ones simply continue to destroy the earth and enslave its inhabitants. They are deliberately weakening the ecosystems of the planet in a constant mad-dash pursuit for wealth, power, and glory—totally unmoved by the adverse consequences they cause to the global population.

The emergence of modernism brought many new political difficulties with more complex socioeconomic challenges to human society. For example, although many of your 'advance countries' have apparently, successfully created some viable administrative and representative institutions, yet, even such supposedly 'law abiding states' are unable to stop the continuation of widespread violations of human rights—their own or around the world. In fact, these exclusive clubs of self-styled 'democracies,' which claim to be the 'beacon of justice and freedom', have completely failed to uphold the values for which they purportedly stand. They have been corrupted under the spell of the dark ones. They are morally bankrupt and unsalvageable, thus incapable of arresting the massive abuses and crimes against humanity, or uphold the basic principles that protect moral decency and dignity on the planet. Essentially, the principal ideals, beliefs and visions upon which these states were allegedly founded no longer influence their leaderships. They have practically disappeared from their political and social fabrics. For instance, despite the many legislations formulated to prevent slavery, it is estimated today that around the world more than half of a billion people are forced to work under conditions that amount to abject slavery.

Main Causes of Human Leadership Failure

-Why has human leadership failed so badly to achieve the fundamental and universal aspirations of mankind; such as peace, justice and equality?

Well, theoretically, there are certainly diverse answers to this question; it all depends on one's perception on the matter. But we choose to consider the following two observations:

- [1] Irrespective of inherent faculties and talents, men are significantly limited in various domains of character and aptitudes. Consequently, whatever type of representative government or form of leadership they may institute automatically reflects those limitations.

- [2] A wise leadership always encourages unity and fosters cooperation; it is categorically inimical to corruption, bribery and intolerance. It knows that the supreme duty of any respectable representative government is to serve and protect society; any attempt to deviate [it] from these noble obligations is a severe and flagrant violation to the sovereignty of the law, and constitutes a treasonous act.

As an intelligent evolving animal, man is naturally anxious and bellicose. He does not organically recognize the spirit of *peace and love* within himself. Therefore, unless he is enlightened intellectually and spiritually, he is, likewise, unable to perceive and appreciate that holy presence in his fellow kind.

The highly delusional and vainglorious modern potentate does not relish ruling over his subordinates with mercy and kindness. Because of their deeply rooted personal insecurities mixed with many superiority complexes, coupled with their aggressive tendency to oppress and tyrannize others, most human rulers find it hard to govern their people justly and fairly, much less to love them.

Challenges to World Peace

World peace will remain a fantastic utopian ideal on your planet until there is an international consensus to abolish warfare, adopt a global language, and transcend the self-deluded belief of a 'chosen people.' To commence this great initiative, there need to be first a resolution forbidden all military hostilities between any two or more states. Moreover, conscientious efforts must be made to consolidate the capabilities of all nations to ensure sustaining and lasting harmonious international co-existence. As we view it from our vantage, most Urantians would willingly relinquish the legendary concept of isolated national sovereignty to a single planetary government if these revolutionary changes do occur; and if they are fully respected and observed by all countries, without exception.

Simply stated, from our perspective, the legitimacy to lead and make decisions on behalf of a country by any government invariably lies in its people. *Cosmically, the human personality is a sovereign entity; its rights to self-determination are inalienable and absolute. The cabal's success relies on its continuing suppression of this universal truth. But today the control system is failing, for it is known throughout all creations that the power to rule and govern is always inherent in the people!*

Naturally, the political, sociological and economic conditions of Urantia's diverse countries are indeed quite different. But all of them are confronted and affected by scores of common global problems; such as crime, greed, intolerance, unrests, chauvinism, injustice, violence, delinquency, immorality, racism, poverty, diseases, corruptions, dysfunctional politics, etcetera. These ills conversely provoke many other dilemmas, which together overwhelm your institutions and consequently prevent real progress. For example, despite that today is widely considered as the most prosperous epoch in the history of humanity, poverty, pandemics, misery and despair are still rampant global phenomena with no feasible end in sight. In various regions, hundreds of millions of people are totally destitute, and in most cases, the worse affected victims are completely abandoned and forgotten.

The modern industrial revolution also precipitated an excessive abuse of nature—particularly by the most heavily urbanized countries. At the onset of this technical age, for these states, the principal motivation and the bottom-line of commerce became accumulation and consolidation of wealth and power; augment the volume of their GDPs; accelerate transnational exploitations and increase domestic consumptions. Presently, even amidst a severe global recession with the potential to become a global depression, the amount of resources consumed daily by these powers is projected to continue to increase annually.

True, some technological inventions have significantly increased the capacity and proficiency of society to manage and control its regular affairs. However, these ambitious projects supported by the dark cabal are usually pride-driven and self-serving. They are executed irresponsibly to the detriment of ethics and the natural environment, which consequently increases the social degradation of civilization. Many of these apparently great endeavors are morally negative and practically destructive in their impacts on the eco-systems of the planet and its indigenous species.

Obstacles to Planetary Sustainability

Again, today it must be obvious to all thinking people that Urantia is plagued by several dangerous problems that are far worst and more difficult to solve than any previous time on record. As we've seen, the natural order of this world was severely altered by the Lucifer rebellion, and up until recently, it was in cosmic quarantine throughout its strife-torn and bloody history. Hence, typically, there has never been a single peaceful and trouble-free moment here ever since. Yet, the predicaments have been increasing and intensifying lately. Nowadays, issues such as sectarian conflicts as well as geopolitical tensions between your most powerful nations are escalating quite rapidly. One of our gravest concerns is that another devastating World War between these countries is gradually looming in our radar. For even though the overall collective energy of the world's Lightworkers has successfully shifted its energetic body into a higher frequency, the dark ones have yet to suspend their nefarious agenda for global domination. The cabal, in collusi∴n with unscrupulous politicians and a special cartel of larger-than-life tycoons, is still currently largely leading the parade of world affairs. Having at their possession the most sophisticated and lethal weaponry systems ever devised by men, these highly conceited, self-serving villains have set themselves against all true values of human dignity, and they are determined to reorganize the world after their own diabolical design. Noble virtues and enriching ideals such as peace, justice, fairness, equality and altruism, which constitute the foundation for a strong and lasting civilization are scornfully discarded by those miscreants. But beware! *Rich or poor, developed or emergent, powerful or weak, white or colored, no nation, no people, no race is immune or will be exempted from the consequences of their ultimate defeat and catastrophic failure.*

Nonetheless, despite their steadfast defiance against love, in due time, everything shall be restored into their original conditions here. Thus, we urge you to carry on in truth, and to trust in your inborn creative abilities to cause and manifest your reality. We know that for many of you, this statement bears little to no meaning. Understandably, that was expected, for, as we've said before, since birth you have been manipulated into a 'fabricated reality-construct' that controls your perception of who and what you are.

Even the basic innate powers of your being have been kept secret from you. If you don't think so, then tell us when was the last time someone told you that your life was actually the product of your creative spirit – the unfolding drama of your own imagination? Still, even now that we just said it, do you really believe us? Either way, we absolutely respect your opinion, whatever it is. We did not come to this world to engage in a popularity contest, or to prove to anyone whether we are right or wrong. Remember, our main objective is to teach, inspire and guide you into the next upcoming dispensation, to help you realize your new earth. And so...naturally, as your friends, teachers and counselors, we are also very eager to exchange our energy signatures with humanity by visiting with many of you as often as possible.

To us, the current synthetic paradigm in which you are living is a gross distortion of the natural order of things as the Gods anticipated for your kind, and as such, it cannot withstand the transformational changes from the Correcting Time's manifold programs, which are unfolding now. Those of you who are courageously advocating for the emancipation of mankind from this corrupt order are setting the foundation for the coming new era. You are the trailblazers for a future generation—the actual forerunners of a *Golden Age* to-be on this planet.

Nowadays, it is quite obvious that people are waking up to the realities behind the dark cabal's evil global control network, everyday. The long well guarded scheme to rule the world 'unchecked' is losing steam and momentum, for it is being deprived of its most powerful ammunition—*its secrecy*. And...apart from a few aristocratic beneficiaries, their '*big idea*' has a very unfavorable rating among all who knows about it. The dire repercussions of its malfeasances have long reached worldwide. They are visible in several planetary dilemmas, such as lawlessness, terrorism, corruption, diseases, environmental disasters, and nuclear proliferation. It's no coincidence that many of your respectable scientists and experts believe that these men-made problems are essentially the most dangerous global challenges of the 21st century.

As civilization continues to expand physically, the quantity of energy necessary to sustain the life quality of developing nations will exceed the available amount of any given energy resources the earth can provide. Thus, it is essential to identify various alternatives to continue to fuel this rather rapid material expansion and urbanization. Fortunately, many of your authorities are beginning to realize that it is a grave error to rely on a single resource for energy and power, no matter how convenient and massive it may be.

For the past several decades, there has been a race between the world's potent states to accumulate and secure vast quantity of energy resources—primarily oil and gas, to respond to their high volume of industrial activities and the continuing rising demand of their populations for energy consumptions. This dynamic has provoked serious politico-economic frictions between them, though this tension is now cleverly mitigated and diplomatically controlled for the sake of their mutual interests and securities. Their socioeconomic interdependence and shared prosperity have, thus far, relatively overshadowed and eased their profound political disparities. However, don't be fooled! Beware; this diplomatic approach is not to be trusted. It is deceiving and deeply malicious. Underneath their negotiating tables, the most ferocious war yet to be declared is being softly ignited. In effect, this form of sophisticated political hypocrisy is one of the biggest threats to modern civilization.

Today, many once green regions around the world are rapidly developing, thus increasing the need for energy demand to sustain their populations. The stronghold of the hegemonic states over the world's natural resources and energy materials is no longer foolproof and secured. Actually, it has been gradually decreasing in recent years.

It is impossible to objectively assess the global energy crisis without factoring America as the planet's first economic and military superpower. Being the capital of the industrial and financial world, America itself, of course, is the focal point of the problem. However, America's potential rivals and challengers have been increasing as well over the past few decades. In addition, the country is suffering from severe internal problems due to wide economic and social inequalities. It is dangerously affected by growing political enmity around the world primarily because of the failure of its foreign policies and military engagements. Presently, it is no secret that there is a strong will among some of its formidable opponents to support an alliance against this young and resilient imperial power.

In the coming years, if these superpowers fail to agree on a resolution for lasting global peace, stability, and cooperation under International Laws regardless of their manifold differences, then the world may rest assured of a possible confrontation between them at some point in this century.

With the manufacturing of ever more powerful and destructive weaponry systems, humanity can no longer afford a full-scale war between two, three or more of your most militarized countries. With their current arsenals, a military conflict between these nations is unthinkable – for this would be no less than sheer 'madness.' Such a horrendous eventuality would practically ensure their *mutual destructions.*

And... as you well know, the development of this particular situation on your sphere consumes a great deal of our time and occupations, as we seek to alleviate a variety of tensions, foil plots and curtail other actions to provoke, what we see as an "absurd potential world conflict" that humanity will not be able to endure. This has been indeed a very "nerve-racking circumstance" for us as we work secretly to prevent this catastrophe from manifesting into your reality, especially in times of crises that are often orchestrated by the dark cabal to instigate it.

Throughout the last two centuries, and notably following the Second World War, we became gravely concerned about the course of Urantia's political and social order, not necessarily because of the new liberalism and blind materialism that were promptly embraced by society, but rather because of the more dangerous arms race that was unleashed for scientific, technological and military supremacy between her two most powerful confederations.

The Roots of Global Unrests

Any objective social analyst would most probably agree that since the rise of secularism as mainstream philosophy of modern life, human civilization has not only embarked on a journey of unfettered expression and irreverence, but also of greed and debauchery. As we see it, based upon the values of the "Golden Rules" of an advance culture, true modernity is [yet nonexistent on earth]. It is clear to us that the domination of capitalism, the declination of morality, the spiritual stagnation of religion, and the misguided scientific developments of the last three-and-half centuries are essentially the roots of today's continuing global unrests, violence, and wars. There is ample evidence to support the veracity of this observation.

Since the debut of the new secular pragmatism, revolution practically replaced evolution in your world. As a result, political turmoil, widen economic disparities and social dissatisfactions have sharply increased throughout the globe for the past three hundred and fifty years. Unfortunately, largely, the disastrous consequences of these events have tremendously exceeded the positive realizations of your time. Historically, the causes for these sorts of dilemmas are usually bold and diverse, but they've become more secretive and centralized in modern time.

Civilization does not spring from nature. It is rather the evolutionary outcome of intellectual, moral, social and spiritual developments. Primarily, to survive and endure, it relies on the three fundamental faculties of the human mind, which are causality, morality, and spirituality. No social order is entirely safe and secure so long the manifold problems issued from these mental constituents, are not resolved. Inevitably, any civilization will eventually collapse if the values of its main institutions—such as the family, government and religion—are not recurrently upgraded with novel and progressive philosophies of living. To remain in pace with the speed of humanity's ongoing collective intellectual, moral and spiritual evolution, global authorities must never be fixated on dogmas. A society should not be reluctant to change and improve its value system when necessary. Generally, the longevity of an organized culture is invariably dependent on its flexibility to transcend itself periodically in accordance with the changing episodes of time. To ensure the continuity of any nation, every new generation must not only increase its efforts to produce fresh problem-solving techniques for itself, but should also make provisions to accommodate the aspirations and facilitate the progress of the next.

The ongoing antagonisms between Urantia's various nations are chiefly caused by the abject lack of ideals and wisdom of their leaders. A great number of those officials blindly continue to look into the past for solutions to existing problems. They persistently draw their courses of actions from the historical rationales of their predecessors. They are flooded with all sorts of ideas, but are poverty-stricken of ideals. Most of them persist on following ancient ideologues whose doctrines of governance are incompetent and unfit to face contemporary challenges.

Nowadays, the influences of civilization's most fundamental institutions—namely the family, religion, and government—are steadily declining as these establishments are being seriously confronted and undermined the world over. People are increasingly becoming distrustful and apprehensive of the authoritarian state leadership, disloyal to family responsibilities and independent of theological conventions. In most countries, "legal authorities" are severely defied; their relevancy and legitimacy are overwhelmingly rejected. Thus, because of this representative leadership crisis, more and more, governments are relying on extreme coercive measures as a deterrent to curb social uprisings.

Lasting political stability and national peace in any country greatly depends upon the dexterity and wisdom of its administrators to successfully harmonize the unvarying principles of its constitution with the ever-changing mentalities, pursuits, and activities of its people. Peace cannot be achieved absent from a nation's goodwill to uphold the "rule of law." And…this relies predominantly on the strength of the relationships of its diverse public and private institutions. It is the legal duty and the most sacred responsibility of government to provide the means and to create the conditions by which its citizenry can co-exist peacefully. A government truly begins to endorse peace when it chooses to lead by virtue instead of force; when it functions according to the fundamental values of human dignity. That is, when it encourages decency, supports justice, facilitates education and development, solves domestic and international issues diplomatically, promotes cooperation between its people and institutions, so they can effectively fulfill their obligations, without favoritism.

Overregulated political organizations and highly demanding societal standards may be efficient methods of segregation, but they are lousy techniques to secure domestic order in an ethnically diverse country. The supreme duty of government is to preserve peace, order and the integrity of the rule of law. Thus, it must always be impartial in all national relationships.

Peace and social justice cannot prevail when the legal institutions of a country are privatized and function at the behest of specialized interests. Under the control of an affluent elite minority stomping on a neglected, marginalized and frustrated mass, government automatically becomes a threat to civil harmony and progress, not a facilitator of justice. Such a corrupt and illegitimate leadership is highly detrimental to lasting peace and stability. In the long run, it can only provoke unrests and severe hostilities between the different classes of a society, which may lead to [revolution] or even more serious national crises.

Saying "no one is above the law" is essentially pointless and irrelevant if this assertion can be violated. And… a law that relies on retribution and violence to ensure its sovereignty, can never produce a harmonious society. Law becomes oppressive and thus, redundant, if there is no collective or popular agreement to obey it. To be positive, the legislative policies of a country must be designed in the best interests of its population without discriminations.

If it is not cautiously exercised for the betterment of the people, what you call "legal authority" can be the most powerful enemy of any nation when it is frequently, arrogantly used by a few to the detriment of civilization.

Much of the current hardship the inhabitants of Urantia are experiencing, are the results of long years of systematic abuses of political power, civil injustices, and unfair exploitations of its resources by an intrusive, centralized cartel of heartless criminals. Though this model of men's domination over their weaker fellows has been around for millennia, its recent heirs have taken the concept to a totally different level. Their justification to abuse and brutalize the vulnerable peoples of the world, which sprung from their self-deluded sense of superiority, is grotesque and shameful. Such a deceitful and affected attitude is utterly unbecoming of a civilized inhabited realm.

In a truly progressive society, it is an utter nonsense to regard the right to lead as a special privilege granted only to those of a particular race or gender. The concept of racial superiority and sexism are insignificant in such an ethnically blended, culturally diverse, socially linked and geo-politically inter-dependent world as Urantia. It is true that every race is endowed with different natural potentials, and does manifest dissimilar psychological propensities. However, collectively, the entire human family is equally embraced by divinity. Bear in mind, regardless of the magnitude of their intellectual, social and economic discrepancies, it remains forever true that all men are created equal in spirit and matter.

Most of the differences of the mortal races are usually eliminated during the Adamic planetary dispensation on all normal inhabited worlds. Spiritual power is always the result of God-consciousness. It is founded on the immutable cosmic law of unity, not conformity.

The agelong history of human leadership, as we've seen, has not brought any significant, positive and definitive development to the human race. Rather than progressing toward real change, mortal rule has mainly exacerbated the already desperate condition of your species. Worse, unlike other evolving planets, time has not helped transformed the situation either. Today, optimism has all but disappeared in the collective consciousness of the global population. Hence, naturally, there are good reasons to be concerned about the future of government and civilization here. And...it is precisely in light of this precarious state of affairs that the Correcting Plan was designed, and is being implemented at this time.

Thus ends the initial part of our co-creative assignment regarding the development and activities of this great cosmic undertaking. We shall begin the second part as soon as you are ready to commingle our energies and receive us again. I will now bid you farewell for a short season. Stay in the light little one.

Part 2

THE ACTIVITIES OF THE CORRECTING TIME PLAN:
The three major celestial programs to restore the Creator's will on earth

The first part disclosed the primordial cosmic events and situations that adversely affected Urantia. The archenemies of creation and the countless problems of their revolt, which continue to beset the earth even today, were exposed. The second part will focus on the diverse aspects of the Great Correcting Time Plan to rectify these ills; notably, its three major programs, which were designed to help salvage the planet from the sinful legacies of the Lucifer rebellion. The main topics discussed, succinctly, are: [1] identifying and honoring the Master Architect and the Senior Executives of the Correcting Time Plan; [2] present the Urantia Book and its value; [3] disclose the Teaching Mission; [4] reveal the Magisterial Mission; [5] acknowledge several of humanity's celestial helpers; [6] Explain why the Correcting Time is happening now; [7] expose God the Father's interference on Urantia; [8] counsels to embrace the higher self; [9] empowering words of encouragement to imagine and co-create the future. This set of revelational transcriptions were also transmitted by the celestial teacher—Abomaly, through the receiver or channel—Joseph Elie.

Read on...

Paper 10

The Master Architect Of The Plan

HIS URANTIA BESTOWAL AS JESUS OF NAZARETH

The Senior Executives of the Plan's Major Programs on Earth

Celestial Teacher: Abramaly – Channel: Joseph Elie 11-07-2012

IMMEDIATELY AFTER THE LUCIFER MANIFESTO on Jerusem, Michael took counsel with Immanuel concerning the best course of action to follow in light of such a bold defiance against his rule and the Father's will. He was advised to adopt an attitude of "non-interference"– to allow the outbreak to pursuit its course freely – thereby ensuring the quick and certain defeat of the rebels. Upon Michael's decision to remain clear of the rebellion, Gabriel, the Chief Executive of the universe, took the initiative and mobilized his staff to defend the Creator's cause in Satania. However, though he chose not to interfere with the rebel forces, Christ Michael was not necessarily indifferent to the situation. He was fully ready to meet the challenges.

As the rebels were structuring their illegitimate government, the Creator Son had hitherto designed a wise, far-seeing, and comprehensive plan to retrieve the worlds that were affected. And…

even then, preparations were already being made in anticipation of the time when it would be implemented. Much of the activities of what is now known on your sphere as the Correcting Time, were fully considered and expected more than 250,000 years before.

In fact, Michael's first step to counteract the rebels' mendacity was the conception of the Great Correcting Time Plan, which he officially launched over 2000 years ago on your planet by his miraculous incarnation as Jesus of Nazareth. As the mastermind of the greatest cosmic rehabilitation project ever undertaken by a Creator Son in the Superuniverse of Orvonton, we deem it important and honorable to dedicate this transmission mainly to the unusual personality of this extraordinary Christ. The Senior Executives of the plan's major programs will also be disclosed. No matter how doubtful Urantia mortals may be about the veracity of his bestowal, we are humbled and delighted to say that the miraculous Jesus, who lived among you for 36 years not too long ago from our perspective, was truly the Creator of this vast universe – a bona-fide Paradise Son of the Universal Father.

Christ Michael as Jesus of Nazareth
The Son of Man & the Son of God

Jesus of Nazareth was a physical manifestation of Christ Michael, the Creator Son of the local universe of Nebadon. He was not a man associated with God, but instead, *God incarnated in man.* He lived a full human life just as this is required of all men in the cosmic ascension journey to Paradise. He experienced the hardships and dealt with the vicissitudes of the earthly existence just as fully as any other mortal of his time had to cope with these common circumstances. As we see it from our vantage, the human experience must be observed and understood from a qualitative perspective in order to determine its real value.

A mere thirty years of positive living consecrated to love,

faith and service, is more valuable than a hundred years of brutal and selfish experiences. Accordingly, we believe Jesus' life offers the perfect example to support our assertion.

Jesus lived a short but wholly consecrated life to God's will. His commitment to the Paradise Father's business was steadfast and superb. Since the inception of Nebadon, never before was there such a loyal and devoted mortal personality to the cause of divinity before the incarnation of Joshua Ben Joseph on your planet. He allowed nothing to distract him from his unyielding decision to do the will of God, *at all cost*. Throughout his life and public ministry, whenever he was challenged to assert himself, he calmly replied with a firm and an unbroken assurance, *"Not my will, but that of the One who sent me—my Father in heaven."* To his enemies, he fearlessly continued to demonstrate this by responding to all their attacks with love and mercy, even during the savage and tragic death that were unjustly inflicted upon him.

In this matchless creature experience, Michael of Nebadon thoroughly depicted the divine love of the Paradise Father for all living intelligences that populate the vast domains of his universe. He demonstrated that there is never any divergence or estrangement from the Creator's standpoint; that all guilt and disagreements with the Father were derived from men. In one short mortal life, he managed to portray the limitless affection of the Eternal God, not just for the races of your world, but also for all the inhabitants on the numerous evolutionary planets of his vast creation. Thus, through himself was established the spiritual path to attain the highest reality of the universes—recognition of sonship with the Universal Father of all. By consecrating his entire life to the pursuit of the uppermost cosmic destiny attainable by any will-endowed creature, Jesus completely defeated all temporal challenges and emerged triumphant with the Spirit of the First Source and Center—the Eternal, Absolute and Infinite, I AM.

Jesus is the infallible and certain path to divine perfection. He is our eternal assurance of salvation, and the Living Truth leading to the Universal Father on Paradise. He is the supreme model of perfect personality for all evolving souls on all inhabited worlds throughout the universe of Nebadon. He was indeed a revelation of the living God to all the progressing realms of his vast creation. By that event, he provided a safe and sure route to attain the Father, and to realize the Truth of your Sonship with Him. It is literally true that whoever had seen Jesus – now sovereign of Nebadon – had actually seen the Universal Father of all creations.

The Certainty of the Triumph of His Gospels

The materialistic concept that scientists involuntarily led modern men to embrace for the past one and half century has more or less destroyed the influences of medieval superstitions, and somewhat retarded the moral and the spiritual progress of civilization on Urantia. However, this revolution has left the profound meanings of the truths of Jesus' real teachings totally intact. And… we know that the Master's revelations of love will eventually triumph over the illusions of evil by redeeming men from all temporal imperfections, be they physical or spiritual. When Jesus and his Gospels are finally understood by most Urantians, all nations will co-exist harmoniously. Races will abide and work together peacefully in reverence of love and service. For all will know that they are in truth and in spirit, children of the Most-High.

His Denunciation of False Religion

Jesus fearlessly denounced the frauds and deceptions of the religious leaders of his time. He wisely and eloquently exposed their misrepresentations of man's relationship to God by revealing the true character and nature of the Paradise Father to his hearers.

With the stunning revelation of man's sonship with God, he did indeed set new and higher spiritual standards for all generations. Although most of his ideals and visions remain yet unfulfilled on your planet, they have, nonetheless, significantly improved your understanding about the quality of your relationship with the Paradise Father. His life and teachings were essentially divine, even though he was also a real specimen of human origin – a mortal of the realm. The profound love of God for humanity was fully revealed and epitomized in this single short sojourn of Christ Michael on your world as the Son of Man.

His Twofold Natures

After his magnificent life on earth, Michael of Nebadon rose to the headquarters of his universe fully invested with all powers and sovereignty over his creation from a new experience as the Son of Man and the Son of God. You now have in him not merely a God of divine origin, but also an understanding and sympathetic fellow human being. Someone who is an expert in the manner you live on your own sphere of nativity. Thus, you must now and forever settle in your philosophy that God is approachable by all, the way into the divine kingdom within is widely open to whoever shall seek entrance therein.

Anyone who sincerely wishes to do the will of the heavenly Father is duly qualified to partake of the divine water of life, and thus, shall drink abundantly.

If one has any doubt or concern about the spiritual achievement of Jesus on Urantia, then one must ponder over the fact that now every new generation possesses the perfect model that establishes the path leading to the true living God. And... rests assured that this revelation will not fail; it shall eventually deliver and enlighten all mankind. Jesus could not have invented or imagined the God he proclaimed, for he was himself a representative of the Creator revealed to mortal men.

In essence, spiritually, he was indeed a revelation of the majestic character, divine nature, and sublime personality of the

Universal Father. That is why those who fail to recognize the divinity of Jesus also do not acknowledge the Father as a reality, and are thus, unable to appreciate the cosmic source of his Gospels.

› His Unshakeable Faith

Jesus' devotion to God and ministry to mankind were the highest forms of faithful commitment to divinity possible in the life experience of a mortal personality. For the pessimist who declares that he must see to believe, let the life story of the Son of Man on earth, which was thoroughly delineated by the revelatory corps of your Urantia text, serves as a physical testimony of the existence of the Paradise Creator.

Jesus unequivocally showed the truly divine way by which men may transcend their evil tendencies and addictions, and elevate themselves spiritually as mature faith-sons of God. For him, the spirit-born believer is to live as if he or she was already on Paradise - at the bosom of the Father. He urged his Apostles and disciples to remain faithful to God through prayers and regular communions with His indwelling Presence. His religion was a relentless living experience. His faith was both steadfast and supreme.

From our understanding, the quality of his devotion to the cause of Deity was so replete and absolute; it is not surprising that he was the very manifestation of the divine nature to men. In reality, God incarnated upon the mortal races of your world.

The Necessity for a Renaissance of His Teachings

Today, as the Correcting Time Plan unfolds, we are encouraging all dedicated truth-seekers to join in spirit and consolidate their efforts for a rebirth of *Jesus' true teachings* on Urantia. There is a great need at this moment to rekindle the light of the Master's Gospels in the hearts of all men. In fact, as we see it from our vantage, a global resurgence of his genuine Gospels as he really taught and lived them, is now crucial to reorient and re-energize the bewildered spirit of the human race. This is actually paramount to secure the continuing survival of your kind. Honestly, as things are now, the future of civilization here greatly depends on rather every successive generation will have the courage to strive to improve itself according to the eternal values of Jesus. Put blatantly in other terms, from our observations on this side, we are absolutely convinced that a planetary revival of Michael's real life experience and teachings is imperative in order to avoid unthinkable and irreversible catastrophes on your sphere at some point within this century.

Today's world desperately needs to see Jesus live again. Humanity needs to observe the faithful, benevolent and charming personality of the Son of Man in the lives of his professed followers. There is a desperate need to comprehend and appreciate the profoundly touching relationship that may exist between man and God, when man truly elects to do the Creator's will.

Accepting and Embracing this experiential connection between humanity and divinity is the only definitive manner to bring about lasting positive changes in your world. Comprehending and embracing the meanings of the sublime expressions and actions of Jesus in perfect union with God is the sole effective way to arrest the ongoing moral and spiritual degradation of your global society today. His supreme affirmation of man sonship with God must no longer be ignored or overshadowed by an unprogressive, dogmatic, self-serving, and corrupt church that refuses to bear the fruits of his spirit.

Now is the right moment for all authentic Jesusonians to rigorously and fearlessly propagate this great truth throughout Urantia. Irrespective of creeds or denominations, all sincere believers, truth-seekers, and Light-Workers are called to participate in this extraordinary undertaking as they obediently adhere to the values of the Master's teachings.

The Youths Are Ready to Welcome His Religion

As we said, Jesus' religion was essentially predicated on two basic and inalienable cosmic Truths: [1] The universal fatherhood of God; [2] The planetary brotherhood of men. From our observations, most youths on your planet today would have little to no difficulty accepting this profound reality because unlike previous generations, they manifest a remarkable penchant and desire for global peace, liberty, justice, equality and social unity.

Many thinking young people are ready to accommodate and even adopt the genuine religion of Jesus if only it was presented to them as the Master originally taught and lived it. These intelligent, open-minded and truth-seeking souls are the hope for a possible future restoration of the Son of Man's revelation in your world. They are the potential *Light-Carriers,* who will steer humanity into the next age of true intellectual and spiritual liberation.

Christ Michael ensured the destiny of this world forever by his incarnation here as Jesus. However, his ideals and vision for the planet will not be fulfilled until the full participation and honest cooperation of all mankind. Being absolute, eternal and infinite, the will of God does ultimately prevail on any evolving sphere, but men also play a pivotal role in determining their temporal and spiritual fate in the universe.

His Non-Resistance to Evil

Jesus taught his followers not to resist evil. But instead, to live unconditionally dedicated to the doing of the will of God. He admonished them to walk in the light of Truth. They were to strive to emulate and project the goodness of God in all their earthly activities. Always, would he say to them, *"Be perfect even as your Father in heaven is perfect."* He encouraged them to be an exemplary society of emancipated, spirit-born souls by entering completely into the joy and peace of loving service to all men.

Again, as we stated before, Christ Michael thoroughly revealed the divine character and the loving personality of the

Paradise Father in his magnificent human life experience as the Son of Man. However, unfortunately, his revelation has never been really understood by any generation on your planet since then. Sincere believers may grasp much of his real teachings from the inner ministry of the Spirit of Truth. But alas, humanity has yet to comprehend the fundamental meanings of the Master's Gospels— especially his peculiar *nonresistance* attitude towards evil.

The Keynote of His Gospels

The principal message of Jesus was his momentous declaration of the universal fatherhood of God coupled with the planetary brotherhood of men. The core information of his entire bestowal mission on Urantia was all mortals, by virtue of their indwelling spirits, are the children of the Paradise Father, and they are, by that presence, spiritually brothers and sisters. Relentlessly, and joyfully, he proclaimed this glad tiding to the peoples of his time. And... today, the propagation of this sublime truth is more important than it has ever been. As the Master taught his early interlocutors, present generations of his alleged followers bear the responsibility to resurrect the spirit of his message in the world. You must, by your exemplary lives centered in faith and motivated by love and service, demonstrate the immortal nature of the truths he revealed and the values he promoted.

The Distortion of His Gospels in Christianity

When it was initially founded after the eventful Day of Pentecost, Christianity had already deviated from the main teachings of Jesus. Neither his Apostles nor his common followers remained loyal to the veritable truths and spirit of his Gospels. Jesus taught that everyone was a child of the eternal living God. He declared love as the supreme relationship of God with every soul, and Truth is the revelation of that relationship. To confirm his assertions, he lived a unique and exemplary life consecrated to the business of the Universal Father.

However, almost immediately after his departure from the world, the true spiritual meanings and purpose of his mission were virtually lost in confusions. His entire bestowal was converted was widely viewed as a newly emerging religious sect, which promised redemption through faith in the sacrifice of the resurrected Christ. Though this new gospel was a serious deviation from the authentic teachings of Jesus, it resonated to thousands of souls and spread rather quickly throughout the world. Conversely, although millions continue to preserve the traditions as such today, there has also been an ongoing massive worldwide disillusionment with the church for several decades now. Vast numbers of once loyal adepts are either openly or tacitly questioning its spiritual authenticity, legitimacy and authority. Nevertheless, a decision to clarify the ambiguities surrounding the events and circumstances that transpired after the ascension of Jesus, which culminated in the creation of the religion is yet to be taken. Like any other institutionalized faith, dozens of questions could be raised to challenge the official narratives concerning the spiritual origins and veracity of the church's precepts and theologies, which it claims to be from the Master's Gospels. However, we think a few are sufficient to elucidate this artificial religion, which was founded upon the story of the risen Christ, but utterly failed to acknowledge and honor the religion of Jesus as he taught and lived it.

For example, consider those two: was Christianity founded by Jesus? Did Jesus teach celibacy? If not, then why has the Catholic Church so fully embraced the Pauline doctrine of sexual abstinence contrary to the Master's real teachings? Is Paul a wiser and superior teacher?

We are not sure, but it seems that the church is not interested in answering many simple questions as they are put forth by concerned individuals, though they are also quite common even among their adepts. We are certainly not an isolated voice asking these questions. Many before us have done that, and many more will continue to do so as long as they remain unanswered. While we don't know why the church refuses to answer and clarify its position, but the hidden motive of its peculiar attitude is quite easy to detect and understand. In reality, the church can't answer these plain questions objectively and truthfully without damaging its preponderance and jeopardize its authority. Doing this would cause it to raise other questions about the very foundational values of its dogmas, and thus, destroy the myth of its spiritual origin and legitimacy – this would be detrimental to its own existence and suicidal to the status quo.

The reality is that there are many distorted versions of Jesus' Gospels in the creedal philosophies of diverse factions of Christianity. A few centuries after his ascension, these falsified translations of the Master's sayings and doings were adopted as mainstream values throughout the Western World. As you know, up until recently, in modern history, much of the Western hemisphere was largely subjugated by the clergy – Europe and America mainly languished under the hierarchical authority of the Catholic establishment. Even today, scores of nations remain subservient to the dictate of the medieval church, especially in Latin America. However, as we've said in prior messages, this era of religious despotism is passing away.

Now the cat is already out of the proverbial bag. Bear in mind that Christ Michael's Truth Spirit pervades the hearts and minds of all receptive souls on your planet. The true meanings and values of his Gospels are fully accessible to all from within –, and this knowledge is rapidly spreading throughout your sphere today.

Unfortunately, many of the Truths the Master taught the men and women of his generation—especially the core of his message, which was the universal fatherhood of God predicated on the planetary brotherhood of men, were quickly twisted and largely misrepresented by his Apostles and disciples soon after his departure from the world. Hence, these erroneous interpretations of his teachings were integrated within the creeds of the early movement of his devoted followers that eventually became

"Christianity," which was founded in his name, predominantly by the illustrious Apostles Peter, Paul and Philo of Alexandria.

Yes indeed, Christ Michael's veritable teachings were initially innocently and later, deliberately revised by his Apostles and pretentious followers after his ascension to the heavenly Father. And most of those distorted, rearranged, and misinterpreted versions of the Master's utterances unavoidably became part of the fundamental doctrines of Christianity. Nevertheless, let us reiterate if we may, since the bestowal of the Spirit of Truth upon all flesh on the memorable Day of Pentecost, all morally conscious Urantians, generation after generation, are endowed with the contents of the Master's Gospels as he revealed and taught them to the people of his time. And... this complete permeation of his Spirit in all hearts prepares the stage for the coming *dispensation of enlightenment* on your planet. Yes, a grand global jubilee of fellowship and unity.

The Futuristic Meaning of His Incarnation

Symbolically, the incarnation of Christ Michael as the Son of Man on earth was a futuristic characterization of a highly developed and spiritualized human race in divine association with God. The mysterious Man, Jesus of Nazareth, was a revelation of a future generation of God-conscious personalities. It was a disclosure of the quality of the souls, which will inhabit the earth when the human race becomes fully conscious of their true relationship to God.

The Son of Man was a cosmic revelation of a future planetary event that unequivocally depicted the reality of man's sonship with God, and ascertained the eternal existence of mankind as an evolving spirit in the universe.

Jesus did not only affirm man's sonship with God with mere words. He also lived this sublime truth as a factual personal reality. He never doubted it. This is why he required his followers to be perfect like the Father, for to him, that supreme mandate was a true living experience, not a fantasy. The Master taught and commanded his Apostles to live permanently in accordance with the divine ordinances of Paradise – to consecrate themselves to the will of the Eternal Creator. When this is done, he asserted, one is automatically received as an effective citizen in the glorious abodes on high. He declared, "Even though, you, as faith Sons, must still await natural death to join your progressive brethrens on the mansion worlds, but you are already conscious of the Truth of your sonship with the Universal Father, and that is, in and of itself, sufficient to picture some of the glories of the divine kingdom within yourselves."

Essentially, Jesus was the depiction of a future spiritual epoch of a perfected generation; a society of spirit-born, God knowing and Truth abiding souls. But all of you may experience his presence and ministry at any moment. In fact, all right-minded Urantians are endowed with his Spirit—known as the Spirit of Truth—the promised "Teacher and Comforter." By virtue of this spirit, each and all of you possess the perfect guide who will lead you into the source of all Truths. Indeed, the Master's spirit is gradually recreating, elevating, and perfecting humanity, ushering the world into a better future, an ideal reality, and a greater   It works tirelessly to spiritualize and elevate the quality of your thinking, to increasingly transform you into bona-fide, self-realized, faithful sons and daughters of God.

The Sovereign Planetary Prince of Urantia
Machiventa as Vice-Gerent Prince

After his magnificent human experience and his success in terminating the Lucifer rebellion, Christ Michael was immediately recognized as the official Planetary Prince of Urantia by his Elder Brother, Immanuel—the Union of Days who represents the Paradise Father in the universe of Nebadon. Hence, he is called the Prince of Peace. However, following his ascension to Salvington, the Capital of his universe, Michael appointed Machiventa Melkisedek as his Vice-Gerent Planetary Prince. Melkisedek was also selected as a member of the twenty and four elders assigned by the Master to oversee the affairs of Urantia and the 36 other worlds in spiritual quarantine within Satania.

As far as we know, Christ Michael has never openly revealed or discussed his intention for appointing Machiventa as the temporary acting Planetary Principal of Urantia. Given that, he now reins supreme over everything in Nebadon; it is hard to perceive this as a gesture to compensate for his absence on the planet. Nonetheless, some of us incline to believe, at least partially, that this might be one of the reasons behind this action.

Being one of his bestowal realms and the one on which he obtained the full sovereignty of his universe; Michael's objectives and plans for Urantia are essentially unsearchable. Aside from his immediate associates – the Senior Executives of his Correcting Time Plan, and, perhaps a few of the highest rulers of the universes, we seriously doubt anyone truly knows or understands Michael's final purpose for your world. As for the rest of us, in order to discover the real motive behind his seemingly strange doings, we must patiently wait as we attentively follow the unfolding of his divine plan.

Even though Christ Michael is always transparent and candid with us in all administrative matters of universal jurisdictions, our receptions and understandings of such cosmic transactions are wholly up to the extent, we can appreciate their spiritual imports and values.

The Creator is never tempted to satisfy the curiosity of his inquisitive creatures by disclosing informations that are utterly beyond their intellectual capacity to comprehend. However, that doesn't quash the prerogatives of will-creatures to ponder upon and speculate about the meanings and purpose of his manifold universe activities.

We incline to believe that the decision to appoint Machiventa as Vice-Gerent Prince of Urantia was taken because of several technical situations, which could not be ignored or dealt with otherwise. Some of these minor inconveniences we perceive only vaguely, hence, we can hardly trust these assumptions. Nevertheless, we are almost fully convinced of two, in particular, and they are:

- *The fact of Michael's personal absence in the world*
- *The fact of Melkisedek's material incarnation*

~After the bestowal of his Truth Spirit upon all receptive souls on this planet, Christ Michael was, incarnated in the soul of every rational Urantia mortal. However, he is neither personally present on the planet nor did that gesture made up for his absence. Thus, it is perfectly logical to deduce that our beloved Father-Creator-Brother wanted his final bestowal world to have its own immediate personal representative in the heavenly councils on high by appointing Machiventa Melkisedek as vice-gerent Planetary Prince of Urantia to replace the unworthy and now-deceased Caligastia.

~The fact that he was indwelt by a Thought Adjuster during his incarnation in the flesh, Machiventa had completely altered his Melkisedek career, and thus, he had joined the rank of ascending sons of God in the universe of Nebadon.

~As the Sovereign and Supreme Chief of Nebadon, Christ-Michael's administrative headquarter are on Salvington, the main capital of his universe. Though he may move freely throughout the master universe, for unlike the Mother Spirit, he is not confined to the domains of his respective creation, but he cannot be personally present in two places simultaneously. Christ Michael is a highly personalized Being; he cannot fragmentize himself as do the Paradise Father and the Infinite Spirit. Although his Truth Spirit permeates every positive intellect on earth, but his glorious personality is to be found at his regular residence on Salvington. This is why we believe that it is to make up for his absence on Urantia that he designated Machiventa to represent him as Vice-Gerent Planetary Prince.

No one knows exactly for how long Melkisedek will stay on this post as a representative of Michael to the service of this planet. We believe he will probably remain assigned to this realm until the future ages of Light and Life. But again, we are not certain. Since Michael pledged to return on earth, and recent situations seem to signal his readiness to fulfill this promise, there are many who think that Machiventa will probably be released from his planetary duty in such an occasion. But this is just one among the least popular speculations on this matter.

You would be certain about your salvation and the fate of your world, if you really understood the true spiritual imports of Michael's bestowal mission on your planet over 2000 years ago. If you could see past your physical limitations and observe this mighty Creator Son as the official *Sovereign Prince* of your Planet; if you could visualize his equally powerful and brilliant associates—the Senior Executives of the Correcting Time Plan on earth, then all your doubts would instantly disappear.

The Senior Executives of the Plan

As we have mentioned throughout the book thus far, the Great Correcting Time Plan is a systemic, multifaceted project with three major programs aiming to restore the Creator's will on the 37 rebellion stricken planets of Satania. It was designed by Christ Michael primarily with each of these worlds in mind as it is tailored to meet the needs and responds to the challenges of each, specifically. There is an untold number of celestials involve in this astronomical undertaking, but it is implemented on every sphere under the supervisions of a few main personalities as Senior Executives who were especially chosen by the Creator Son.

On Urantia, besides the numerous high celestial figures that are participating in the execution of this plan, such as Gabriel of Salvington, Immanuel, and Lanaforge, there are two Senior Executives, who are overseeing the entire project. [1] Machiventa, a Melkisedek Son who incarnated on earth around five thousand years ago to preserve the light of Truth in the hearts of men following the miscarriage of the Adamic Dispensation. [2] Monjoronson, an Avonal Son of Paradise-origin who was designated by Michael to undertake a Magisterial Mission on your planet.

Although their works are exquisitely coordinated, Machiventa and Monjoronson maintain their own unique staffs of celestial personnels and ministers to implement their programs. Being the Vice-Gerent Planetary Principal acting on Michael's behalf, save for some minor details that were seized upon by the Constellation Fathers after the Caligastia revolt, Melkisedek practically oversees the entire cosmic government of your world. He has jurisdictions over the whole angelic and super-angelic ministerial army that reside here. In addition, as a member of the council of the twenty-four elders on Jerusem who were appointed to supervise the affairs of the quarantined worlds in Satania and a one time incarnated mortal of the realm, he exercises even more power in the matters of this planet – both in his own stead and as Michael's protégé.

For his part, Monjoronson is ably assisted by a vast corps of experienced celestials hailed from all levels and dimensions of this universe, the Superuniverse of Orvonton and beyond. He is also scheduled to be incarnated soon on your world to officially inaugurate the *New Era of Spiritual Enlightenment*. Urantia has never been visited or judged by a Magisterial Son before. Hence, he will be the first of his order to ever do so on your planet.

Ever since he was selected by Christ Michael to take on this enormous task, Monjoronson has been painstakingly working along with his staff in preparation for their great assignment. He has taken a deep interest in practically all aspects of your world's history – from its origin to its recent condition. He has interviewed scores of former mortals of this realm and familiarized himself with all your cultures, languages, and civilizations – past as well as present. He now embodies in his being your entire evolutionary history as a species since Andon and Fonta. Thus, he is fully prepared to assume the challenges of this exceptional mission on your sphere as a bestowal Son among men, which is to begin soon. In fact, his work has already begun on your planet for several years now, for he and his staff have been actively and diligently teaching, rehearsing and preparing scores of human beings who are willing to participate in the Magisterial Mission.

Monjoronson's adjudication of your world has nothing to do with destroying sinners as reported in many of your religious annals and traditions. The Magisterial Mission has come to your planet, mainly to offer and minister the mercy of Paradise to your kind, not to judge or punish mankind for his misdeeds as these concepts are understood here. The problem, which perpetuates this erroneous belief, is that most mortals of this realm are yet to understand that judgment is not an aspect of the divine nature. Since the new dispensation of enlightenment is scheduled to begin officially soon, we are more than ever, pressed to make this as clear as possible today. Again, let us repeat this if we may, *God does not judge you!* The Creator never seats in justice over his universe children. Karma is innate in the very order of creation in which you exist. It is a direct, proportionate energetic response to your own attitudes and deeds. It is an undetectable but inherent property of the function of energy itself, but it invariably manifests in the processes of all sentient living beings. What many of you call "*divine Judgment*" is not a conscious act of a personal Deity against you. Rather, it is the karmic repercussion of your own misguided attitudes toward divinity. Sin is a fatal spiritual poison, and so is the judgment that annihilates it.

You have been taught there are three major programs that define the activities of the Correcting Time Plan on your sphere. It has also been communicated to you that these programs were all designed to be implemented co-creatively with humanity. They were customized intentionally to help you participate in the spiritual healing and restoration of your world. The first serious act that was taken to kick-start this recovery project was manifested by the revelation of the text known to you as the Urantia Book, or the Fifth Epochal Revelation, as it should be properly recognized. Several decades after the publishing of the Urantia Papers in 1955, a second major step was made by launching the Teaching Mission around 1990-95, which was promptly followed by the recent disclosure of the Magisterial Mission.

We've now reached the end of our transmission for this evening. We shall delve quite extensively in the circumstances surrounding the Urantia Book in our next session – namely its mystical origin, uniqueness, authors, purpose, and significance. We shall speak about it not only as the beginning of the Correcting Time, but also as the precursor of the approaching new age of peace, goodwill, harmony and cooperation on earth.

I will now close this session and return to my domicile, farewell.

Paper 11

The Fifth Epochal Revelation

THE URANTIA BOOK—A PRECURSOR TO THE NEXT DISPENSATION

A Celestial Revelation to Humanity

Celestial Teacher: Abennally ~ Channel: Joseph Elie 11-17-2012

AS WE'VE MENTIONED IN OUR previous interactions, the *Great Correcting Time Plan* is a massive cosmic undertaking in its visions, dimensions and implications. It essentially incorporates several strategic programs, which were specifically designed to liberate the 37 quarantined planets of Satania—not just your world, but all of those that were badly affected by the Lucifer rebellion. About a century ago, this astronomical enterprise was started upon your planet under a threefold celestial program as indicated in our title: the *Urantia Book*, the *Teaching Mission*, and the *Magisterial Mission*.

Although this plan was initially conceived and launched eons before, it was not officially disclosed to humanity until the end of the 19th century, precisely in 1898, when the decision was made on Uversa to dispatch the original celestial Revelatory Corps of Light and Truth to your world [Urantia]. This commission had the mandate to prepare and deliver the text known as the Urantia Book, an extraordinary action that formally commenced the enfoldment of the first major cosmic revelation to this realm since the bestowal of the Creator Son here.

The Urantia Book
A Celestial Revelation to Humanity

During the early years of the 20th century, or more precisely in 1933, a mysterious revelation was disclosed to humanity by a group of celestial personalities hailing from diverse sectors of the universe—notably Uversa—the capital of the Superuniverse of Orvonton. The revelatory commission conveyed their messages to the world through a few souls of destiny who were used as channels or Transmitters/Receivers [TRs]. Very little can be said to explain how this process was achieved, and, perhaps even less is understood about why those particular mortals were selected as terrestrial liaisons to the angelic delegation. The book itself does not reveal anything about their personal identities. It simply remarks that they were members of the world's *Reserves Corps of Destiny*.

However, one thing is clear from its short and somewhat ambiguous descriptions. Those individuals had to demonstrate certain spiritual traits and qualifications prior to their selections as reliable conduits for these profound and unusual communications. But except for being members of the Reserve Corps of Destiny, little else was ever disclosed concerning these unique personalities through whom the narratives of the Urantia Papers were inspired. Suffice to say, regardless of who they were, they faithfully and successfully performed their responsibilities as temporal receivers, custodians, and trustees of the revelation.

The Reserve Corps of Destiny

The Reserve Corps of Destiny is a peculiar group of forward-looking human beings, who are ordinarily selected by some celestial agency/ies to function as planetary liaisons for the spirit realms, or in some other supernatural capacities. This fraternity of secretly rehearsed and spiritually endowed mortals has been in existence on your earth since the days of Adam. The number of its members varies in every generation. Although it is comprised mostly of average individuals, it is nonetheless, a cluster of spirit-conscious personalities who are highly receptive to the divine light, and who can perform various unusual tasks without affectation or pride. Those unique light-anchors are not preoccupied with the world's prevailing political, socioeconomic or even religious affairs. They are primarily intended to uphold the light of Truth, peace and love in the hearts of men, or when necessary to perform some other service, such as "*Ambassadors of the spirit world.*" This special corps was established eons ago, though it has seldom functioned in its full capacity on earth. But its existence was never disclosed to the world prior to the revelation of the Urantia text

Today, this rather obscure and mysterious circle of spirit-contactors, though is rarely employed in the conduct of world affairs, has been nonetheless, quite active lately in preparation for many yet undisclosed future activities on earth.

Epochal Revelations are Recurrent Events

The transmission of the Urantia Book's 196 Papers was entirely a supernatural process. But that was not, by any mean, a first-time event on earth. As the book itself affirms, humanity has received four previous Epochal Revelations since Urantia was registered as an inhabited planet in the universe of Nebadon. In the universe, when an evolving world is ready, providing it with new revelations to expand the consciousness of its inhabitants, is a cosmic tradition and a priority of the Gods.

As far as we know, the celestial administrators have always ascertained that every mortal inhabited planet receives adequate revelations periodically, not only to enlarge human consciousness, but also to ensure that every successive generation increasingly become more receptive to divinity and eager to find God. Apart from a few and rare exemptions of planets with serious abnormal circumstances, every new dispensation is usually open either by an incarnation of a descending Son of God, or by direct interplanetary communications of novel revelations—like your Urantia Papers.

Long before the time it was initiated, some of the celestial personalities who participated in this special endeavor were already stationed on earth in service duties. But essentially, the corps of messengers had officially begun the transmission process in the year A.D. 1934, following their contact with the selected human personalities who were to help them fulfill this extraordinary mission.

After the reports were completed, the original copy of the text was organized and published for the first time in the year A.D. 1955, under the title, "The Urantia Book"—the formal cosmic name for the planet earth according to the records. Unquestionably, the transmitting and assembling processes of the book were certainly a highly confidential matter, known only by those few special men and women who were secretly kept in solemn communication with the Revelatory Corps. But the secret was to be temporary, for the revelation was meant to be disseminated to humanity.

Beyond Mortal Imagination

We strongly believe that any objective analysis of the Urantia Papers would unfailingly disclose that such a phenomenal work of pure intellectual genius and spiritual brilliance could not have been the realization of mortal imagination; hence, it must be, indeed, *a revelation*. Actually, this is clearly proven by the fact that the book needs no interpreter; as any *truthful* information, *it absolutely speaks for itself.*

The majority of its various assertions are timeless, and therefore, supermaterial. They are incomparable to any other philosophical or sacred writings that can be found in the world. Most of its contents utterly exceed the literary concepts, meanings, and qualities of the noblest of men's intellectual achievements. The spirit of its declarations highly transcends any other inspired scripture known to mankind. Its superb descriptions of the nature, attributes, character, and personality of God, His equal Associates, with their exquisite and perfect universal administration, are certainly indicative of its divine origin. But above all, it is the brilliant depiction of the entire life history and teachings of Jesus that unequivocally confirms the transcendental source of this one-of-a-kind document. Moreover, the flawless harmonies of the sequential patterns in which its Papers are delineated, organized and presented, also suggest its supernal quality and demonstrate the sophistication of the technique that was used to create it.

One of the most peculiar characteristics of the Urantia Book, in our humble opinion, is the perfect symmetry and consistency of its narratives, irrespective of their broad disparities, origins, authors, and timelines. The perspectives from each of its 196 Papers may be different, but they are so well coordinated and organized that they perfectly overlapped and complement one another.

To us on this side, it is undoubtedly a universal revelation to your kind, which was intended to be the forerunner of a new dispensation of enlightenment on earth. It reveals the reality of the personality of God and the superb administration of His limitless creations along with the debacles of the Lucifer Rebellion. Essentially, save for the chronological delineation of Urantia's evolutionary ages and the life history and teachings of Jesus, the text mostly treats transcendental matters of eternal imports. Among some of the finite subjects of terrestrial meanings, it deals with are: science, philosophy, time and space, evolution, knowledge, race, art, civilization, government, religion, and family. Additionally, it eloquently harmonizes *the supernal values* of religion, *the true ideals* of philosophy with *the temporal facts* of science. It categorically asserts that the postulated *First Cause* of science and the hypothetical *Primordial Being* of philosophy are, in essence, one and the same loving *God of religion*. And it certifies that this inclusive, infinite, and absolute Deity, is also the Eternal Ancestor of all material, mindal, spiritual, and personal realities. Moreover, it explains the origin and history of your solar system along with the cosmological birth and developmental processes of its comprising planets, particularly the earth. Furthermore, it sequentially outlines the most decisive natural events, such as the ecological and biological transformations, which transpired on the planet throughout its long ages of evolution. All of that and immeasurably more, the text explains and substantiates with pristine clarity and commanding authority.

Nevertheless, notwithstanding its celestial origin, it is humanly graspable. Though it is unarguably, the most mysterious inspired literature to ever been penned and published on earth, the Urantia Book is amazingly intelligible to all sincere truth-seekers who truly aspire to know God and do his will. Most of its contents are unquestionably in a league of their own. By and large, as we said without prejudice, they greatly transcend the concepts, meanings and values of all mortal philosophies. And yet, they are completely understandable by any honest believing individual. The book unequivocally affirms that the genuine religious experience is nothing more or less than one's conscious loyalty to God—the Universal Father.

Apart from its first two sections which mainly describe the nature, attributes and personalities of the Eternal Deities along with depictions of Paradise, Havona, and the local universes of space, the book is essentially a summary of the major events that occurred on earth during the four previous dispensations; hence its name the Fifth Epochal revelation. The depths and scopes of its manifold narratives are profound and extensive, but it mainly focuses on revealing the true relationship of humanity with divinity. Personal acknowledgment of sonship with God is the central call and the predominant theme of its message to mankind.

Among its numerous assertions, it emphatically declares that man's realization that he is indeed a son of God is wholly dependent upon his faith and trust in the reality of the Father's presence within himself.

All mortals that honestly aspire to know God will always unfailingly find him in themselves. And provided that they are wholeheartedly consecrated to this quest for the divine maker in their own mind, they simply cannot fail to attain a certain degree of personal contact and communion with the Heavenly Father.

Speaking freely from our evaluation of the Urantia text, we firmly believe that any thoughtful and sound examination of its contents would most likely show that they are transcendental in nature — spiritually originated. We are convinced that an objective analysis of its narratives will unfailingly demonstrate that, in fact, they grandly surpass the intellectual capacity and the creative imagination of even the most brilliant minds on earth.

This is Joseph: Honestly, I often believe that humanity was probably not yet ready to receive and appreciate let alone apply the teachings of such a sublime celestial revelation. I often think that much of the cosmic actuality, Truths and spiritual values revealed in the Urantia Book actually exceed our current level of consciousness and capacity of understanding. However, I also know that by virtue of the divine presence in the human mind, deeply that's not true. I don't suppose the Gods would have sponsored such a revelation if mankind were utterly unprepared to receive, understand and effectively apply it. But regardless of my occasional doubts and concerns, I'm sure about one thing; comprehending the messages and implementing the teachings of the Urantia Book is impossible without the help of ones indwelling spirit, or the assistance of some other supernatural entities—such as the Spirit of Truth, the Holy Spirit or an angel.

My opinion that this angelic revelation exceedingly transcends our current level of comprehension may or may not be true. But I'm certain that without the ceaseless ministry of divinity within the mind of every rational mortal on earth, this revelation would not have been appropriate for our time, for no person would have been able to decipher and understand the significances of its narratives. The very existence of this book is sufficient evidence of the factual presence of spirit agencies operating in and around us.

However, it remains a test to humanity as to the degree we will accept and adhere to the values of this startling new revelation. Only the future will tell if, in fact, the human race is fully ready to study, embrace, and apply the teachings of such a supernal scripture. As for me, I'm praying for the arrival of the time when this revelation becomes universally known on earth. I don't believe I will witness this great achievement during my lifetime. Even so, I shall continue to look with interest and follow the progress of this magnificent endeavor as it unfolds, even beyond the grave.

As Abomaly mentioned in slightly different phraseologies, despite its divine origin, the book is remarkably intelligible to any Truth-discerning and progressive soul. A sincere heart with a receptive mind is all one needs in order to appreciate the importance of its message and grasp their meanings and values. All genuine truth seekers who are determined to expand their consciousness and spiritual understandings, will undoubtedly find the Urantia Book extremely captivating and profoundly inspiring. It will definitely illuminate their inquiring minds and feeds their hungry souls.

I encourage and praise all those wonderful souls, which are devotedly studying and laboring to disseminate this superb revelation throughout the world. You have remembered who you are. That is essentially, why you have undertaken such a great work for the spiritual edification and upliftment of all humanity. And may the Heavenly Father guides you and protect you from all that could potentially jeopardize or handicap your noble efforts.

Nevertheless, as we seek to understand the profound truths enclosed in this supernal revelation, it's imperative that we remain mindful of its divine origin and always look for the spiritual meanings of its declarations. It should be borne in mind that the authors of the Urantia Papers were celestial personalities, some of whom hailed from the very presences of the Eternal Paradise Deities. The human beings through whom they transmitted their messages were merely used as channels in the process. Although its 196 fascicles were transmitted using a material language, the bulk of informations enclosed in this peerless work predominantly derived from the spirit realms on high. Therefore, they can be truly understood only with the assistance of our Inner Guides, the Spirit of Truth or other celestial helpers. A certain degree of affinity and cooperation with these magnificent spirits is vital to comprehend the veritable meanings and embrace the real values of the eternal truths and the cosmic realities contained in this great revelation.

Origin of the Urantia Book

Abomaly: As we mentioned earlier, the Urantia Book is primarily a divine revelation. Its 196 Papers originated from several orders of celestial beings that were dispatched on a special mission to reveal universal truths to the inhabitants on this planet. This revelatory commission was instructed to upgrade and enlarge humanity's spiritual perceptions and understanding of Deity and reality. It was also envisaged that they teach humankind about the Gods' vast domains of creations and perfect cosmic administrations. By and large, they have successfully carried out their assignments. Though they were approvingly instructed to remain within the range of your current planetary development, but that mandate did not preclude or affected the fact of the presences of the Spirit of Truth and the divine Adjusters operating in the human mind on the planet. Thus, knowing this, the corps faithfully took the liberty and disclosed, for the first time, many profound cosmic truths that are completely beyond the scope of existing religious philosophies.

It is widely believed that the Urantia Book was written and created in less than a decade, but the precise amount of time it required to transmit and organized the entire revelation was never disclosed. This is generally unknown save perhaps for those who were directly involved in the receiving process. However, many among us think that given the enormity of this extraordinary task, the Revelatory Corps conveyed their communications to their mortal receptors rather very quickly in a conscientious effort to begin quickening the minds of modern men in preparation for the current unfolding Spiritual Renaissance on earth.

The members of this special delegation hailed primarily from four particular cosmic levels of existence, and they are:

Paradise: the eternal abode of the three existential Deities, God the Universal Father, God the Eternal Son, and God the Infinite Spirit.

Uversa: the Capital of Orvonton—the name of the seventh superuniverse of time and space. This central domain of Orvonton is presided over by three Ancients of Days.

Salvington: the Capital of the local universe of Nebadon, which is, presided over by Christ Michael—the Sovereign Creator Son, who once incarnated on Urantia as Jesus. In union with his immediate divine assistant, Nebadonia, Michael confers administrative authority to Gabriel, the head administrator and Chief Executive of Nebadon.

Jerusem: the Capital of Satania—the Local System of inhabited worlds in which Urantia belongs. Jerusem is currently presided over by Lanaforge—the System's Sovereign. He replaced Lucifer after the latter's fierce and sinful rebellion against the authority of Christ Michael as the supreme Chief and God of Nebadon. Lanaforge is a fully tested and loyal Son, who has always supported the spiritual sovereignty of Michael as the absolute personification of the Universal Father in Nebadon.

One among the many remarkable factors showing the divine authenticity and uniqueness of this book is that despite that its authors were recruited from various cosmic domains, and though they hailed from different orders of universe intelligences, their narratives and presentations are, however, exquisitely coordinated and superbly unified. This is indeed a testimony of the spiritual unity of the Gods who sponsored the revelation.

Together, the celestial messengers that authored the Urantia Papers were all assigned to function under the jurisdictions of the three presiding Orvonton Ancients of Days on Uversa and Gabriel of Salvington. Their informations were fully endorsed by the Paradise Trinity in accordance with the mandate of the Universal Father and His Creator Son – Michael of Nebadon.

It Confirms the Truth of Man's Sonship with God

During his memorable sojourn on Urantia, Christ Michael asserted that every human being was an offspring of God; a unique personality upon whom the Universal Father bestows his loving spirit. And... that by virtue of this indwelling presence, the body of man was essentially a divine temple.

Nineteen hundred years later, the Urantia Book reaffirms this revelation and unequivocally substantiates the Truth of Michael's sacred declaration. It brilliantly describes the reality of those Mystery Monitors and their ministries as they indwell the mortal minds of men. This gift of God—a parcel of Himself to each human being—is also depicted in the book as the Thought Adjuster, the Divine Presence, the Indwelling Spirit, and the Guiding Light of each child who comes into the world.

Although the Thought Adjusters' activities are, for the most part, mysterious in nature, but the Urantia Book graciously portrays and summarizes their preoccupations, both as indwellers of the mortal mind and otherwise. It highlights their dedication to spiritualize the minds and immortalize the souls of their human hosts. You are taught that those divine gifts of God work incessantly to ensure the eternal survival of their indwelt subjects.

The belief in a spiritual presence within the human body is quite an old tradition on earth. But in this revelation, much, very much was indeed disclosed for the first time about this profound and mysterious relationship between humanity and divinity.

In his mortal life experience as Jesus, Christ Michael had thoroughly revealed the universal truth of the fatherhood of God and proclaimed the planetary fact of the brotherhood of men. It is literally true that in Jesus, the world had witnessed a manifestation of the divine word made flesh—God the Son was incarnated in man. The Son of God truly became the Son of Man. However, unfortunately, by and large, the world has failed to comprehend the veritable significances of this sublime revelation. Today, humanity is still a long way from grasping the real meaning and purpose of that event.

It is altogether impossible to decipher and explain the secrets of the bestowal techniques by which a divine being—even the Creator Son of a universe may be personified as a mortal of time. The spiritual procedures of those incarnations of the Gods are one of the seven great mysteries of the Paradise Deities. Nevertheless, we can all rest assure that these mysterious embodiments of the Paradise Sons are fully possible, and occur regularly throughout the cosmos.

Essentially, the world's great failure to understand the profound significance of Christ Michael's mortal incarnation can be attributed directly to the gross perversions of his legacy of a lifetime consecration to God and service to men soon after his ascension to Salvington—the Capital of the universe of Nebadon. The divine concepts, meanings and values of the Master's teachings were intensely distorted and misused since his return to his central abode as the Sovereign of this universe. Today, they are still grossly mischaracterized and misinterpreted in the creedal philosophies of many self-proclaimed religious organizations, including the one that was created in his name. They are largely overshadowed by the orthodoxies of a rigidly controlled and institutionalized, hierarchical church. However, contrary to this clerical dominion with its pretentious claim of salvation in the risen Christ, the Urantia Book actually discloses the authentic story of Jesus as he lived, taught, worshiped and ministered to the world. It recounts the entire human bestowal experience of Christ Michael, as the Son of Man on earth. The fascinating declarations and teachings of the Master along with all the extraordinary events that marked his unique mortal life on Urantia are superbly relayed and illustrated for the edification and enlightenment of all generations.

Moreover, the book also reveals the biological origin, the planetary purpose, and the cosmic destiny of humanity for this *universe age*. Furthermore, it affirms that every spirit-born human being experiences the divine presence exclusively, hence discovers God individually, and recognizes sonship with Him as a personal spiritual reality. According to this revelation, belief can be a collective subject, but a believer must be actively and earnestly engaged in true spiritual communion with God in order to develop genuine faith. Indoctrinated religionists may be staunch and loyal supporters of creeds or mystical traditions, but only authentic faithers are personally inspired and spiritually motivated to do the will of the Paradise Father as his planetary sons and daughters.

There are indeed serious differences between genuine spirit-born faithers and mere conceptual believers and creedal worshipers. For example, belief may incite passion for loyalty to some religious convention, but only faith can lead to true worship, and may provide total assurance of spiritual survival beyond the grave. Essentially, a believer becomes an authentic faither merely after discovering and experiencing the divine presence within his own spiritualizing mind. In other words, when the evolving soul of this believing individual finally develops adequate capacity to discern and commune with his spirit monitor—the divine gift of God, which dwells within his mortal tabernacle.

Following this extraordinary spiritual attainment, such a faither goes on worshiping God freely, joyfully, peacefully, faithfully and personally irrespective of his traditional religious beliefs. There is indeed an inexpressible feeling of great inner peace, inner assurance and survival security that unfailingly accompany the realization of sonship with God. The serenity and joy of faithers are indescribable once they become conscious that they are really God's evolutionary children on earth. Once they are made aware of this by their indwelling spirits, believers are so deeply uplifted and inspired that they live on earth as if already in Paradise. And those who have truly discovered and experienced the divine presence in themselves, and who have therefore entered into a sincere betrothal with their Thought Adjusters honestly know God as a factual spiritual reality; even as the Infinite Maker and the divine Father of all.

It is both disturbing and pitiful to observe how some misguided individuals foolishly continue to deny the existence of

God while his spirit actually lives in their very pessimistic and incredulous minds.

As a personality, man can be positively gregarious or even ethical, but he becomes genuinely altruistic, moral, and unselfish only when his evolving soul is guided by the indwelling spirit. A believing person can be absolutely sure of God solely in the reality of his own personal spiritual experience with the divine monitor who dwells within his physical tabernacle. And that experience for every faither constitutes the only veritable and undeniable proof of the presence of divinity in humanity. For it completely erases all doubts about the possibility of contact and communion with God. And to all such inner spirit-contactors, discovering the divine presence is indeed the most blessed and rewarding of all possible human experiences. There is simply no other form of religious insight comparable to the personal realization of God within one's own mind.

In order to redeem themselves from their slavish subordination to traditionalism, the suffocating yoke of theological injunctions, the blunders of mortal philosophy, the narrow perceptions and detrimental values of materialistic science, it is imperative for modern Urantians to establish good and frequent communication with their indwelling Thought Adjusters.

Traditional slavery to stagnant dogmas and imposing beliefs and philosophies is one of the greatest setbacks to the intellectual, sociological, and spiritual evolution of mankind. In order to discover and comprehend the veritable purpose of life beyond our conventional beliefs and prevalent planetary wisdom, to discern and differentiate truths from our theological deceptions, to find God personally and learn about his universal plan for mankind free from the backward philosophies of institutionalized religion, I honestly believe that all genuine truth-seekers must read, study, and conscientiously meditate upon the Urantia Book.

The Urantia Book is the Fifth Epochal Revelation of Truth unveiled thus far to humanity. Like its predecessors, it is a unique cosmic revelation whose purpose is to elevate and spiritualize us. It embodies materials and informations from all previous authentic revelations that were ever disclosed to mankind. In reality, the Urantia book is not explainable or decipherable using any particular human method of analysis and reasoning. In a nutshell, the depth, quality and veracity of its contents boldly transcend all current predominant theological philosophies known to men.

Though it can hardly be described as a prophetic document, for its narratives are primarily concerned with revelation, but, to the extent one is interested in discovering the future probabilities of time, the book can definitely stimulate the imagination. In a sense, the Urantia Book may be regarded as a summary of the most stupendous past cosmic actualities along with insights on many likely fated universal and planetary events. However, as we delve into its mysterious papers, it should be borne in mind of their revelatory purposes to avoid any distortion of their meanings and values. The most important thing to keep in mind when reading the Urantia Book is that it was delivered to us under the direct order of God the Universal Father himself. Hence, to all practical intents and purposes, its narratives are absolutely true.

Additionally, we should also remember that as we continue to traverse the outer circuits of the universe, increasingly pushing towards its inner trajectories, we are always following the ordained cosmological path of the Universal Father to his eternal residence — the magnificent and glorious Isles of Paradise.

The universe hosts have kindly called upon modern Urantians to cease your petty religious discords and resolve your spiritual differences in the light of the most complete universal revelation that was ever unveiled to the human races of this world — the Urantia Book. You are encouraged and invited to amiably receive this revelation; to heed its message and earnestly apply its teachings. Especially at this moment, as the drifts of world events continue to decline for the worst, slowly but surely moving humanity toward a major and decisive planetary transition. Presently, your sincere commitment to adhere to the values of this supernal revelation is crucial to ensure the ultimate triumph of peace, and to improve the quality of worship and religious fellowship on earth. In effect, every living personality on Urantia has been summoned to participate in a global effort to propagate this superb revelation for the spiritual elevation of all mankind.

Much more could be said about the Urantia Book even from a purely material perspective, but like all sacred scriptures one must read it in order to discover and appreciate its message. Therefore, it is futile that I attempt to describe it any further here. Though it is my design for this book to be primarily a promotional document for the Urantia Book, but it would be presumptuous to assume that I can fairly describe such a supernal work of pure genius with watertight analysis as to convince you [the reader] of its divine qualities, meanings, values and universal Truths. These things, you must realize on your own. If you are a truth seeker, and if you are naturally persuadable, perhaps I might have already convinced you of its importance. Although I seriously doubt this could be sufficient information to guide your decision. Hence, you are responsible to transcend any personal handicaps that could potentially hinder or prevent your access to this exceptional revelation of our time. Finally, above all, the Urantia Book needs no interpreters; it absolutely speaks for itself.

In the quest for Truth and spiritual enlightenment, devotees must always remember that faith is imperative to any success, and your will to attain God consciousness must be supreme. Your desire to discover the Creator and learn about his universal administration has to be solid and unremitting if you wish to be at least partially successful in this supernatural enterprise. You must relentlessly nurture your faith to such an extent that you become predispose to rise above any immediate obstacle and move forward, or rather inward every time your soul is stirred by a bit of truth, irrespective of where it may have originated. God is not approachable with a half-hearted commitment to his divinity. The Paradise Father requires wholehearted loyalty and absolute allegiance, or none at all.

The Forerunner of a New Dispensation

Today, the world stands in desperation for a spiritual renaissance. Humanity needs to be empowered with *truths* in order to avoid an unthinkable looming planetary catastrophe. At this point, quick action is vital because that potential global mayhem is fast approaching. The current generation is facing the most formidable challenges mankind has ever encountered in history. And no amount of intellectual dexterity or technological ingenuity can possibly remedy or resolve all the existing problems.

More than ever before, humanity is in great need for celestial assistance to ascertain the future of civilization on the planet. Every peaceful, liberty-loving person needs to seek for his or her own truths from within. You must transcend the deceptions of this passing era. Once again, this generation needs to be invigorated with the true Gospel of *Sonship with God* as Jesus revealed it while yet on earth.

Jesus was indeed a miraculous incarnation of the divine word made flesh. A revelation, which he declared, was established on two fundamental and inalienable cosmic Truths: 1] the universal fatherhood of God; 2] the planetary brotherhood of men.

It is self-evident that the world is now dangerously crossing the threshold of a very gloomy and decisive period, which will drastically change the current course of human history. The sharp escalations of warfare, social unrests, bigotry, greed, etc. without exaggeration, indeed suggest even more dangerous times ahead. Nevertheless, almost unnoticeably, this moment also embodies the prospect for a new and better global community. It is latently carrying a novel spirit that will, in time, revolutionize the current international order and utterly transform the world for good.

In the midst of all the present troubling and tumultuous circumstances of this precarious global transition, the hope for spiritual enlightenment through the restoration of Christ Michael's Gospels has never been greater. Humanity now has the opportunity to redeem itself finally from the traditional bondage of institutional religion by learning anew the authentic teachings of the Master, which is thoroughly provided in the Urantia Book. Since its publication, many once captive and dejected souls have been emancipated as they found peace and joy. Scores have regained their strengths by studying this great revelation.

Essentially, the veritable religious experience is primarily absolute, wholehearted acceptance and embracement of the sublime truth of the universal fatherhood of God and the planetary brotherhood of all mankind. No more should religion be limited to culture and conventions, or rigidly subjected to the influence of some ecclesiastic authority.

In its real expression, religion is purely a personal spiritual experience. Its derivative social fruits are fundamentally moral and just. And... as such, it is therefore, always unique and original for every believing individual. The authentic faith or religious devotion cannot be transformed into creedal philosophies. In fact, worship is such a transcendent activity that it cannot be described with mere dead letters or symbols. It utterly originated from the inner association of the evolving soul of man with the indwelling spirit of God. Faith is the absolute assurance of profound connection with the divine presence of the Universal Father. Throughout all times, religion was, is, and shall remain an unfathomable, yet experiencible spiritual reality to all progressing souls. It is an original practice for every honest mortal who may come to believe in God by choosing to do his will. Traditional submission to theological injunctions effectively impedes the spiritual development of mankind, and consequently, delays religious progress on Urantia.

One of the most peculiar and remarkable developments that is occurring in the world today is the emergence of a Truth-curious generation even amidst all the present despairing situations. As you face this critical moment with the looming challenges ahead, it is encouraging to acknowledge also that many spirit-endowed minds around the globe [particularly young people] are now ready to embrace and appreciate higher spiritual possibilities than what is known conventionally, or currently accepted as the word of God on earth. Undoubtedly, a growing number of thinking individuals throughout the planet are gradually escaping the theological confinement of institutional religions. Many honest and genuine believers are increasingly becoming objective truth-seekers than indoctrinated followers and worshipers. Through information, revelation, and faith, they are steadily maturing morally and spiritually. Those progressive personalities are empowered to differentiate truth from deception without ambiguity. They are rapidly acquiring enough spiritual insights to participate in the attainment of their own cosmic destiny. There are tremendous talents in this group that can transform the religious landscape of this world by outshining all nonprogressive creeds if those faithers would earnestly allow the divine seed of love to germinate and flourish within their souls.

Now, humanity can no longer afford to continue to observe and cherish static and fruitless creeds in order to preserve and honor traditions. You have arrived at a juncture when it is no more conducive to be fixated ideologically on any matter pertaining to religion and spirituality. Your blind loyalty to culture and tradition has severely damaged your intellectual and spiritual capacity to achieve true greatness. Good thinking and sound actions are the fruits of a morally balanced individual—a rationally stable human being. Man must be set free to worship God in the knowledge of divine truth as this is revealed to him by his own mind indwelling spirit. The traditional approach to God through sacrifice and ostentatious subordination to some ecclesiastic authority is now obsolete; it's rapidly passing away. The approaching new world will be emancipated from the spiritual darkness of the current, for much of the pervasion of the annals of religion will be clarified or eliminated. A normal minded human being should never be coerced to live strictly according to the precepts of any particular religious institution under any circumstance.

To be objective in your perceptions and evaluations of religion, you must first recognize its mysterious nature as a personal spiritual experience. Man becomes conscious of God as a factual spirit and a loving Deity personally, through recurrent interactions with his inner Guide, not by his affiliation to a cult. This realization is primarily dependent upon his capacity to recognize and commune with the divine presence in his own heart. To the son-conscious soul of adequate spiritual maturity, religion is the most private and confidential of all possible human experiences.

Man's spiritual liberation from the natural handicaps of time begins with his wholehearted disposition to do the will of God. By responding favorably to the callings of the Father's immortal spirit, which lives in him, man is slowly but surely transcending his material nature, gradually shifting his personality from the localized consciousness of time to eternity. And this transitioning process, no matter how incomplete, irrespective of the theories of his religious convictions, constitutes the essence of his faith—his religion.

Genuine spirit-born individuals naturally desire world peace and fellowship among all mankind. They live by faith, worship and commune with the Universal Creator while patiently waiting for the ultimate triumph of Truth in the hearts of their fellows. Love and service are the prime motivations of their illuminated soul. Those divine qualities unfailingly dominate all interactions among progressive believers.

The true faith essentially liberates men from the bondage of traditions and institutions. It illuminates the soul and expands the consciousness beyond the precincts of the material world. It delivers the mind from all evils, which derive from superstitions, earthly prejudices, and mortal handicaps. It safeguards the intellect from all animal fears and effectively suppresses all temporal doubts.

Spirit-born individuals deeply understand the real nature of religion. They know it is their personal experiences with God, which are always inspiring, uplifting, and enlightening. This is why they are so appreciative of all authentic and meaningful expressions of any religion, irrespective of its origin and kind. They can easily differentiate inspired truths from mere fabricated mortal theologies. A liberated soul is fully aware that he or she needs no creed to approach and communicate with God. To him, theology is but the psychology of evolutionary religion; it does not portray the true connection of the soul with the indwelling spirit. The nature of the filial relationship of God with man in the inner association of the Thought Adjuster with an evolving soul cannot be explained psychologically or sociologically. This subtle affiliation of the Eternal Creator with the finite creature is essentially unfathomable to virtually all orders of created intelligences. It is original and personal for every evolving human being. It is above and beyond the understanding facility of the material mind, and thus, it evades all finite intellectual examinations.

At its best, organized-religion should be regarded as a noble endeavor of believers to socialize their personal spiritual experiences. Therefore, their derivative creeds and precepts are always subjective. When he sincerely and respectfully shares his religious thoughts with his fellows, man epitomizes the proper attitude of the veritable faith. But when he sets out to transform his beliefs into sacred doctrines for everyone else, he fails immeasurably to discover the liberating spirit of the authentic religious life. The dogmatization of any concept, be it true or not, automatically results in its spiritual degradation - its subordination to a temporal authority. The living faith unfailingly transcends the circumscribed realms of dogmas, and elevates the evolving soul to the heights of the eternal glories of Paradise.

The spirit-born faither deeply knows that most of the rules and doctrines of organized religions are illusions and lies. Frankly, it is disconcerting to observe the pathetic efforts of some misguided religionists to replace the real values of religion with the dead letters of traditions. Again, faith is strictly a living experience. It simply cannot exist in any material will-creature without continuing personal interactions with God. What the world mostly needs today are the great Truths, which lead to this dynamic and living faith. Since 1934, the transmission of the Urantia Book as the Fifth Epochal Revelation to mankind started a comprehensive process to disseminate these truths. However, we have been advised that it is now time to increase the momentum of this movement. We firmly believe that humanity's planetary deliverance from the dark cabal will not come from any established traditions or so-called New-Age teachings. Instead, this will happen by a rigorous worldwide dissemination, studying, and application of the Urantia Papers

Accordingly, we pledge to do our utmost to fulfill our part in this global undertaking as it is faithfully entrusted unto all potential Jesusonians by our divine parents. And this, we unreservedly choose to do because we believe that every sincere and devoted truth-seeker, no matter how or where he or she started out on the quest for enlightenment, with perseverance in faith, shall eventually discover the supreme truth upon which established the foundation of religion, which is concisely sonship with God and fellowship with all mankind.

This has been a rather lengthy session pertaining to the Fifth Epochal Revelation, which is commonly known as the Urantia Book. We covered many aspects of this, the first among the three major programs, which constitute the overall activities of the Great Correcting Time Plan. Our next exchange shall be about its second main component, which has been revealed to you as the Teaching Mission.

I will now take leave for a season of rest and rejuvenation. Good evening.

Paper 12

The Teaching Mission

THE INFLUX OF EXTRATERRESTRIALS ON EARTH

Preparation for the New Era of Spiritual Enlightenment

Celestial Teacher: Abennalg ~ Channel: Joseph Elie 11-26-2012

AS THE URANTIA BOOK WAS the precursor to the ceremonial beginning of the Correcting Time Plan, the Teaching Mission [TM] is the successive program designed to fine-tune, elevate, and expand humanity's collective consciousness for greater reception of divine love and Truth in preparation for the New Era of spiritual enlightenment on earth. In fact, it is a continuation of the Fifth Epochal Revelation, hence its concurrence with all the activities of Michael's Plan. Though they were conceived together, this project was not revealed to your world simultaneously with the Urantia text. The Revelatory Corps made contact with their human hosts in 1933. The book was first published in 1955. However, the initial communications that launched the TM activities started in 1991, by Abraham of the Old Testament.

Since its disclosure in Switzerland to a Urantia reading group, over two decades ago, the Teaching Mission has quickly expanded throughout the world. New groups of sincere truth seekers who believe in the co-creative process of channeling and working with spirit are forming across the globe regularly now—

especially in North America, Europe, and Africa. We are witnessing a splurge of truth-hungry and inquiring souls that are seeking for answers to many questions, which are practically outside the perimeters of normal human perception and understanding. And... we are amazed by your extraordinary diligence and passion to grow and attain spiritual enlightenment despite the vicissitudes and hardships you must often endure on this lower plane of existence. In general, humanity's response to this enterprise has been tremendous, and your enthusiasm has sharply increased the power of the divine light upon the world. As a result, this phenomenon has so elevated man's collective consciousness that, it changed global society's previous destructive course and shifted it towards a more peaceful and stable future. We are delighted to have been able to work with you in this marvelous co-creative process to bring about that great victory through the Teaching Mission's efforts even before the official inauguration of the Magisterial Mission. We celebrate and rejoice with you!

No more are mortals of this realm ever to fear the future because of some ominous prophecies of doom. Now humanity is called to wake-up from the deep slumber of spiritual ignorance. You have been subdued in servitude for too long. Today, you are being prepared to receive the full revelation of your true cosmic identity, which will not only confirm your affiliation to Deity, but also empower you to experience this sublime reality. The recent momentum for world peace is the result of that subtle but powerful calling from on high to all dear hearts here. Our main exhortation to you is to begin searching for *who and what you truly are* from within through regular stillness and meditation, for this is the foundational knowledge to your complete awakening and enlightenment. You must first discover your relationship to the Prime Creator of the universe, *to all that exist,* in order to be totally liberated from the handicaps of the mind and the flesh. We believe it is due time for you to reflect seriously upon and embrace the revelation that you are indeed made in the image of the Gods. It is imperative to delve in yourselves to find the real meaning of this profound Truth. We are here to encourage and inspire you to continue the battle of faith on this confused world. And again, we honor your sincere efforts and perseverance to keep the flare of light and love burning bright in the midst of all the difficulties surrounding existence on this strife-torn planet. Believe me my friend, we never cease to marvel at your courage and audacity to stand for a noble conviction and even die for a truth deeply enshrouded in your heart. During our many ages of planetary service here, we've learned a lot from this experience, and we've developed an exquisite affection for the human race.

The Universal Mobilization to Approach Humanity
Influx of Celestials for the Teaching Mission

For almost a century now, by Michael's direct order and under the immediate supervision of Machiventa Melkisedek, [the vice gerent Planetary Principal] there has been an influx of virtually all types of supernatural entities from various domains of the universe arriving regularly on this world to minister for the success of the Correcting Time Plan. Those foreign volunteers along with the staff of your local angelic helpers and millions of forward-looking humans are functioning in unison to shoulder the enormous responsibilities of this superb cosmic enterprise. Today, there is an ongoing *universal mobilization* to approach humanity with a greater revelation of Truth, and that is quite effectively conducted through the Teaching Mission. These activities are coincided with the presence of Monjoronson, an Avonal Son of Paradise origin who recently arrived on earth in a Magisterial Mission to adjudicate and close this age. He and his staff came to facilitate the rectification of the deplorable conditions on this planet due to eons of systematic evil, neglect and abuses.

The executive methods of this celestial project upon your world are so subtle and effective that millions of humans have responded to *The Calling*, even though most ignore its existence, and they too, are also unknowingly contributing to its success and completion.

As you know, together, the three major programs that are being implemented to rescue this sphere from spiritual darkness, i.e. the dissemination of the Urantia Book, the Teaching Mission, and the Magisterial Mission, are formally known on high as "The Great Correcting Time Plan." It is an astronomical agenda, which not only includes the salvation of this world, but also all the other planets that were affected by the Lucifer rebellion.

Inasmuch as we are conversant with, and up to the limit, we may discuss the circumstances of this supernatural project, there is serious diligence here and on high to help humanity prepare for the looming eventualities ahead that will officially terminate the current dispensation. As we mentioned earlier, many celestials from various sectors of the universe have assumed the enormous task to mentor all willing and teachable Urantians, who desire to expand the horizon of their spiritual awareness. Many of these volunteers were once mortals of the realms themselves; former humans in advance stages of their ascending careers who relish serving their fellow kind. They have temporarily postponed the Paradise ascension activities to offer their help and assistance or to witness the proceedings of Christ Michael's prodigious recovery plan. They want to be part of an incredible cosmic history in the making.

Today, there is a massive mobilization on high to support and assist every Urantia mortal that is sincerely thirsty for the Living Truth offered by the Creator. Our conscientious efforts, particularly the broad educational and teaching programs to uplift and prepare mankind for the next dispensation, are functioning excellently in the world at this moment.

The main responsibilities of those of us who are concerned with this unprecedented ministry are to teach, inform, train and advise all believing and receptive mortals on this realm who aspire to know and do the will of God.

Bear in mind, our mission to this world is basically a co-creative endeavor between humanity and us; it is wholly a mutual process. We work in conjunction with you. The level of our success will ultimately be measured by the degree of your cooperation. With sufficient of you onboard the *"love ship"* as we sometimes characterizes this ministry, the ultimate goal is to design and create a new global society wherein peace, love and fraternity truly prevail in the hearts of all mankind. We are here to help you aggrandize your awareness and clarify your understanding of self and reality, thus redefining your boundaries and limitations. We hope to inspire you to embrace the truths of life; to transcend your mortal handicaps; to acknowledge your higher spiritual nature; to communicate with your divine selves, and to begin to live in appreciation of all that you truly are. Unfortunately, with the prevailing menial comprehension of self-identity, most of you are practically unable to access much of the creative powers of your inner selves as multi-dimensional, will-endowed personalities.

Each of you was created complete, which literally means potentially eternal, perfect, and infinite. However, you only perceive and experience a fraction of what you are capable of at your current level of consciousness and understanding. Frankly, without being disrespectful or judgmental, after thousands of years of human evolution, the scope of intellectual and spiritual awareness on your earth is extremely limited and pathetic. Thus, to help you fully actualize your higher potentials and realize the sublime truth of your boundless indwelling divine nature is our main goal. Assisting you in building a forward-looking and peace-loving global family according to the will of the Universal Father, is one of our most important and cherished tasks.

Like the four previous dispensations, this one is intended to enlarge the frame of your spiritual perception by disclosing new revelations and teachings to increase your capacity to realize and interact with the Presence of God within yourselves. As you know, the main purpose for these periodic celestial revelations is to elevate mankind morally and spiritually; to encourage soul growth and increase your awareness of the Father's Spirit. And as you do so progressively, collectively you are gradually approaching the shining of the glorious age of Light and Life, when all of humankind will readily embrace the divine will.

Some of us can even now visualize the light of this wonderful epoch on your world; and it is with great joy and anticipation that we extend ourselves to assist you in creating this paradisiacal time for all future generations. Verily, we regard it as an honor to be a part of, and a privilege to play a role in this magnificent project that will ultimately usher your planet into a new path of peace, righteousness, and brotherhood. We are very excited about the progress we are making in reaching and communicating our messages to those of you who receive us. The goal is to reach and have contact with all of you. As our little brothers and sisters of this realm, we are very fond of you.

True, your world and many others were gravely affected and disoriented by the catastrophe of the Lucifer rebellion. But as we've said before, this is behind you now. You are entering a New Era. You can start over and rectify your mistakes. You can rebuild your lives on higher values that reflect and reveal your true spiritual nature as children of God. You can willfully embrace truth, beauty, and goodness. You can cultivate good intention and benevolence. You are all members of the universal divine family. The secret to realize peace, unity and happiness among your races is not enshrouded in gold, pride or power, but in love, mercy and joyous service to one another.

Some of the current global challenges will not disappear immediately after the official inauguration of the new era. There will be an interval period of relative chaos before this world regains its equilibrium—before order is restored completely. However, you can rest assured that as the Correcting Time's activities continue to spread and intensify over the world; the divisive attitudes that beset this world will increasingly fade out of your collective social fabrics. Eventually, all the negativities of the Lucifer rebellion will ultimately disappear from your planetary consciousness. For example, racial and transnational animosity will become practically obsolete during the advance stages of the new era. And… such ignoble tendencies will no longer exist in the human psyche during the Ages of Light and Life on earth. In effect, it is encouraging to observe that many who welcome our presence and work with us have already transcended these lowly, abhorrent inclinations, and are learning to appreciate the diversities of their fellow mortals as they passionately engage in this stupendous endeavor to retrieve their planet from the legacies of a sinful rebellion.

I commend you for your ongoing efforts and determination to continue to make yourself available for this kind of contact with us. As difficult it may be sometimes for you to muster the faith and trust necessary to allow our communications to flow freely into your physical mind, you always manage to defeat doubt and rise to the occasion because of your humility and passion to draw near God and interact with us. I can clearly perceive that from my point of observation. So, as Michael would say, "*be of good sheer*," your faith will always guide you to the source. I will now bid you farewell, good afternoon.

Paper 13

The Magisterial Mission

THE FUTURE INCARNATION OF THE AVONAL SON

The Return of Jesus with Melkisedek and Adam & Eve

Celestial Teacher: Abmmaly - Channel: Joseph Elie 12-07-2012

WHEN THE SUDDEN OUTBREAK OF the Caligastia secession started around 250,000 years ago, there were several immediate plans of action proposed by diverse celestial councils to deal with the unusual uprising. Many concerned personalities offered to prepare a contingency of Melkisedek Sons with other emergency ministers to seize jurisdiction of the planet by *Fiat Power* or by divine decree. Some even considered replacing the traitorous Prince promptly with another worthy ruler, thus bypassing all the established protocols of the universe in the manner of dealing with such situations.

Those who had ideas about how to solve the crisis were permitted to present their proposals and plans before the body of authority that was responsible to mitigate the Luciferian insurrection in Satania. However, because the offenses of the rebellion were so severe, as the rebels' transgressions were so egregious, which made them liable for personality extinction, the Ancient of Days—the Supreme Justices on Uversa—had to intervene to mend the situation. Accordingly, it was decided to allow the miscreants freehand to prosecute their nefarious agenda on the 37 planets that were aligned with their government.

After conferring with Immanuel, Gabriel and the Father Melkisedek, Christ Michael had decided not to interfere with the rebel forces directly and permitted them to continue with their spree of blasphemy and sin unmolested. However, as we said at the onset of Paper 10, he did not remain inactive.

He did immediately devise a comprehensive plan to eventually retrieve those lost worlds from the control of Lucifer and his accomplices. And... as you know, besides some other unusual actions that were intended to be taken to correct the problems resulting from the upheavals, such as Michael's own incarnation, the bestowal of the Fifth Epochal Revelation and the Teaching Mission, that plan also included Magisterial Missions – the bestowal of Avonal Sons of Paradise origin to adjudicate these troubled planets. Thus, the celestial personality widely known among those who are acquainted with the Teaching Mission as Monjoronson or Soraya was designated for this special assignment on your world. It is interesting to mention that this will be a first-time event for all the 37 rebellion stricken kingdoms.

The Future Incarnation of the Magisterial Son
The Coming Fifth Dispensation

Since the disclosure of his presence on the astral plane of Urantia, Monjoronson has painstakingly labored to share his energy signature with humanity through frequent interactions with scores of receptive light workers and channels. Like Christ Michael, this Son is fully motivated by mercy and compassion, and he is eager to begin his exceptional mission as one among you. Though the precise time of his anticipated incarnation has not yet been published, he has personally revealed many circumstances that will characterize his arrival and sojourn upon your sphere. And he has also hinted at the imminence of his arrival here. So we urge you all to remain vigilant, and be ever ready to meet and visit with him. Since he intends to remain for a very long time on earth, perhaps many centuries, the Magisterial Son has devised a long-term global program that will be systematically implemented to cleanse and restore Urantia from the remnants of the legacies of the Lucifer rebellion, and lead [it] to the Ages of Light and Life. As the divine adjudicator of a dispensation, Monjoronson is, of course, mostly preoccupied with the spiritual development, progress, and ascension of the human soul. However, his Magisterial Mission will also address all significant earthly circumstances; hence, his emphasis on planetary sustainability. This is precisely why creating sustainable institutions—starting from the family to the state—is his priority, and one of the most popular topics many have discussed with him over the past few years since his arrival here.

Monjoronson has recently submitted himself to the morantial energy directors to undergo the preliminary changes that will allow him to incarnate soon as a human being on your world. He will not be born from a woman as did Christ Michael over 2000 years ago. His being will not be subjected to the natural processes of physical and mental development, for he will incarnate as a full-fledged matured personality. He has not revealed in which of the planetary races of Urantia, he will appear. He has stated that he will materialize as a male. However, being an Avonal Son of divine origin, we doubt that he will marry or beget any offspring during his life in the flesh.

Additionally, unlike Michael, Monjoronson's personal staff of earthly helpers and assistants will be quite large – numbering around 144 dutiful personnels. He will travel extensively with many of his close associates. And…as he has declared, when they arrive, he and his crew will avail themselves of all the social media networks available on the planet to communicate their messages and interact with mankind.

Now, since the announcement of the Magisterial Mission to some of you, there have been many transmissions from various celestial entities, including Monjoronson himself, emphasizing the importance that the world be made ready for this extraordinary event. It is imperative that conditions are right and suitable to accommodate the arrival of this new Messiah on your planet. This is an extraordinary event that will profoundly change humanity's social and spiritual paradigms; that will greatly clarify Michael's revelation of the fatherhood of God and the brotherhood of men.

The principal slogan guiding this magnificent pending event will be: *Peace, Harmony, and Spiritual Unity on Earth.*

During this new upcoming dispensation, it will be paramount for your societies to begin to stop seeing themselves as separate clusters of peoples that must compete for global clout, position, prestige and power. You will be asked to lift up the veil of mortal ignorance and prejudices, which, from our viewpoint, merely fuel division and intolerance among your races. Most of you on this sphere have been taught to live in fabricated generalities; to respect and identify only with your native cultures and races. This form of planetary experience has been strongly encouraged and sometimes forced upon you by the dark cabal to keep you divided and weak, thus unable to muster any effective resistance against their rules and domination. It is now extremely important for you to realize that this model of segregating and classifying yourselves into different antagonistic factions has only worked to the detriment of your global society and benefit your real enemies.

Beloved ones, simply put, the times have changed drastically when you can no longer afford to remain ignorant of your true nature and cosmic identity. Thus, we are urging you to open your minds and hearts beyond the scope and horizon of these temporal illusions, such as that which you call state, religion and nationality. Dear hearts, it is now imperative for you to know that these mundane references are not only illusory, but they no longer serve you in this journey. It's time to let them go and embrace your true selves – begin to get familiar with the real you as we perceive you on high. You are all beautiful evolving souls of personality dignity; finite manifestations of the Eternal I AM who is *Infinite Love*. You are children of God albeit the smallest among myriads of other created intelligences in the universe. So please, seize upon this golden opportunity to claim finally your divine inheritance.

The Projected Return of Christ Michael
An Anticipated Event on Urantia

As it was published many centuries ago in various annals of your religious philosophies, and as it has been revealed in recent transmissions from the Teaching Mission, Christ Michael is returning on your planet soon. However, like the anticipated bestowal of Monjoronson, no specific date has been projected for this event yet. But virtually all of us on this side are inclined to believe that their appearance upon your sphere is imminent. The latest events that occurred in the development of the Correcting Time Plan are unprecedented, and we think they confirm our speculations. The direct interference of the Universal Father to balance the negative energies that beset Urantia along with the sudden announcement of the opening of a new dispensation and Michael's recent visit to Paradise for a special conference with the Father seemed to indicate that the Creator Son is getting ready to fulfill his promise of revisiting this world in the flesh.

Nevertheless, it should be made clear that Christ Michael has visited Urantia several times since his departure from your midst, especially since he began enacting his correcting plan here about a century ago. But those visits were only registered on the astral or spiritual plane of your world, for he did not manifest in physicality. We are cognizant of the ambiguities and confusions that surround the prospect of this great pending event on your world as many are clinging to erroneous beliefs pertaining to the second coming of the Master. Some of these misconceptions are being removed, and a significant number of you have been quite elucidated about the subject as you become more receptive to the energies of the divine light, which now surrounds your planet. In effect, we wish for you to know that the spiritual energies that are being poured upon your sphere today are purely from the First Source and Center of reality. Hence, nothing that is valuable, meaningful and necessary for the development and growth of your souls can be retained from you now. Actually, this is always so. And if you sincerely wish to see Christ and learn about his promised return on Urantia, then you cannot fail to inter in contact with him spiritually provided you truly desire such a connection. Yes beloved, it is as simple as that! As it has always been, the only obstacle to your realization of Christ Michael's presence in your heart at this time is your own *unbelief.*

The old planetary grid through which your collective thoughts and emotions are filtered has been removed and replaced by a new one to anchor the light and the love of the Father on your world. As this was revealed to some of you, the previous grid was severely contaminated by Lucifer and Caligastia in their efforts to retain all deceased souls within the lower levels of reality and prevent them from ascending to the Source of all that is. This anomaly has been dealt with effectively, and now all souls of survival potentials are immediately transferred to their respective mansion worlds following natural death.

Michael had to come personally to Urantia to ascertain the success of the removal of the Luciferian grid, for it was so heavily coded with energetic imprints of fear and despair. In fact, that was the situation, which prompted the Universal Father to intervene directly to accelerate the cleansing process and facilitate the continuation of the Correcting Time. And… it is just after this momentous event, we began to observe several changes in the cosmic administration of Urantia, which to us are indicative of something extraordinary in the horizon. There is now almost total unanimity among those of my order regarding the imminent return of the Creator Son to your sphere as he had promised over 2000 years ago. And, according to the latest information broadcasted from Salvington to Urantia, he will probably be accompanied with Machiventa Melkisedek and Adam & Eve.

Although, as Michael stated while yet on earth, only the Father knows the date of his return, but we believe that his latest personal conference with the Father on Paradise was a big hint signaling that such a time has arrived. Many of us think this was the last private meeting that invested him with the final authority to materialize once again on Urantia, except this time, as the Sovereign Lord of Nebadon and the official Planetary Prince of your world. There are duly a lot of speculations concerning the precise moment this might occur, but all are excited to see this day and to feel the imminence of this highly anticipated event.

We are fully aware of the importance of such an event for many dear souls on this planet. We know it will bring you tremendous joy and happiness. You must know that you played a great role in bringing about this day that is now virtually upon you. Your honest prayers and supplications have not been discarded. No, they were all heard and considered even when the responses were delayed or adjourned for another life. Yes, whether or not you can believe it, part of the reason why Michael is returning is you, his children who have never ceased to request his presence on earth. If only you relinquished your doubts and accept the guidance of his gift of the Spirit of Truth, then you would be sure of this, for you would have the knowingness that Michael has never left you alone in the world.

This concludes our transmission on the Magisterial Mission today. We shall commingle our energy signatures again for a similar connection in the coming days. But we will slightly deviate our attention from the procedures of the Correcting Time to discuss certain of humanity's immediate celestial helpers as you requested. We kindly thank you for your attention and service, good-bye.

Paper 14

Humanity's Immediate Celestial Helpers

NEBADONIA—THE HOLY MOTHER SPIRIT OF THIS UNIVERSE

The Seraphims, Adjutants, Midwayers & The Indwelling Spirits

Celestial Teacher: Abonnady ~ Channel: Joseph Elie 12/12/2012

AS YOU HAVE BEEN TAUGHT, spiritually, humans are never alone during their short sojourn in the flesh on their native planets or throughout their long ascending careers in the universes. Besides the indwelt spirit, the evolving soul of survival potential is ably and sympathetically guarded by volunteer angelic personalities. These benevolent creatures are normally appointed to serve in this and many other capacities on behalf of humanity. And they are indispensable in the ascension program for the mortal races of time and space. Although many orders of universe intelligences are attached to the planetary service of men, and are thus, also respectively classified as celestial helpers, the seraphic angels have been the most widely recognized on earth due to their unique ministry of guardianship to human beings. Seraphims not only watch over their mortal subjects in the flesh, but they also serve as the temporary custodians of their souls after natural death. It is the custom of the universe administrators to provide two angels, normally a Seraphim and a Sanobim as wardens for the safekeeping of every soul of destiny. Traditionally, the Seraphim angel serves as the official guardian of the subject, while she is skillfully assisted by her Sanobim sister. But both angels are necessary to ensure their success in this intricate task, which is to protect and guide man's earthly paths while supporting the growth and evolution of his immortal soul. In this ministry of grace and salvation, the Seraphim angel is always partly responsible for the survival of her subject.

Man's admission to seraphic guardianship is conditional upon certain requisite moral attainments. In principle, technically the ascension program requires that mortals should be morally balanced and must manifest adequate spiritual disposition before they can be assigned personal guardian angels. Accordingly, only those of you who possess the undeniable potential for eternal survival; who sincerely desire to be led by spirit are effectively qualified to receive the intimate assistance of these affectionate celestial helpers. Otherwise, prior to their qualifications, individuals are ordinarily guarded by a pair of angels in clusters of one thousand, one hundred and ten. Nevertheless, it should also be noted that, in reality, the spiritual progresses of man cannot be technically monitored or scientifically evaluated. Therefore, no one can know for certain when someone is qualified to receive the gracious ministry of a personal guardian angel.

The concept of a spirit world originated early in the minds of men on earth in quite contrast to a few other evolutionary planets in Satania. At the dawn of cultural civilization on Urantia, every race had already developed various cults that, to some measure, supported the existence of celestial entities capable of interring in contact with human beings. Though early men were terrified of ghost and the dream world, that did not affect their sense of reverence for the extraordinary. The urge to worship is innate in man. Thus, since these primordial times, successive generations did subsequently evolve fairly suitable religious philosophies. And many of the enigmatic informations that were revealed throughout these consecutive epochs were properly recorded in several of the planet's traditional scriptures; such as the Torah, the Bible, the Q'uran, and the Bhagavad-Gita.

The belief in guardian angels originated since the dawn of human evolution on your earth. Long before the emergence of culture and civilization, their existence and influence were already widely accepted throughout the planet. Initially, the beliefs about a spirit world and angelic ministry were vague, crude, and utterly fraught with superstitions. They were essentially conceived and driven by the countless apprehensions of primitive men — particularly from their fear of ghost and the dream phenomenon. Though these peculiar notions became increasingly clarified by subsequent celestial revelations throughout the age-long struggles of evolutionary religion. But unfortunately, the natures, functions and messages of many angelic orders were grandly confounded with those of other celestial groups of intelligences, and thus hugely misrepresented in various religious documents throughout history.

There are a number of different causes for the continuing distortions and falsifications of inspired revelations on Urantia, particularly regarding humanity's immediate celestial helpers — the guardian angels. However, not all of them are necessarily related to religion.

Since the global ascendancy and dominance of secularism over the past three and half centuries, modern men have given birth to a new and unparalleled breed of pessimism and irreverence that virtually overshadowed and diminished the importance of moral and spiritual values in society. And this unprecedented degradation of ethics and total absence of faith have consequently, produced a generation of egocentric, pride-driven and self-seeking materialistic social automatons. Additionally, it provided a platform for an increasing number of incredulous people [atheists] who categorically deny the belief of angelic existence, and reject the idea of their assistance and ministry to humankind.

Rationality compels thinking individuals to find some form of logical or scientific explanation for everything. But in our last analysis, the proceedings involve in the services of angels are beyond the material concepts of human understanding. Science, principally astronomy, does certainly enable scientists to explore and study the physiological phenomena of the universe. However, it is totally inadequate to discern the actualities that are transpiring on the supernatural levels of the human mind, spirit domain, and the personality circuit. The natural world can be examined scientifically; its physical laws and principles are detectable, and energy-matter can be, to some extent, technically metamorphosed. But the spiritual realities of the universe are beyond the finite analyses, judgments and comprehensions of men.

The activities in the higher dimensions of creation are not intellectually discoverable or conceivable by mortal man, unless they are directly revealed to him by his celestial helpers. Man is simply unable to conceive or imagine anything of the veritable spiritual world without some kind of transcendence or elevation of his consciousness. In other words, if he is not born of spirit, man cannot possibly, consciously interact with the divine realms. Neither science nor metaphysic can even partially identify the glorious presence of God, which incessantly patrols the circle of the Master Universe. For heavenly realities greatly transcend the limited scope of human perception.

The Seven Adjutant Spirits
Mind Circuits

Besides the guardian angels, mortals are also helped by another group of ministerial spirits, which was revealed to Urantia as the Adjutants. But unlike the angels, the adjutant spirits are not personalities. They are more fittingly classified as mind circuits, and they do not operate on the outer sphere of the human mind as do the angels. And no prerequisite moral achievement is required to benefit from their ceaseless ministries. Actually, they are freely bestowed by the Mother Spirit of the local universe upon every normal minded evolving individual human being without prejudices. The primary objective of the adjutants is to fine-tune the human mind, and prepare it for the reception of a Thought Adjuster and the Spirit of Truth.

Although the adjutants are not usually categorized as true personalities, they are unconditionally so regarded by the Universal Mother Spirit. Notwithstanding that, they are widely defined and understood as circuits of the mortal mind, their activities and influences are always in accordance with the cosmic plan and purpose of their source—the Divine Minister—who is personality. Their ministry is invaluable for the initial preparations of the human mind to its eventual reception of the divine gift of the Universal Father—the Thought Adjuster. Like the Adjusters, the adjutants are mind indwellers, but they chiefly function on the lower levels of the mortal intellect.

There are seven of these tireless mental ministers in the mind of every rational human being. And they are universally designated as *courage, intuition, counsel, knowledge, understanding, worship, and wisdom.* The adjutants toil incessantly to uplift the thought quality and sponsor superior meanings in the mortal minds of men in order to facilitate, subsequent contacts with the Spirit of Truth and the Mystery Monitors.

Mortals naturally start out in the struggle for mind perfection under the influence and command of the adjutant spirits sequentially. In principle, these circuits are crossed orderly starting from the highest to the lowest number. You begin from the seventh, the spirit of courage, and gradually attain the first, the spirit of wisdom. Starting from courage, which is followed by intuition and counsel, you are then assigned personal guardian angels. Your first direct intellectual contact with the mind of the Universe Mother Spirit occurs when you reach the adjutant of knowledge. Next, you move up to the circuit or the spirit of understanding. The last two adjutants, worship and wisdom, preside over the others.

Every human being with a normal mind can feel and appreciate the divine presence of the Holy Spirit through the ministries of the adjutants and the seraphic angels. This is possible provided such an individual is submitted to the spiritualizing influences of these entities. Those spirit beings are indeed the direct ministers of the Holy Spirit to the mortals on the evolutionary worlds of time. They are her offspring. Their tireless and sympathetic services to humankind clearly demonstrate her affectionate nature.

The New United Corps of Planetary Midwayers: *Mobilized to Restore the Integrity Of Their Order*

As it was revealed in your Urantia text, the planetary Midway Creatures are physically the closest and the most akin supernatural entities to men. When serving, they are normally classified in two groups—primary and secondary. They are universally known as your cousins on high for they had somewhat of a human origin. Those of the primary order are the progenies of the one hundred former ascending mortal personalities who constituted the corporeal staff of Caligastia. The secondary ones are descendants of Adam's children. Midwayers are not angels, but they do possess many angelic attributes and share much in common with humanity. For instance, naturally, most tend to be exquisitely sympathetic like angels and manifest several human emotions, such as humor, joy and love.

But unfortunately, scores of these highly serviceable beings were corrupted by Caligastia. They had joined the Lucifer rebellion. Out of the 50,000 who were created under the rare conditions that were reported in the Urantia Book, more than 40,000 were lost. Most of the myths and traditions about demons and evil spirits on your planet are dated since that antiquated tragic revolt, which caused the massive desertion of these entities from the light.

Following Michael's seventh and final bestowal on Urantia, the majority of these strayed creatures were temporarily interned by a decree of the Ancient of Days on Uversa to await the adjudication of the Lucifer rebellion. Many were eventually set free on probation as they manifested some intention to repent from their folly during the two millennia since the Master's incarnation. Recently, all those who sincerely chose repentance and desired to continue their services were assigned to special Melkisedek schools to undergo a period of rehabilitation before they could be fully reinstated into the universe's administration. It is worthy to note that most decided to discontinue their disobedience to the divine will and gladly accepted Michael's mercy, which was freely and unconditionally given to these misguided beings. Even Beelzebub, the one-time notorious Commander in Chief of the infernal army of the secondary Midwayers, repented and embraced the rehabilitating program of the Melkisedek under Michael's order. That event was greatly celebrated on high as it was completely unexpected. It was simply too difficult for some of us to imagine or contemplate this sudden shift after observing the furious attitude of this personality against the divine will for ages. This widely known secondary Midway personage became an icon of mischief and evil on Urantia mainly after the dispensational failure of Adam & Eve, when humanity was basically thrust into an abyss of superstitions and darkness. His status was hoisted in the infernal hierarchy on earth when he was appointed by Daligastia, Caligastia's lieutenant, as the Commander In chief of all the disloyal midway creatures—those miscreant entities which most of you, largely refer to as "demons."

Now more than ever before, the combined groups of the loyal and repentant Midwayers of your world, which comprises of personalities from both, the primary as well as the secondary order, are fully mobilized to accomplish their original mission. Their new motto is "whatever we undertake we shall finish." Most of them have renewed their pledges of allegiance to the Creator and reengaged themselves wholeheartedly in their planetary services. As you know, there are a number of circumstances in which the presence and ministry of the Midwayers are indispensable to achieve any success. For example, they facilitate direct communication between spirit with mortals and performing quasi-physical tasks when necessary, like protecting the material existence of souls of destiny.

This rather new United Corps of Urantia's Midwayers is now fully mobilized to serve the true purpose of their kind. They have renewed their pledges as permanent planetary helpers, recorders, transporters and spiritual catalyzers of human civilization. They have completely embraced Michael's Correcting Time Plan as they are now determined to restore the integrity and repair the damages done to their wonderful order. You all can finally rest assured that those peculiar beings, which permanently share the planet with you, are benevolent, and they do have your best interest in mind.

Mortals of this realm should no longer be leery and fearful of the Midway creatures because of the past mistakes some of them have committed. For all the negativities have been mitigated, and justice was fully served to those who were found in contempt of any divine law. Now, you are called to feel free to interact with these amazing beings, which are very similar to your own kind. They are eager to communicate and even visit with you if you can handle such an experience.

Nebadonia
The Holy Mother Spirit of the Universe

Essentially, a local universe is the space dimension occupies by the conscious presence of a Paradise daughter of the Infinite Spirit. When they embark on the enthralling adventure of universe creation, these unimaginable beings are normally designated as the Divine Assistants of the Michael Creator Sons. One of those Holy-Spirits volunteered as a collaborator of Christ Michael upon his entering into the career of universe building. She is cosmically known as Nebadonia.

To all extents and purposes, as a Michael Creator is the Father-God of his created universe, the Divine Assistant is the Holy Mother-Spirit of that particular creation. As a personification of the Infinite Spirit to a finite creation, a Mother Spirit pervades her entire universe of dwelling. During the early periods of her ministry in time and space, she bears allegiances and loyalty only to the Paradise Trinity. In creative union with a Michael, a Mother Spirit functions to bring about the innumerable realities of things and beings within her cosmic domain of actions. Additionally, she bestows mind upon all living creatures that dwell on the worlds of her respective space of manifestation.

The Holy Spirit of this local universe is indeed a perfectly loyal associate and Divine Assistant of the Master Christ Michael. Like the latter, she maintains headquarters on Salvington, the capital of Nebadon. Principally, her cooperation with the Creator Son is essential to the existence, functions, evolution and maintenance of this creation. Ever since their collaboration in the gigantic enterprise of universe building, Michael and Nebadonia have painstakingly labored for the material welfare and spiritual enlightenment of all their offsprings, the natives of Nebadon. There has never been a lapse in their diligent efforts to sustain their creations, and to elevate the overall status of their well nigh numberless celestial and planetary children.

Normally, the Creator Son and the Creative Spirit of a local universe equally share the countless responsibilities of their creation. However, the Divine Minister usually cedes all powers to the Son subsequent to the latter's seventh bestowal mission as a revelator of the Universal Father in the likeness of his mortal creatures. This subordination of the Holy Assistant to a Michael's sovereignty is entirely a spiritual affair. It is a voluntary act of loyalty and devotion to an eternal loving ministry. And thus, it must never be interpreted arbitrarily, for it is not an act of diminishment to her universe authority. Having said that, I also want to point out that it is nearly impossible to explain or illustrate correctly the nature of divine association between perfect personalities to the mortal mind. Therefore, it is not to be thought that such supernal matter of universal relationship between the Creator Son, and his Divine Assistant is communicable and fathomable from a human perspective and understanding. Suffice to say that like themselves, the natures of the Gods' relationships are also mysterious and impenetrable.

The final bestowal and triumph of a Creator Son as a planetary mortal usually qualify this Michael as the indisputable

Sovereign and Chief of his created universe. In Nebadon, our local universe, this event occurred a little over two thousand years ago, when our beloved Father-Creator incarnated on earth as a helpless babe born of an ordinary virgin of the realm. While for the most part, his life proceeded as a normal planetary experience, but the whole universe of Nebadon was then completely mobilized to witness the most remarkable approach of the Universal Father to reveal his infinite loving nature to his evolving mortal grandchildren on the material worlds of time and space. After his triumphant human life experience as Jesus of Nazareth on Urantia, our Father-Creator had practically finished the last of the required bestowal assignments to achieve personal sovereignty over his creation. Even before the termination of his mission on earth as Jesus, Michael was fully recognized by the Ancients of Days on Uversa as the Master-Christ of Nebadon, and was confirmed on Paradise as the Sovereign Chief over his vast universal domain of more than three million inhabited worlds.

You have been taught that in all matters concerning life creation and maintenance of the universe, the Mother Spirit functions cooperatively with the Creator Son. However, the Divine Minister never directly or autonomously conducts the administrative affairs of the universe. The managerial and executive decisions of a finite universe are the responsibilities of its Creator Son with his numerous created Sons. Nevertheless, the Holy Spirit is always supportive of a Michael's governmental plan, and is ever ready to assist him in all his undertakings to execute the will of the Paradise Father in their creation. The Michaels are also usually ably assisted by a host of higher personalities who function in diverse capacities in the local universes, such as Paradise Observers and Counselors, Trinity Teachers, Dispensation Adjudicators, etc.

To all extents and purposes, the Creator Son is the spiritual Father; the Divine Minister is the Holy Mother of all native creatures within an evolving universe. However, there are some minor technical differences in the method of administration between the two. For example, unlike the Creator Son, the Mother Spirit cannot leave her universe of assignment until it has been perfectly stabilized within the gravitational circuit of its respective superuniverse. Michael of Nebadon can depart from the universe's capital or central headquarters as he often does in different occasions on periodic visits to Paradise. In fact, as we mentioned in the previous Paper, he was recently summoned by the Universal Father for a private conference, and not too long ago, he attended a special conclave of Sovereign Creator Sons - aka Master-Christs–,which are those Michaels, who have finalized their seven-creature bestowal experiences in full accordance with their Paradise oaths.

Once the primary circuits of gravity of a newly organized local universe have been sufficiently stabilized, it continues to revolve within the cosmic orbit of its respective superuniverse safely with or without the presence of the Creator Son. However, the continuing creation and organization of the manifold star systems with their countless forms of life and sentient intelligences are utterly dependent on the actual presence and consistent actions of the Holy Mother-Spirit. Thus, the Divine Minister is eternally assigned to her universe until the latter has fully reached the limits of its potentials, and exhausted the capacity of its physical, mental and spiritual evolution.

There are probably several other unknown or yet unrevealed reasons for the confinement of a Mother Spirit to her domain of manifestation and creation. But we believe there are two that basically explain this quite satisfactorily. First, she is the primordial source and circuit of mind in her universe – meaning all intelligences, high and low – are encircuited in her Being. Hence, her absence would immediately provoke an unimaginable intellectual pandemonium throughout the universe. And second, though a Creator Son imparts life to his creatures, but he does so only in union with and through a Mother Spirit. Therefore, her steadfast presence is central to the animation, evolution, maintenance, and perpetuation of life in the universe. Simply stated, if the Divine Minister of Salvington should ever leave her headquarters, her absence would instantly trigger an indescribable cosmic upheaval that some believe would completely obliterate and terminate all material and mental existences within this universe.

The Spirit of Truth
The Promised Teacher & Comforter

As we've seen mainly in paper 2, the Creator Son's choice of Urantia for his last self-imposed creature incarnation to finalize his bestowal career literally changed the cosmic status of this realm forever. However, Christ Michael's mortal life as Jesus did not only reveal God to men and modify the destiny of this world. He did also greatly elevate humanity by pouring out his Truth Spirit upon all flesh. This now enables all sincere believers to become son-conscious —to faith-grasp that they are indeed children of the Universal Father on high.

When he was yet on earth, the very presence of Michael's personality brought about many changes in human thinking and relationships. Jesus accomplished several extraordinary things, many of which were seen as impossible prior to his bestowal. He delivered mankind from the possibility of demonic possession and opened for him a direct personal avenue to God the Father. He made two main promises to humanity: [1] to bestowal his Spirit of Truth, which he designated as the divine Teacher and Comforter that will substitute for his physical absence in the world. [2] To return to the planet. He has already fulfilled the first. We now await the execution of the second with great anticipation, for there are clear signs on high indicating the imminence of such an event. Moreover, he also promised a future age of spiritual enlightenment and renaissance on earth. This era will come, he asserted, as a result of the eventual triumph of love and light over fear and darkness in the hearts of all mankind. Even though no one, save God the Father, knows for sure when that dispensation will begin, but we can all be certain of these promises and rest assured that he will, in due time, fulfill them all.

However, before these great transformational events can materialize, the current growing, spiritual renaissance must reach its climax. Humanity's collective consciousness must be sharply elevated. Your character and intention must be refined—meaning that more of you must become peacemakers and truth-seekers to increase and fully anchor the divine light upon the earth. And, as more of you do that the momentum of the transcendent energies that you have been receiving will be accelerated. Thus, the existing global consciousness will be shifted from predominant fear and evil to love and goodness. Again, as we perceive things from our vintage, soon, the nations of Urantia will learn to abandon the culture of violence and dispel all ignorance peacefully as one planetary family. The number of open-minded light-receivers in the world will continue to increase exponentially. Our objective is to see you become a majority. And...we can see this happening soon, as more and more of you, as you say, are waking up!

You are now entering the last phase in this stupendous and dangerous transitional period. As you move onward to the final stages reaching the fulfillment of Michael's promises, principally his second coming, please bear in mind there are inexorable, and that your fear and doubts are the only obstacles preventing you from being absolutely sure of this. As far as we are conversant with the affairs of your world, it is our understanding that there is presently a growing worldwide development of mind-elevation and spiritualization that will eventually spurn all evils and eradicate all arbitrary authorities from the planet. This global awakening movement may be fraught with many ambiguities and confusions now, none the less; it is a formidable force that is carrying humanity forward with the initial current for eventual sweeping and drastic changes in your planetary affairs. We are in no doubt that you will be finally liberated from the gross imperfections and illusions of dualism at some foreseeable time in the future. But to open this new paradigm, you must first be emancipated from the oppressive control of the dark cabal. And... it is with great joy that we announce to you that this shall occur before the passing of the present generation. While all parties involved are freely voicing their opinions, yet the real purpose and direction of this peculiar planetary activism are primarily free and independent of all centric and localized ideologies.

Though it may become necessary to structure and organize this emergent society of truth-seekers in the future. But we believe that it would be unwise to do this prematurely.

With the Spirit of Truth permeating the human mind, every Urantia mortal is fully endowed with the perfect guidance to lead a positive and even divinely motivated life. One who heeds and follows the leadings of the Spirit of Truth cannot be duped or led astray from the path of their destiny. As a teacher and a comforter, the Spirit of Truth is mainly preoccupied with the edification and consolation of the human soul. Your inner encounters with it should always leave you with a deep sense of joy, courage and fulfillment.

After the pouring out of the Spirit of Truth upon all flesh on the Day of Pentecost by Christ Michael, it became unnecessary for mankind to wait until the arrival of another epochal dispensation in order to obtain new spiritual revelations. Since that event, in every generation successively, all believing minds on Urantia have been encircuited into the divine source of Truth, there are capable of receiving, understanding, and applying revelations regularly. You are empowered to be conduits of Truth and light in the world; to discover who you truly are and move upward in your quest to find God within your souls.

No longer is the observation of a creed necessary to show loyalty and devotion to God. This Truth Spirit that was bestowed by the Creator Son primarily elevates humanity's level of consciousness. It is by its sole presence an energetic sustenance, hence its name the Comforter and Teacher. For it does greatly sustain, edifies and energizes all genuine believers in Jesus' Gospels of the fatherhood of God and the brotherhood of men.

The prevailing social condition on a life-planet, as we view it from our vantage point, is usually relative to, or dependent upon the degree of its inhabitants' intellectual, moral and spiritual development. In other words, the level of maturity of a planetary civilization, both individually and as a collective, mainly ascertain its overall situation and its position vis-à-vis the rest of creation. Stated differently, the consciousness and quality of its people predominantly determine the types of social, political and economic paradigms that will prevail on any given mortal inhabited sphere. However, the transcendent phenomenon we call God-consciousness remains absolutely a personal experience to every single mortal regardless of all existential circumstances.

Mortals that willfully accept the invitation of the Spirit of Truth to love God and serve humanity have essentially freed themselves from the confusions of all the established theologies and socio-political ideologies of their days and generations. The faith of such Truth-abiding souls may be affected occasionally by the unpredictable circumstances of life, but only temporary, and those times are always inspiring, educational and enlightening. Genuine believers profoundly know the source of their spiritual convictions; their own level of consciousness will never allow them to venture too far from the light.

As far as we are aware of, there is no force in the entire universe that can prevent a dedicated truth seeker from entering the portal of Paradise provided such an endowed soul is really thirsty for the water of life and righteousness - honestly desires to do the will of God. Absolutely, nothing that we know of in all creations, high and low, can alter the course or change the spiritual destiny of a human being who is sincerely seeking for Truth and willingly go wherever it may lead. To our knowledge, there is no power that can spoil the fate of a believing creature that made the solemn resolution to do the will of the Eternal Creator.

Immortality of existence is a gift from God. However, to receive it gracefully man must fulfill the Father's mandate of perfection, "Be you perfect even as I am perfect." And to do this effectively, we believe you should commence by first realizing the inalienable truth of your sonship with Him. We encourage all of our liaisons to do their best to *"spread the word,"* to borrow your vernacular. The liberating truths of Michael's revelation of the fatherhood of God and the brotherhood of men must now be propagated throughout your world with more zeal and power. For it is only by recognizing and embracing this spiritual reality that humanity may come to experience the fullness of the Father's infinite love, the Son's endless mercy and the Spirit's eternally compassionate and ministry.

The Mystery Monitors
The Mighty I AM Presence in the Human Mind

While human beings are guarded and guided by a number of spiritual agencies operating in and around them, the Mystery Monitors are the nearest entities of light to you. There is simply no adequate explanation to describe the nature of their attachment to the human mind. Suffice to say, their technique of function and relationship to mortals are impenetrable. Nevertheless, those of us on this side with a higher and more accurate perspective of humanity – who see your beingness and discern you as you truly are—can perceive the luminosity of these marvelous spirits as they indwell the mortal tabernacles of men.

These divine fragments of God work incessantly to spiritualize the human mind and immortalize your evolving souls. Though they are completely independent in their sphere of action, nonetheless, their ministries are always in perfect harmony with the Spirit of Truth, the Adjutant Spirits, and the Guardian Angels.

As God's gifts of Himself to humanity, the Thought Adjusters bestow infinite goodness and perfection upon you just because you exist. You are all children of love and light by the sole virtue of this majestic presence of divinity within yourselves, whether you can appreciate this or not. The Mighty I AM presence in the human mind is the inner link between you and the personality of the Universal Father on Paradise. In addition, it is the absolute guide, teacher and Father of the soul as well as the guarantor of its spiritual survival following natural death. Nevertheless, unlike the guardian angels, they never have to answer for the failure of their subjects to survive. For they are absolutely perfect entities whose method of service greatly transcends all finite judgments and operates above all possible criticisms.

Simply put, the Mystery Monitors are, to all extents and purposes, sparks of *God,* which are bestowed in the hearts of men. Each embodies a comprehensive life program for their chosen mortal subject. These tireless Father-Fragments, as they are sometimes referred to on high, are the essences of the divine nature bestowed upon man as a gift to recreate himself and attain perfection in the universe.

From the ministries of the seraphic guardians to that of the Adjutants, the Midwayers and the Spirit of Truth, humans are lovingly assisted by several celestial agencies. But the most profoundly and divinely touching of them all is the mysterious innermost relationships that exist between the evolving soul of man and his indwelling immortal Mighty I AM Presence.

The soul, being the "eyewitness" of the divine presence, has little to no difficulty with faith. She is naturally faithful and expectant. But the physical mind, in which reside the seat of will and action, is fundamentally fearful and too often pessimistic. Hence, attaining any kind of meaningful, mutual expression with the divine vibration of the spirit is virtually impossible.

By virtue of the presence of the Thought Adjuster in the mortal mind, there should not be any divergence between the constituents of man's personality. Yet all sorts of personal disorders, dis-eases, and imbalances exist as permanent circumstances on Urantia. That is mainly because, unlike the indwelling spirit, the human intellect is conditioned to the universal phenomenon of temporal causes and effects.

Finite life and its meanings take place between the mortal psyche and its environment. As this mutual association functions to reach higher perception of universal possibility and consciousness, it increasingly attains the idealistic and perfecting levels of morantial and spiritual values. That should end our session for this evening. Until next time, good-bye.

Paper 15

Why The Correcting Time Now?

A NEW DISPENSATION ORDERED BY DIVINE DECREE

The End of Urantia's Cosmic Isolation

Celestial Teacher: Abonnady - Channel: Joseph Elie 12-19-2012

CHRIST-MICHAEL'S CORRECTING TIME PLAN to heal and salvage the 37 quarantined planets of Satania from the ills of the Lucifer rebellion is essentially a co-creative project between humanity and divinity. As we've mentioned to you many times before, it is an astronomical undertaking; an unprecedented feat that requires the full cooperation of mankind to succeed on your world.

This is primarily why the wake-up call to this sacred enterprise has been made to the global population. It will ultimately bring about a new era of peace and harmony on earth. There is now an urgent need to propagate this great news of celestial encircuitment and divine rehabilitation to all nations and peoples upon your sphere. Life on an evolutionary planet such as this is full of unexpected incidents—surprises. But dear friend, this project is anything but a coincidence. It was designed long ago, and it was intended to be implemented at this very moment in time.

Today, your world is dangerously drifting and approaching the shores of a 'new dawn' with profoundly drastic transformations that will lead you to a Golden Age. As a species, you are facing many unique problems that exceedingly surpass your collective awareness, ingenuity and understanding to resolve affirmatively and peacefully. It should be abundantly clear to all thinking people that you are living in critical times that call for the succor and assistance of supernatural forces or celestial intervention.

The current global transitioning events cannot be managed and much less directed successfully using merely your ordinary planetary resources. Consequently, in light of this precarious and decisive moment in your planet's history, we have come to help and assist you through the difficulties.

We are here to co-creatively work with you to rehabilitate and save your species from the looming catastrophes that we can see befalling your sphere. We beg your attention and crave your recognition. We pray for the time when you shall collectively acknowledge, feel and appreciate our presence on the planet. We are patiently yet enthusiastically waiting, for the moment, when most of you will heed and honor our counsels.

We are delighted to be part of this great undertaking to help you build a safer, friendlier and more prosperous world. Seeing you all co-existing peacefully and harmoniously as a global family is our main goal, for you are all sons and daughters of the Most-High on this wondrous little blue planet.

The Correcting Time Programs
The Divine Decree for a New Dispensation

As you know, the Correcting Time Plan for the spiritual rehabilitation of humanity comprises of three major different but coordinated programs that are unfolding simultaneously on the planet as follows:

- [1] The worldwide dissemination of the Fifth Epochal revelation—*the Urantia Book*.

- [2] A comprehensive *Teaching Mission* to answer   human concerns and encourage global spiritual unity starting by the recognition of this great truth: *Sonship with God is a Personal Reality.*

- [3] The bestowal of a *Magisterial Son* to inaugurate a New Era of spiritual awakening and social progress following many cataclysmic events that will drastically change this world forever.

As he had promised during his bestowal on Urantia, Christ Michael, now Master and Sovereign of Nebadon, has dedicated vast resources to retrieve this planet and 36 others from the clutches of sin, and reintegrate them into the fold of the normal evolving realms within his universe. The implications of this tremendous plan-- notably the three major programs along with many other activities and personalities involved to recover these lost worlds, are profound and comprehensive. This is by far the greatest and the most remarkable spiritual mission in this universe since the Creator's incarnation on this planet 2000 years ago as Jesus of Nazareth.

The need for this cosmic intervention to salvage these sin- perverted kingdoms should not be difficult for anyone to recognize. This is, in fact, the fulfillment of thousands of years of ardent prayers and supplications from their inhabitants. However, in order to fully appreciate the wisdom behind this recovery effort, many previous situations of these strayed worlds must be acknowledged and understood initially. Considering, for example, up until recently, for over two hundred and fifty thousand years, your earth was in cosmic quarantine, basically existing outside of the universe's family of normal planets since the outbreak of the Luciferian revolt. As it is depicted in your Urantia Papers, at the onset of its first dispensation, this planet was immediately cut off from the communication circuitries of the universe soon after its traitorous Lanonandek Prince had espoused the Lucifer rebellion. You were practically isolated and deprived of many regular cosmic services, e.g., periodic extraterrestrial broadcastings and free interactions with other life-spheres. To stop the rebellion from spreading, earth and the other troubled planets were severed from the spiritual network of the universe by a decree of the Most-Highs of the Constellation of Norlatiadeck. All the strayed worlds were duly prevented from sending information beyond their shores and from receiving normal universe broadcasts. This strategy [an unfortunate but necessary decision] greatly undermined Lucifer's efforts to corrupt more worlds, and did effectively restrain the capabilities of the apostate Planetary Princes to propagate their sinful doctrines to other evolutionary kingdoms, but it was a severe and trying experience for the inhabitants and the loyal corps of celestial ministers of these quarantined planets.

Today however, as Christ Michael has said, your earth is in a spiritual renaissance. The long unpleasant period of isolation is over. It is behind you. It's history. Now, a new age of self-discovery and spiritual progress is dawning upon humanity. And, all of you are being called to rise to the occasion by joyfully receive the love and graciously accept the mercy of your divine Parents; by learning to forgive yourselves and one another. Rejection of this timely offer will only ensure that you continue to tarry on the road of darkness with no feasible end to your plights and sufferings.

This generation is invited to seize this extraordinary opportunity to embrace this period of grace wholeheartedly in order to cure the wounds of your world and lead it into a better and brighter future of peace, prosperity, and harmony. This is a unique time with a golden prospect for the children of Urantia to break free from the bondage of fear, vanity and spiritual ignorance. This is an empowering moment to rise above the dark forces of division; to realize you are actually *a finite expression of infinity; you are one with all that exist.* You have a mandate to dispel ignorance with knowledge, to destroy suspicion with understanding and to change division and competition into union and cooperation. Your favorable response to this great calling is of the utmost importance to cleanse your world spiritually, and stir it towards the Days of Light and Life.

Ever remember my brother, love is the most powerful energy in the universe. It can easily appease all tensions and solve any problem between all kinds of personable beings - mortals as well as celestials. Whenever love is applied in any life situation, it automatically changes the dynamics for goodness, harmony and peace to shine and prevail. Abiding in love always enlightens and glorifies a personality in God whom is its true Source. Simply put, love is your only gateway to freedom from the vicissitudes of time to the beatitudes of eternity. It is your passport to traverse the frontiers of space and attain the Eternal Isles of Paradise. Learning to cultivate love now and forever is man's sole option to transcend himself from a mortal to an immortal creature in the universe.

As we said before, today, there is an influx of divine energies that are being poured out upon your world at an unprecedented velocity. These spiritual pressures bring valuable concepts such as peace and unity to the forefront of the human mind. Scores of truth-hungry souls are gladly responding to these heavenly blessings. They are wisely aligning themselves with the vibrational frequencies of this outpouring of divinity. Consequently, they have placed themselves in a unique position to benefit from it. Regardless of circumstances, these benign forces fosters love, joy, peace, wisdom, and protection. It is wonderful to observe the promising immediate outcomes of this cosmic emanation upon your world already. Now most spirit-receptive and thinking Urantians are disillusioned with the societal criterions of the current system of things. They have awakened! They are becoming aware of personality's innate powers to attain God-consciousness and willfully create reality. And more will realize the fact of this natural human ability as the Correcting Time's activities unfold.

Many profound truths pertaining to personality that were once considered mysterious and concealed by your decision makers must now be disclosed, known and understood by all who sincerely desire to know them. *The creative powers of all personalities are like those of God Himself; and you humans are no exception.* But in this current menial class of consciousness, you are yet to discover and live by this sublime Truth. You will grow, traverse many horizons, and live countless lives, as you ascend in the universe to your ultimate destiny. Yet, never will you grasp the full spectrum of universal reality. Your level of consciousness will remain inadequate to visualize the entire vista of potential realities or possibilities contained within your own beingness up until the time you attain Paradise. For it is a spiritual fact that as persons, you are all like God; creative, mysterious, and infinite.

Nowadays, many transcendental as well as scientific informations are being disclosed to all receptive and thinking mortals of this realm. Some of you have already discovered and learned a whole lot. We commend your efforts and diligence. Many of you are learning to approach and communicate with your indwelling Father Fragments more consciously and frequently. This is a phenomenal event. We are very pleased by this development. And whenever possible, we do also impart our energies to this process in an effort to increase your potentials for greater attunement to that *Divine Presence* in you. We know that your faith and perseverance will ensure your success in this endeavor. And eventually you will be redeemed from all temporal handicaps; such as fear, anger, lust, and avarice.

Whether or not this is conceivable to you, the truth is, all mankind do actually possess the power to transcend matter, bear spiritual fruits, and live as spirit-conscious children of God on earth. As personalities, it is entirely true that you are endowed with the capacity to create your own realities, to determine the quality of your experiences. You are the light, the consciousness, the creative spirit that animates the void of infinite possibilities to bring into concrete forms what once existed only as potentials. You impart meanings and purposes to the process of life. Truly, you are fully equipped and empowered to run the course of your cosmic destiny, respond to God's call to perfection, and fully attain immortality.

We encourage those humble souls who gladly receive us to be patient and resolute in your quest for Truth. We urge you to remain steadfast and faithful until the end. For this is only the beginning of a new and better paradigm of existence on your native planet. From this point on, God and man shall no longer be set apart as two incompatible mysteries. Neither will you be hailed as his slaves and servants any more. But rather, you shall be known as his children and as brothers and sisters. Finally, the supreme reality of mankind's affiliation to God will cease to be a mystery. All open-minded and teachable persons will discover the sublime truth of their *sonship with God* in their own spiritual experiences. Today, those who are conscious of the extraordinary creative powers of the [human] *personality,* such as its ability to transcend time sequences of events, visualize eternity, choose perfection, and make a gift to God, may be in the minority. But it will not be so in the future, for this knowledge shall spread and permeate the collective consciousness of humanity as the oceans cover the surface of the earth. Otherwise stated, during the upcoming dispensation, most if not all of you, will become fully aware of your innate potential *mystical powers.* You will know the true meaning of being created in the image of God. But for now, you must continue to transition from your current marginal state of self-awareness to that moment in time when you shall regain the complete consciousness of your real *cosmic identities.* And so, we urge you to carry on in faith, have the courage to exceed the limits of your 'physical selves' by letting go of old habits and attitudes that no longer serve you in this laborious process of self-awakening.

The human family on this planet is presently undergoing what many of us on this side characterize as a *"Tremendously profound dimensional shift of consciousness."* Nothing can or will escape the impact of such a drastic transformational development. All aspects of life as it is in the world today will be affected, some way or another, by that radical change in awareness.

As the Correcting Time's activities, notably the Teaching Mission and the propagation of the Urantia text, continue to increase throughout the earth, its multiple civilizations will gradually undergo sweeping revolutionary transformations. Humanity's noble aspirations; such as liberty, justice, and equality will continuously intensify as more people cease to comply with the old paradigm of authority, while embracing the leadings of their Inner Guides. Eventually, this latent movement will grow into a fantastic global phenomenon. A greater consciousness promoting peace, tolerance, harmony, goodwill, and benevolence shall emerge here. This will completely catalyze the overall quality of life in your world. However, to open this New Age officially, many substantial and comprehensive reforms in the management of your planetary affairs will be made as the initial steps, which must be taken before the divine campaigns for the general rehabilitation of this realm can be fully implemented.

To you personally my friend, and to those who shall peruse these lines, I say open your minds and hearts, and faithfully receive this shifting energy. Submit yourselves to the Father, abide in his love; be patient and carry on fearlessly. Remember, you are not alone in the struggle of the hour—especially during this crucial epoch. We are here now to guide and assist you through this momentous time in your planet's history. Do not be afraid to step forward and explore this new territory; to avail yourselves of this supreme opportunity to usher your world into the days of light and life. Instead of fearing this change, you should rejoice and give thanks to God. You should see this transition for what it truly is – a blessing from the Universal Father who planned your existence and designed you to be perfect as Himself. And the sole requirement for you to attain that perfection is to continue to expand your consciousness and grow spiritually. Thus, to do this you must ascend inwardly towards your super consciousness—your consciousness—your omniscient Higher Selves—in order to reach your ultimate destiny for this universe age.

Let me remind you that dispensational transitions are basically divine orders for an evolutionary world to move forward and progress. We hope you embrace this tremendous opportunity more joyfully than your predecessors have done in the past. And remember, notwithstanding the planetary isolation, mankind was never totally deprived of spiritual watch-care and assistance. Much was given to you despite the unfortunate status of your world, and now, even more will be given as you demonstrate a willingness to grow and progress.

This is Joseph: May I interrupt you with a couple of questions? 1] if you are able to, can you please specify the time the sanction was lifted on high? 2] Were the planet's spiritual circuitries of communication reopened simultaneously with the end of the quarantine period, or was that a separate event?

Abomaly: To be specific, the quarantine period technically ended in 1985 of Urantia time, following the closing procedures of the adjudication of the Lucifer rebellion. But the planet was not yet officially realigned with the communication circuitries of the universe because Lucifer, and some of his associates had contested the verdicts. They could not be executed without their agreement that this was the best thing to do, since they would not accept Michael's mercy. Hence, there was a delay in reopening the circuits because these rebels were still alive.

In January 2004, however, Gabriel, the Chief Executive of Nebadon, formally announced the end of the trial with the annihilation of Lucifer, Satan, and Caligastia with many of their unrepentant collaborators. That was basically the first universal broadcast transmission to this world in 200,000 years, indicating that its spiritual circuits had been officially restored and realigned with those of the universe. This momentous event occurred pursuant to Michael's prosecution of his Correcting Time Plan to reclaim the 37 planets that were strayed into darkness by Lucifer's secession, which included earth.

Let me say if I may, that we are already seeing tremendous transformations and progresses as this plan unfolds on these troubled worlds, and we are waiting with great anticipation to see the final results of its execution upon your beautiful planet. This endeavor is humanity's greatest opportunity in generations to grow into full consciousness of who and what you truly are, to realize *sonship with God.* Please seize upon this unique chance and occasion to transcend your selves; to enhance the quality, meaning and value of life upon your world, and move it closer to the Ages of Light and Life. To you personally my friend, I say this is the time to let your light shine for the edification of others, so they too may come to know, honor and glorify the Father. Let even your silence be heard to resuscitate your native world from its long nightmarish slumber of spiritual darkness.

Delays in the Correcting Time
February 21, 2011

As you know, lately they have been a few unexpected issues that basically delayed some of the activities of the Correcting Time on Urantia. But today, it is my pleasure to announce to you [personally] by the decree of Christ Michael and under the supervision of Machiventa Melkisedek in concert with the Magisterial Son, Monjoronson; the Correcting Time programs to rescue this world from spiritual darkness are in full swing.

From the permanent celestial ministers of your planet to the countless volunteered student visitors and helpers, all of us are mobilized to reach out to humankind and teach you a safer and better way forward.

We wish to help you mend your current international difficulties peacefully and effectively to pave the way for a brighter and securer future. There is a massive effort to approach mankind and interact with you on a personal, social, and global level more than ever before.

Each of you is being nudged up to the limit of your spiritual capacity and receptivity; spirit is at the door of your hearts. Many legions of benevolent light entities are standing ready to draw near you momentarily for mutual recognition and cooperation. We await your invitations to be of service.

The Perilous Course of Global Civilization
The Divine Decree for Human Liberation

As we mentioned in our last conversation, presently this planet is undergoing many big and radical changes in practically all domains of its many cultures and diverse civilizations. As you can observe from your news networks or the Internet, life is changing rapidly in virtually all the societies upon your world. Those reforms are permanent; there is no turning back. Global society will continue this frontward transition progressively until the current prevalent international but highly corrupt institutions and centers of authorities are completely dismantled. This is the result of an ongoing process of an extraordinary transition, which your world must undergo now in order to be corrected from ages of disruptions and malevolence.

From our dimensional awareness or point of observation, which significantly transcends yours, we are able to perceive quite accurately, where your civilization is headed. Thus, we can, to the limit permitted by our superiors, assuredly anticipate the future of your world. However, we usually do that in full accordance with the mandate of our assignments, and in much consideration for your personal prerogatives. We highly respect your free will. Hence, we will always abstain from saying or doing anything that would deprive you of the precious experience of discovering and creating the future yourselves.

That said, however, as your personal teacher, here is what I can share with you today:

A lot of spiritual pressure is being applied upon this planet at this moment in order to increase human awareness and help you decipher, "who and what you are spiritually as sentient beings." It has been decided on high that the time has come for you to begin to discover and know yourselves, as we perceive you - evolving spirits of personality dignity - ascending children of God. Much of that divine energy - [creative power] - you receive cognitively as information, intuition and occasionally, revelation. To help you become more receptive to this transcendent force, which springs directly from the Mother Spirit of the universe is, succinctly my brethren, one of the fundamental objectives of our mission on your planet.

As we perceive your world at this moment, civilization is generally on a dangerous course of self-annihilation. The current contentious political trajectory of the so-called United Nations, particular, among the member countries within the body of the "Security Council," if not diverted toward sane, fair, balance and applicable solutions to ensure continuing peace and stability, will inevitably bring about its catastrophic disintegration, with perhaps fatal planetary consequences, potentially including another world war. To be honest, from our perspective, most of your established global institutions that are supposedly designed to guarantee peace and equity in international relationships, with legal authority to act on behalf of humanity's interests, are corrupt. Frankly, their insouciance to fulfill the true purpose for their existence is morally reprehensible even by their own supposed ethical standards. It is appalling to observe the real motive and intention of those who formulated the 'International Laws and regulations' that are imposed on the global community through these institutions. As much as they may be creatively executed by cunning diplomats who are well trained in the art of public relation, people must bear in mind that they were never designed or intended to refine and elevate the average person, but to ensnare, subdue and enslave him.

The Dark Cabal's Worst Nightmare

The few individuals who constitute the elite minority that generally runs the affairs of this world have absolutely no regard for the *Golden Rules* of humanity, nor do they have any respect for the laws of creation or the values of divinity. The perceptions, ideals and motives of this small and detached cartel of overlords greatly differ from the rest of mankind, and they stand in even wider contrast with those of spirit. Their culture of excessive greed, treachery, decadence, irreverence and injustice has basically divested them of conscience. They have lost the ability to sympathize with another fellow mortal, including their own offspring. Driven and dominated by the sophistries of their exalted egos, they virtually lost the capacity to be thoughtful or make moral decisions. Spiritually, they are blinded by their own sense of pride and self-importance. They are prisoners of their ugliness and iniquity; they merely survive on the sinful attitudes they cast. This is why they are so afraid of you becoming aware of who you are or spiritually enlightened. They tremble in terror at the idea that you should ever discover your true relationship to God and the nature of reality.

These two fundamental values are deliberately kept and concealed from you as the highest ranks in the infernal hierarchy of the dark cabal fear a massive global awakening of humanity's collective consciousness, which, when eventually happen, will put them in a direct collision course with the *Planetary Supreme.*

And here, before we continue, let us elucidate our dialogue by defining this new term in the context we use it. The Planetary Supreme is the global soul that embodies the consciousness of all energetic interactions between all life forms of nature; it contains the meanings of all mental and spiritual activities in the human experience. This wealth of information and wisdom allows it to be a proficient catalyzer in the developments of world affairs when it becomes necessary and divinely appropriate to take such an action. In times when crucial and decisive decisions must be made to advance a sphere towards its ordained spiritual destiny, the Planetary Supreme may be volunteered to accelerate and facilitate the task. One-way of imagining what this extraordinary being does without distorting its character and function is to visualize it spiritually. It works in full harmony with the Divine Providence who oversees the general wellbeing and progress of humanity. Think of the Planetary Supreme as an entity, which encompasses the totality of the ideals, purposes, meanings and values of all human relationships; imagine this being with an objectified and qualified identity or perhaps even personality. This entity is real and possesses a formidable degree of awareness that is beyond the current range of your individual consciousness.

You have a saying, 'There is power in numbers,' that is true, but it's unfortunate that   you failed to see the same   about   your thoughts   and   imaginations.   You've   been   manipulated   into abandoning your inborn creative spirit; you have been lied to about your true identity and connection with God and the universe. *The dark cabal has misguided, abused and systematically encouraged you to ridicule and reject your own personal spiritual powers. They have worked to sever any connection between the human and the divine YOU, by either orchestrating or supporting all kinds of ill situations to beset your lives and keep you in a state of fear, desperation, hopelessness and survival.*

Their greatest trepidation of you becoming conscious of who you are, is actually the real motive behind their hollow claim of godhood, dubbing themselves *"the illuminated ones"* and thus, offered a completely different meaning of the concept to your imagination. Primarily, this was done to confuse, deceive, and induce you to believe their lies and worship their infernal god, Lucifer – the Lord of deception.

They carry a lot of pride with this, for it is one of their favorite methods of control against you. But the world's inhabitants are catching up rather quickly nowadays.

Seven Facts of Their Crimes against Humanity
Socio-Political Actualities

There is overwhelming evidence to support our claims that there is indeed a dark cabal of larger-than-life tycoons, delusional sociopaths with unscrupulous politicians – all loyal to the Luciferian establishment – that wield near sovereign influence in the global affairs of mankind. The proofs are all over your planet.

They are inescapable; one can surely find them if they are looking. But we could consider these seven factual crimes they have committed against humanity for a start:

- [1] They have directly worked to undermine rules established to guarantee equality and the good of the common citizen, regardless of race, creed, or belief.

- [2] They have directly influenced the creation of laws in order to further agendas that will only benefit them in terms of increased control and power over the population.

- [3] They have worked to instill fear into the hearts and minds of the population so that they are deceived to willingly relinquish their freedoms in favor of a non-existent desire to provide them with Liberty or Security.

- [4] They have incarcerated and killed many who dared to question the evil Governments, and established laws preventing anyone from denouncing said Governments.

- [5] They have conspired to destabilize populations and entice them into wars based on their racial differences and their beliefs, with the intention of appear on the scene as the "saviors" and be allowed to establish governments sympathetic to those that secretly instigated the wars.

- [6] They have used scientific and medical knowledge in detriment of the well-being of the people, with the intention of enriching those that control the applicable agencies.

- [7] They have lived with evil in their hearts, in memory of the great deceiver Lucifer, and continue to guide their existence based on his tenets of sin and iniquity, while rejecting the Eternal God's Mercy.

As you have been taught, the more real man is, the closer he is to God. Those pride-driven and fear-motivated individuals have isolated themselves from the Creator. They have removed themselves so far away from divinity that they are now virtually spiritually bankrupt; day-by-day they are losing personality dignity. In other words, they are increasingly becoming *unreal* in the universe.

Moving into the Golden Age
The Necessity for a Better System of Things

Today, it is obvious that civilization is confronted with many serious challenges, which beg a number of questions that can no longer be ignored. Consider these two, for instance: Is it possible to improve the quality of your governments to meet the aspirations of their citizenries while they are owned by and work for an exclusive and detached elite minority that dictates their policies, controls their agencies and calls their operations? Can you really change the political and economic situations on your world for the benefit of all of its inhabitants when the international laws that are supposed to guide global transactions and relationships are basically unfair and deceptive? Evidently, you cannot.

First, universal freedom, equality, and justice, which are the basic values of a real progressive and sustainable civilization, are not practical or realizable on a planet beset by violence, oppression, greed, and fierce competitions. These lofty societal progresses are not achievable under the leadership of bloody and arrogant dictators. Second, you cannot build a peaceful and equitable society on the same beliefs and principles of an oppressive and divisive one. You must, perforce change your approaches and reconsider your priorities to bring such a world into reality. You must transcend the prevailing concepts of this order to find better ideas to solve the existential world problems permanently. It is important to forsake the current paradigm in order to enter the new one.

A renewal of your geopolitical and economic structures is crucial in order to move fully into the New Era. Much work needs to be done to improve the quality and ensure the integrity of your institutions. You cannot possibly create a viable and sustainable civilization using the same flawed institutional models and principles of the present corrupt, failed and dying order. As with science and technology, it's important for you to continue to modernize and enhance the qualities of your administrative, business and social organizations; i.e. your governments, your financial, health, and education establishments, not to mention your vast network of corporations.

You need to learn how to build sustainable institutions; starting from the individual and the family to the community, national and global levels. There are plenty of resources available on your planet to help you do this successfully. And remember, we are here to assist you in creating these sustainable and supportive foundations that will accommodate the global relief plan for your planet and guarantee the physical and social wellbeing of all concerned. These changes must come into effect before long for they are indispensable to lead your planet into the Golden Age that will precede the glorious days of Light and Life.

We are fully cognizant that ignorance, fear, division, and warfare are among the main instruments of manipulation that are commonly used by most governments on this earth to pacify and control their peoples. They have been employed and utilized as tools of domination by virtually all authoritarian systems of government men have established upon themselves since time immemorial. This is unfortunately deeply rooted in the cultural fabrics of practically all civilizations that have ever come into being on your planet after the Lucifer rebellion.

With these authoritarian governments in place running the affairs of mankind, the world will never know a day of peace. It is simply impossible for your planet to evolve beyond its current status of a strife-torn and evil-stricken realm to a peaceful, vibrant, harmonious and prosperous sphere, with the present established global political socioeconomic order in command of its destiny. Thus, changing and replacing it are indispensable to move forward.

The Perilous Blunders of the Present Order
'Its Last Days'

As we perceive it from our vantage, among the many errors and misdeeds that were committed, either deliberately or innocently, which will bring about the demise of the current socio-economic order on your planet are:

- [1] Decades of systematic abuses and exploitations of weak and vulnerable nations.

- [2] Total neglects and disregard for the earth environment.

- [3] Persistent abrasive, wide-scale unsustainable industrial and economic practices.

Today, it is abundantly clear to us and to practically most of you that the existing global economic system on this planet is in peril. It is on a steep decline. If it continues on its present course, it will definitely not see another decade because it is severely fractured. It is operating on a dangerously damaged and practically broken foundation. The majority of its markets are highly unstable, unsafe and unreliable for a peaceful and prosperous future. As we perceive this grave situation unfolding, it is rather sooner than later when the last vestiges of this badly corrupt, and disease infected system will be uprooted and forever eradicated from your midst. Most of the international corporations that are integrated into this organization are following a very unsustainable path that will inevitably lead society to a dead end, with many disturbing planetary consequences. They are in a fatal collision course with nature, time, and humanity. Their practices of resource excavations and exploitations unconcerned by the damages they cause are surreal and unprecedented. Their level of insouciance for the suffering and pain they inflict on the vulnerable populations of the planet are overwhelmingly disproportionate in comparison to any past oppressive economic order. They exceed the criminal records of their predecessors from all previous times in history. Though its champions continue to pretend that everything is sound and normal, but the reality is this system is so deeply broken it cannot survive the next 15 to 30 years. Many among us in the recovery mission have conjectured that at some point in the near future—perhaps in the succeeding few years—we might need to intensify our intervention to help mitigate the tensions and balance the pressures that will likely accompany the unprecedented developments which are upon you now. And… since we do foresee a complete and permanent collapse of this system of things eventually, we are fully mobilized and ready to help and assist in the global relief and recovery plans as soon as this final event occurs.

However, we are very cautious in our mode of approach and communication with humanity in order to avoid or at least, reduce the possibility of misinterpretations of our activities. You are our younger brothers and sisters; we honestly love you. We do not want to alarm you or provoke any unnecessary anxiety. Rather, we wish to teach and show you the better way forward. Remember, *awareness is the greatest antidote to fear.*

We watch with serious concerns the world's formidable military preparations and readiness for warfare, while there is no adequate contingency planning in place to respond quickly and deal effectively with many likely future catastrophes that may affect all living species on the planet. Admittedly, the motives and activities of human leadership are subjects of great interest to us on this side. But it is disheartening to observe that after eons of mortal governments, assuming authority to preserve order and peace among men, yet, every country on the earth is plagued by corruption and violence. Generally, the planet remains a very uncertain place of highly divisive races and antagonistic societies.

However, as we've said many times over, this world is now at an unparalleled historical moment in time. It is at a juncture of profound changes that are more decisive than most humans can recognize or understand. You are traversing a transitioning period before the beginning of a New Era of spiritual enlightenment, which will be officially inaugurated here in a foreseeable time. Typically, as with all past epochal transitions, this one has been quite unpredictable, and it will remain unstable and gloomy for a while. This is actually normal. That's the nature of big change and transition. Nevertheless, irrespective of the amount of difficulties and challenges that must be surmounted throughout the process, the outcome is certain.

Many humans have a vague sense that something exceptional and supernatural is unfolding on this planet today, and rightfully so. You are at a crossroad of extraordinary opportunities for profound changes with enormous challenges. An entirely new dispensation is upon you. And it is unlike any of your previous planetary epochs, for it coincides with many extraordinary events that have never been associated with dispensational reform on any evolutionary world in this universe. For instance, its timing is curiously synchronized with some unusual celestial developments: such as the final adjudication of the Lucifer rebellion, the reopening of the planet's universal broadcasting circuitries and Christ Michael's decision to begin enacting the Correcting Time Plan to retrieve the 37 isolated worlds of Satania.

Lastly, we wish to reiterate this important point concerning the immediate future of your planet which we've spoken about before. From our vintage, we do see potential global problems ahead, but naturally, they will be temporary. As the present dispensation fades into history, it is conceivable that 'the last days' will probably witness several decisive events that will strike at the very foundation of the world's power structures and severely fracture the established global control system of governmental –

industrial – financial – media and military alliance. They will cast a dark cloud upon the credibility and weaken these powerful and highly influential institutions. Consequently, there will be a relatively quick decentralization of international authority and national power, which will progressively usher into an exciting new era of worldwide governmental readjustment, social reorganization accompanied with greater scientific discoveries and personal spiritual development.

We ask and encourage those who interact with us to open your minds and hearts to receive and freely share our messages with others. All are welcome to avail themselves of our services. In fact, it is our honor and pleasure to see you do so.

Our main priority in this mission is to co-creatively design with humanity a new global family wherein goodwill, harmony and peace blossom, where every human being can find purpose, thrives and prospers. We want to assist you in designing, creating and nurturing a better world of sustainable living under equitable social principles that guarantee true and lasting liberty, recognition, respect and justice for all. Our goal is to realize with you a refine planetary community that can accommodate the differences and even celebrate the diversities of all mankind. To this end, we strive patiently and ceaselessly. We certainly welcome and appreciate your cooperation. Finally, let me repeat, you are entering a new era of big temporal changes and spiritual transformations—a *Cosmic Age* as some of you are calling it already. And I say to all the beautiful souls of this realm, welcome at last! In the heavens as well as on earth, these are truly historic and unforgettable times for all of us. I thank you for your kind attention. Be in the light little one, I now withdraw, later.

❀ ❀ ❀ ❀ ❀ ❀ ❀

[Interruption]—this is Joseph: why did you choose to explain the reason for the Correcting Time in this particular Paper given that you have already elaborated extensively on many of its phases, programs, and objectives in the previous?

Abomaly: there is no precise motive why we chose to conduct our assignment in this manner. We are not constrained to convey our information in any specific sequences whatsoever. The chronology of our messages has little to no relevance so long they are true. As much as we are cognizant of the human sense of order and logic, our revelations of any transcendent circumstance cannot necessarily fit these linear and circumscribed perceptions of the mortal mind. Hence, it is duly incumbent upon those who shall peruse these lines to decipher the truth of our assertions spiritually, not intellectually.

While we wish to tax your minds and make you think beyond the realm of finite intelligence, our main goal is rather to stir your soul and awaken your spirit to the wonders and mysteries of creation. And this cannot be achieved by remaining rigidly fixated on a finite model of communication and temporal sequences of events. Moreover, remember this is a co-creative endeavor between our [spirits]. Your mind which is still limited to the sequentiality of time plays only a [medium, secondary role] in fulfilling this conjoint assignment.

Paper 16

Prime Creator Intervenes On Urantia

EARTH WILL BECOME AN ARCHITECTURAL PLANET

The New Declaration of Independence for Humanity

Celestial Teacher: Anomaly ~ Channel: Joseph Elte 12-25-2012

YOU HAVE BEEN TAUGHT THAT following the cleansing of the badly contaminated Luciferian grid in 2011—which required Michael's personal presence to achieve—the Universal Father had personally intervened in the managerial affairs of Urantia. This exceptionally rare situation changed everything pertaining to the previous course of the Correcting Time Plan here.

Though the Father's direct intervention did not discharge anyone from their originally assigned posts and services, but it did renew, reenergize, and remind all of us about the great challenges, importance, and purpose of our missions on this planet.

Many of us have served on other troublesome realms before, even beyond Satania and Nebadon. But we all seem to agree that our commission to this world is the most unpredictable and challenging yet. It is probably quite easy for your modern societies to see and classify themselves as advance and civilize since they have recently begun to make some remarkable progress in the arts of civilization. But from our vantage, this sphere remains severely disordered, morally backward, dangerously unstable, and utterly stricken by evil. It seems to us that you have built several hubs of highly competitive, complex, and sophisticated cultures while you continue to embrace and perform the bellicosity of your primitive ancestors. To us, that's a serious contradiction; it is quite a precarious and unpromising dynamic for this world. Throughout our long careers of universe services, we've never seen such a peculiar mixture of modernism with barbarism on any other realm within the superuniverse of Orvonton. Perhaps, there might be similar worlds in the other six superuniverses, but we surmise, there are few like yours.

As much as it may seem to be, the primary issues with your world today that are most dangerous to peace and stability are not necessarily politics, economics or even militarism, but rather the abject lack of ideals, conscience, and altruism in the minds of men. As we saw in Paper 2 particularly, since the Caligastia secession and the Adamic default, humanity has seriously deviated from the proper course of its biological, moral, and spiritual evolution as they were originally anticipated by the Gods. These unfortunate events plunged your world into an abyss of decadence and irreverence. Plus, the delay of mercy that was accorded to the rebels to reconsider their positions severely impacted and hindered the developmental process of your global civilization. You were deprived of many essential tools or values to help you build a viable, harmonious, and inclusive culture comprising of your diverse ethnic or racial groups. And... because of that, your kind has never been able to create and maintain a peaceful, sustainable and lasting civilization.

The joy and satisfaction that were felt by the celestial hosts following the announcement that the Universal Father had deemed your little blue sphere worthy enough to intervene in its situation personally is indescribable. It might be difficult for you to grasp the true significance of such an action by the Eternal Creator. But we believe this is the greatest opportunity for you to grow in full consciousness of your cosmic identity. Hence, we urge you to engage with the Father through your Higher Selves as He now takes charge of your planetary and universal destinies.

As we've said many times before, the Correcting Time Plan is a co-creative spiritual endeavor between humanity and divinity. Remember, the decision to have mankind participate directly in the implementation of this plan was taken by Michael of Nebadon personally. We now know that the Father has indicated He would use any and all of His receptive children on this troubled planet to bring about the essential transformations that are necessary for peace, joy and love to blossom here. And no doubt, it shall be so. Nevertheless, some of us have wondered whether or not the Father's interference on Urantia was not predestined since Christ Michael took the decision to retrieve and heal this world with humanity's cooperation. Many including myself tend to believe that the choice to bring the Correcting Time with its programs to your sphere, especially the Teaching Mission and the Magisterial Mission, which require full human assistance and collaboration to succeed, was the precursor to this rare intervention of the Paradise Creator in the affairs of your world.

The Divine Decree to Alter Urantia's Cosmic Status
Its Transformation Into An Architectural Realm

Like the Lucifer rebellion that precipitated the Caligastia revolt with the Adamic default did not deter Christ Michael from choosing Urantia as the world whereon to enact his seventh bestowal and obtain the sovereignty of Nebadon; the unique problems caused by these unfortunate events have attracted the attention of the Universal Father to interfere and arrest the free-flow of sins that have plagued this planet for too long. He is now in supreme command of all the celestial hosts participating in this grand plan of correction. He is overseeing the executions of the programs that were designed to rescue and salvage your world. This extraordinary phenomenon, of which very little can be revealed to you now, has further elevated the status of Urantia from a modified, evolutionary life-supporting planet to an *Architectural World* for special education. While physically, the planet will remain a mortal inhabited realm, but it will also become the Father's Garden in Nebadon – one of His mercy-reclaimed abodes in time on which his diverse celestial as well as material children may come to study this subject: *The surety of the triumph of light over darkness.*

Furthermore, this drastic change in status will completely transform its natural as well as its supernatural administrations forever. In fact, many unusual steps have already been taken to indicate this. One, in particular, is the recent announcement from Edentia that the current structure of its political and economic powers will soon be dismantled while its global institutions of authority will be seized upon by the super sentinels of the celestial army that is now encircling the planet. When this occurs, it will suddenly disenfranchise and replace the three main existential centers of administrative control over your world with a new structure of governance that will be introduced and supervised by the Magisterial Son. While it remains a fact that mortals must evolve their representative governments, but it is also true that the Most Highs rule in the kingdom of men when necessary. And so, when ample time has been granted to a political order to oversee the development and progress of civilization, if it fails and refuses to move forward as those on this planet have, then, it is within the supreme laws of the Constellation of Norlatiadeck to remove such a sluggish and unfruitful system. This is what's happening in your world today. The entire global syndicate of so-called "*royal families,*" governments and authorities, which ordinarily administer and control the affairs of this kingdom have been judged and found wanting on the balance of divine justice on high. Thus, a decree was made to liberate humanity from their yokes once and for all.

It is also highly expected that Christ Michael will soon fulfill his promise to return on earth accompanied with Monjoronson—the

Magisterial Son, who will officially inaugurate the Fifth Epochal Dispensation. And we know that following these momentous future events, your world will be administered in all fields of life by sincere and benevolent personalities who are both competent and do have the best interest of humanity in mind. Those among you who will be appointed to assume jurisdiction over any planetary affairs will be distinguished by their dedication to service and their capacity to joyfully perform their duties without succumbing to the illusions of self-importance.

As some of you can imagine, all of us are eagerly awaiting the arrival of those times ahead that will see the fulfillment of the Father's promise to make everything new again here. And we are now certain that His recent decree to transform the planet into an Architectural world was a major step towards this end. That announcement basically confirmed our cherished assumption since the final adjudication of the Lucifer rebellion in 1985, that this extraordinary event was imminent. However, admittedly, although we did speculate a lot on this matter, but none of us envisioned this radical alteration in the earth's cosmic status. We always knew that it would require some drastic measures from the Gods to rescue this world from darkness, but we did not expect this tremendous dimensional shift. Many of the profound and marvelous changes that are scheduled to transpire on it soon were known to us eons ago, but its transformation into a special sphere made to order was unpredictable - at least to those of my order.

Now, we cannot emphasize enough on the importance for you to focus on reaching within yourselves to find the divine Mighty I AM presence.

This is the real guide of your being. Honestly, you can never be totally sure of anything outside of the scope of your personal consciousness and experience. Mentally, you may believe in certain concepts, values, and adapt to circumstances, but absolute assurance of reality is a spiritual attainment. The indwelling Father Fragment is your ever valiant and loyal Higher Self who ensures and guarantees the safety and integrity of your soul during this life and throughout your long careers of ascension to the center of all things. We are not asking you to simply believe in us. But rather we would like to see more of you earnestly engage in the enthralling adventure of discovering this indwelling gift of God, for this would greatly encourage us and accelerate the healing and recovering process of your world.

Since the Father has now taken control of your planet's destiny, this should at least appease the anxieties of uncertainty. We advise and encourage you to spend more time in stillness; to live in the *Present* and to communicate often with Him inside yourselves. As far as we know, there is no proper collective method to contact and speak directly to your indwelt Mighty I AM, for this is a highly unique and personal experience for every individual. Nevertheless, we do suggest clearing up your minds of negative thoughts and emotions while maintaining an attitude of love and grace as preliminary acts of intention that invite your Higher Selves for conversation.

All mortals of this realm have been, one way or another, touched or affected by the Father's action, for the divine call after His interference was broadcasted from His central abode on Paradise to every single heart here. Thus, we urge you to prepare yourselves for the coming sweeping changes in your world affairs, which are ordained by Him directly.

Upon this, we will close our session for this evening. Once again, I commend you for your steadfast disposition to cooperate with us in finishing this co-creative project, even though you are not fully aware of its real purpose. I will now take my leave. Stay in the light dear friend, and good night.

Paper 17

Embrace Your Higher Self

Finding and Espousing Your Own TRUTHS

Celestial Teacher: Abannaly ~ Channel: Joseph Elie 12-29-2012

AS DIFFICULT IT MAY BE for the human mind to understand the concept of eternity; nonetheless, all men innately aspire to immortality. Spiritually, you are *immortal* – albeit you are now apparently living what is call a "*mortal existence.*" This is according to the divine plan of the First Eternal Creator to fulfill his universal mandate of creature perfection starting from the lowest teachable mind level of animal consciousness to the heights and glories of spiritual realization.

Thus, from our perspective, though we perceive your perishable physical tabernacle, but we essentially recognize you as evolving souls of light – faith-sons and daughters of God. It is no evolutionary coincidence that among the millions of minded-species, which inhabit the earth, only you mortals manifest such a profound desire to everlasting existence. While most of you are practically unaware and unsure about the realities of a possible afterlife, but in fact, at the uttermost level of your beings, you do feel that, the whole human experience would have been a worthless and meaningless adventure if the end of physical life were actually a definitive cessation of personality consciousness.

In reality, the phenomenon you mortals of this realm generally call "life" is an eternal cosmic quality. Regardless where it appears, in and of itself, like energy, life retains its timeless nature. True, the temporal components of the living human organism, such as the body and the physical mind, are perishable. But the spiritual constituents, i.e. the soul, the spirit and the personality of man persist after natural death. You continue to evolve upward in greater consciousness of divinity, sphere after sphere, life after life, even beyond the confines of the creations of time and space. It is ever true that your material existence on earth is a transient experience, which is but the vestibule of your long career of universe ascension and perfection. The most important task throughout this extensive and fascinating journey is to remember your Higher Self as you seek to find and embrace your own Truths.

The profundity of who and what you are spiritually is impenetrable by any external source from your beingness, for only the *Divine You* fully know the eternal mystery and appreciate the real value of your personality. Thus, finding that Higher Self is not a mere side task, but should be the primary responsibility of every awaken Urantian. Most of you are fully aware of the precarious nature of the present time you live in. The choices that you make now in this juncture are crucial in determining the future realities that will prevail upon the earth. This power of the human will and imagination to create, and direct reality is a well-known fact in your world today. It essentially means that now you can collectively employ this force for the greater good of humanity. We believe that most of you are ready to help co-create the new earth that must come into being during the forthcoming era of enlightenment. There is a unanimous consensus on our side that you are fully capable of overcoming the many challenges of this dangerous transitional time more consciously – with increasing clarity, objectivity, and certainty, provided the proper mechanisms of cooperation are in place.

As a will-endowed, multidimensional being, man possesses many differential personal qualities, such as a body, a mind, a soul, and a spirit. These constituents of the self allow him to function on different levels of universe reality using solely the power of his creative imagination. However, ordinarily, most of you on this realm exert your energies operating merely on the plane of material existence with a quasi-animal consciousness. This is an alarming situation as we see it from our vantage, for it greatly impede the development of your souls, and delay your contact with the indwelt spirit – your Higher Self. The God Fragment that indwells every normal Urantians is neither approachable by any scientific or metaphysical applications, nor can it ever be discovered through ostentatious sacraments of religious devotion. Also, remember, the distractions of contemporary living constitute serious impediments to accessing and acknowledging your Higher Selves.

It is true that there is no precise method to approach the God Presence within yourselves. But the most effective manner known to us for mortals to become conscious of your indwelt spirits is to live in the Now; to be in regular stillness, and to maintain an attitude of faith, grace and love. When there are observed properly and sufficiently, these attitudes cannot fail to ensure contact between the two of you. The fact is the Higher Self's main preoccupation is the fostering and elevation of your soul to divine consciousness. It is absolutely consecrated to spiritualize your mind and immortalize your personality. Whereas, to the contrary, most of you are usually preoccupied with other circumstances than conferring with your Inner Guides.

You spend more time attending to the immediate earthly situations around you than you do in meditation or in reflection of the Divine Presence inside your mind. The vile and misguided liberalism of most contemporary pop cultures, which severely denigrate men morally and spiritually practically consume all your time and energy. The fact is most of you, despite the dark cabal's indoctrinations and manipulations are capable of making better choices that would allow you to retain more of your personal freedom to do what your hearts truly desire. Instead, you have allowed yourselves to become trapped in their web of control by voluntarily embrace their monetary system and embroiled yourselves in the toxic hurdles of their engineered synthetic corporate societies.

Recognize and Claim Your Divine Inheritance
You Are All Souls of Light – Offspring of the Eternal I AM

As we view and judge the general situation on Urantia today, the greatest obstacle to a massive worldwide awakening of consciousness is the sheer ignorance that most humans enjoy pertaining to their cosmic identities coupled with the inalienable sovereignty and inherent powers of personality, which are conferred upon you by God as divine birthrights, just as he does for all orders of will-endowed universe intelligences. Unfortunately, since the Caligastia revolt, there has been such a lack of understanding mixed with a ferocious systematic effort to conceal the transcendent knowledge of *who and what you are* generation after generation, that presently, the desire to know more or venture any further than what you are told by your educators and leaders, has practically disappeared. Frankly, it is quite pitiful to observe that as some of your nations are claiming modernity and freedom, more and more, you are losing your personal liberties to the overwhelming impositions of the authoritarian state.

We know that it is basically taboo to question what is considered normal and acceptable by societies here, especially in most of your so-called democracies, where your basic rights are supposedly protected. Modernism, with all its glamour and enticements, has achieved the dark cabal's sinister goal of creating a nearly hand-free control system that is both attractive and appealing to human pride and self-esteem. It provided them the desired platform upon which to experiment with their manifold techniques of suppression and domination over the world. The network of international institutions that make up their global structure of power constitutes an *iron veil* that has been cast over the world to restrain, manipulate, subdue, and control you, using cunning and tantalizing methods in peacetime, brute and coercive measures during unrests.

You must learn to muster the courage necessary to change the fearful and servile attitude that has kept you subservient to this corrupt world order, which was basically designed to function against your interests and reduce you into passive impotent slaves. You are now at a crossroad where to arrest the continuing spiraling descent of your global society into a bottomless pit of debauchery and insanity, it is imperative that you recognize and claim your divine inheritance. As we've said before, you no longer have the leisure to remain ignorant of your true spiritual identity. The divine decree to open a new dispensation on your planet is actually a mandate for you to break off with the past, expand your consciousness, and realize your sonship with God. Until this happens, you will never be able to emancipate yourselves completely from the residual effects of the Lucifer rebellion.

Therefore, we urge all of you, especially those who aspire to have regular contact with us, to continue your inward progress and ascent to your indwelt spirits, which are your true guides and immortal selves. Recognizing and accepting your affiliation to divinity is not a special privilege granted to a few, but a divine birthright that is conferred upon every sentient living mortal on earth. As we perceive humanity from our dimension, you are all beautiful evolving souls of light – albeit some shine brighter than others. Each of you is truly the embodiment of the sacred flare of the Eternal I AM.

Quite frankly, most of us are very disturbed as many of you are by the overall problematic conditions that continue to prevail on this planet. We watch with great concerns the continuing efforts of many dark forces aiming at precipitating it into an abyss of chaos and hell. But we are determined in our intentions and approaches to work with all of you in order to bring about the healing energies with the transformational vibrations that are necessary for your world to recover from ages of systematic abuses, confusions, strife, and destructions.

Since the decision was made to enact the correcting time on Urantia, scores of truth-seeking individuals have joined us in this astronomical undertaking. We are ever grateful and appreciative of those wonderful souls who do honestly open their hearts and minds to our counsels, and who have offered themselves as planetary liaisons to facilitate our communications with humanity. We need more of you to use this innate power of your personalities to contact and interact with spirit – to speak and visit with us. If we could summarize the general purpose of our commission on this world in a sentence: *knowing and embracing your divine selves as planetary offspring of God*—would be ideal. Much of our resources are committed to helping you realize this transcendental consciousness. Yes, to discover and know the Mighty I AM Presence within yourselves is our most important and cherished goal.

Finding & Embracing Your Own Truths

Discovering and espousing the values of eternal truths is wholly a personal spiritual matter for every individual. Thus, any attempt to influence someone into changing or disowning his religious philosophies is absolutely futile. In reality, such a vain act is an affront to the free will of personality, and therefore, utterly unbecoming of a respectable, open-minded believer.

Religionists, idealists and spiritualists who are zealously promoting their versions of truths should always remember that every individual is responsible to choose his or her own course in all matters pertaining to personal spiritual survival in the universe. Irrespective of its origins, qualities and slogans, religion should never be forced upon anyone. In a progressive society, it must remain optional to all men.

But is it wise to remain subservient and loyal to an organized cult while you ignore the transcendent truth of the presence of God within your own soul? Oh humanity! How long will you remain servile to static, unprogressive traditions before you realize your innate spiritual powers to transcend nature itself? When will you finally redeem yourselves and your children from the abstractions and illusions of a falsely so-called material world? Will you ever take a stand for true righteousness and freedom to blossom?

Again, you are now crossing the most crucial moment in your history as an evolving race on this small planet since the beginning of the current dispensation, which was initiated by the mortal incarnation of Christ Michael. The coming years will likely witness tremendous upheavals and many crises, which may provoke worldwide fear, panic and confusions. And... at some point in this new century, the horrendous day of rectification shall occur. But humanity will not perish. Most of you will survive the global cataclysms that will officially terminate this transitioning period to begin the New Era. Actually, a good number of those who now labor in obscurity to promote truth will be called to serve as guides to help and assist the remainder of your species to move on through these hard and testing times.

Celestial Exhortations

As they have done in the past for previous generations, the celestial hosts have kindly exhorted modern men to expand your awareness of reality beyond the material, temporal world. You are encouraged to recognize and claim your spiritual birthright as sons and daughters of the living God, who is the very source of your personal existences—the secret of your intuitive consciousnesses.

You are sympathetically advised to do your best to evolve spiritually, to transcend your current modalities of engagement: i.e. to learn to resolve your petty secular and religious disagreements peacefully, to repudiate all racial divergences, to stop all transnational antagonisms and abolish warfare. Bear in mind, all matters that only fuel discords and provoke unnecessary conflicts between the nations will not be allowed to continue during the coming dispensation of enlightenment, which, as we've said, is scheduled to begin at some foreseeable time here.

It is pointless to be fearful of this moment, for this is really a time of tremendous global changes that will elevate and transform humanity for the better. Instead, you should be courageous, humble, and receptive to your Higher Selves. Sincerely seek for truth and be willing to go wherever it may lead you. Stop resisting the drawing power of your inner spirit who so desires to guide you to the path of your true destiny. And, most importantly, learn to tolerate, appreciate, and love one another.

To emancipate yourselves from the current control system to which most of you are now subservient, you will have to learn to transcend and expand your consciousness beyond your natural but limited five-sense level of body-mind awareness. This has only conditioned and grounded your perceptions and confined you to the domains of this illusory, holographic, so-called physical reality.

Just as traditions must be challenged and changed sometimes to stimulate social progress, so are your concepts and definitions of personality also need to be revised and upgraded periodically—especially during momentous epochal transition. The present widely accepted philosophy, which basically defines a human being as a purely material creature, totally subjected to nature with no spiritual power, is a far cry from the true universe meaning and value of mankind. It must be transcended!

The notion that the mortal selfhood is a composite of the body and the mind alone, must be changed and replaced with a higher understanding to include the inner presences of the evolving soul and the guiding spirit of man. True, the body and the mind are evidently the most tangible features of the human self, but they are not the exclusive constituents of the entire personality.

The 'Last Days' of the Present Dispensation

Today, you are witnessing the final dramas of the current age approaching the last events that will officially terminate this transitioning period to begin a novel epoch of spiritual renaissance on your earth. This is happening by divine decreed. It is a '*cosmic call*' for humanity to gradually, or rather rapidly learn to transcend the limitations of your present state of consciousness. It is the time of self-renewal and spiritual expansion—the utopian "Golden Age" of peace, harmony and speedy progress that many of your ancient traditions have predicted. This is why more and more people are tuning-in to this momentous awakening process everyday. Scores are gladly responding to *the calling*. Many who use to be indifferent towards spirit are starting to seek for Truth and pay attention to us. At last, they are beginning to manifest the desire to learn and understand the true values upon which all genuine spiritual relationships are founded. This is a wonderful development that we on this side who co-create with you do greatly appreciate.

As you have been informed, this global awakening movement is the prelude of a comprehensive preparation for the future inauguration of a New Era of spiritual enlightenment that will radically transform your civilization. The preliminary governmental changes that will transpire during this changing moment leading to the Golden Age and eventually to the Days of Light and Life, are broad and unprecedented. Society will not readily adapt to them, for most of you will be stunned and dumfounded. Many think they are well-prepared and ready to face what is coming, but we would like to admonish them to practice more humility.

This is why a whole volume to discuss some of these amazing futuristic transformations in world management separately is also part of our co-creative assignment.

You are now at a crossroad between two planetary epochs; one is rapidly passing away into the oblivion of history, while another is about to commence soon officially. A choice must be made at this crucial moment! *You can no longer avoid the responsibility to know and face the fact of who you truly are.* You must seek to discover and embrace your Higher Selves—your true spiritual identities—in order to expand your consciousness of reality beyond the physical limitations and illusions of this world. And, to do that successfully, you need to accelerate the frequency of your interactions and worshipful communion with that *divine presence* in you.

The spiritual purpose and value of your personalities are tremendously greater than what you can conceive or able to understand with your present mental capacity and level of awareness. The five physical senses of the human organism are essentially limited and grounded to the finite world of energy-matter – they do not reach the domains of thought, and much less the sublime levels of spirit. These materially conditioned biological features are hardly adequate to dissect the variances of the material domains of existence accurately, let alone the complexities of the spiritual universe. Moreover, accordingly, the perception of reality they provide is grossly distorted, incomplete and utterly restricted to the circumscribe matters of time and space. However, consciousness is expandable at will; it is not confined to any space. But it can be severely conditioned by perception, belief and ideologies. Because of its perceived relation to the body, unless it is projected and expanded beyond this locality, *"mind-consciousness"* is organically encapsulated and responsive to that bio-chemical system, and therefore, perceives and reads only the so-called "physical world."

It is impossible to achieve God-consciousness by any scientific, metaphysic or intellectual technique. Mortals attain such a sublime level of spiritual realization by repeating mutual encounters with their Thought Adjusters within their own hearts and minds. Man becomes certain of his affiliation to God only after his inner guide has testified and affirmed this to his evolving soul and mind.

There is a vast disparity between speculating and knowing just as there is a tremendous difference between belief and faith. Belief simply narrows and limits one's perception of reality to a circumscribed paradigm of possibilities, while knowing [faith] liberates the mind for the conquest of eternity—to find Deity. Those who truly know God have regular personal contact with him; and they are aware and certain of His reality, personality and supremacy. These recurring experiences with the Father provide those blessed souls with an increasing understanding of the true meaning, purpose and value of the human personality, being itself potentially eternal.

A major epochal transition, which I personally call—*The Truth Revolution*, has been slowly enfolding upon your world for many years now. Though this phenomenon is very real, it's a rather latent and unpretentious dimensional shift of consciousness from the existential global paradigm of the five-sense reality-awareness to a radically greater and better one. It will continue to enfold silently until the current system of things completely vanishes out of existence. And as it intensifies and expands, it will drastically transform your sphere inside out.

The current authoritarian global control system has reached the termination of its time mandate. It is declining quite rapidly, though this may seem slow or not happening at all to some of you. Spiritually, it has been judged and found wanting. From a cosmic standpoint, it has no credibility and legitimacy. This is practically the last century of its reign.

Nowadays, mankind is progressively waking up to the sublime truth of his higher spiritual nature. From our daily observation, we perceive that increasingly, more souls are discreetly seeking and finding the source of all Truths within themselves practically every moment on your earth. And the current control system cannot subsist as an effective power over a world of continuing expansion of transcendental awareness. This is why the lies and sophistries that are its energetic sustenance are being picked on, discredited and rejected virtually everyday now. It's no wonder that it is becoming more and more disagreeable and ruthless, for it has been forced to adopt a defensive approach. Those desperate attitudes are the typical signs of its inevitable defeat and eventual annihilation. Yes, the days are numbered for this old monarchical order. In a few years, it shall pass into history as if it has never been. As for the global community, there is barely any time left for procrastinations and excuses. The spiritual awakening process must continue to expand at all costs! And please bear in mind, you have all to lose and nothing to gain if you persist on that unconscious state of being servile to the formal establishments of an utterly corrupt and vanishing dynasty.

Upon this, we will end our commentaries on this subject in this first volume, for we plan to discuss it thoroughly in the second volume of our trilogy. We are at the final stage of this assignment. As I have already communicated to you, Paper 18 will terminate our transmissions for the initial text of the Correcting Time Plan trilogy. I will now take my leave once again to allow you to rest in attendance of your disposition to receive me for the last session. Farewell.

Paper 18

Imagine & Co-Create Your Reality

THE SUBTLETY OF MANKIND'S SPIRITUAL POWERS

Spirit-Consciousness Precedes and Dominates Energy-Matter

Celestial Teacher: Abonualy - Channel: Joseph Else 1-7-2013

WILL IS YOUR VOLITIONAL POWER, energy is your building material, and your imagination is the link to the indwelt creative spirit that allows you to design and create your experiential realities. That you are the co-creators of your experiences—the products of your own thoughts, intentions and imaginations, is not a mere concept or a fantastic adage.

Truly, imagining, designing and creating the future are neither idealism nor a pipedream, to borrow your vernacular - but a totally doable and practical possibility. In effect, as far as we know, besides life with some of its essential endowments, no value has ever been bequeathed upon any evolving creature within the universe without his or her choice and capacity to appreciate it. Not even a second in time has ever been granted to anyone without their personal desire to live and experience that instant. What you are now and what you are becoming day-by-day are entirely dependent on the choices and decisions you make every moment. By acknowledging and accepting the Truth that you are indeed the co-creators of your realities and destinies, you are, in fact, severing with the prejudices and limitations of duality. You are asserting the supremacy of your true and Higher Selves over the temporal illusions that beset and dominate your mortal existence on earth.

Today, vast numbers of you have liberated yourselves from the political, social, and religious biases of this dangerously polarized world. You have discerned many of the deceptions concerning selfhood that were placed upon you thousands of years ago by the dark cabal. There is now undoubtedly a growing global momentum to seek for higher truths that is increasingly leading humanity to a lot of profound self-discoveries. That inward progress to full emancipation is actually the main goal of Christ Michael's Correcting Time Plan. Thus, we are delighted to observe this development as an immediate effect of its implementation on your sphere. In fact, it is interesting to remark that, though yet latently; many extraordinary and marvelous spiritual transformations have already occurred here since we began our mission a few decades ago. And...as we've said before, the greatest changes are forthcoming.

While we continue to ask for your patience and perseverance in faith, we would like to see you transcend your conceptual meaning of *hope*, which we regard as a loose and ambiguous term. There is nothing wrong with hoping, but it is highly ineffective as a creative tool for your imagination. While it may connote spiritual expectations, hope ultimately stiffens and paralyzes the will to imagine and create effectively. It is literally true that you are responsible for designing and creating your destinies in the universe. Thus, hoping entails that you have forfeited this obligation and relinquished your life responsibilities to another being—be it human or divine. This does not mean that you should not believe or wait on God's promises. Far from that, to the contrary, this is rather to remind you of the Father's all-knowing indwelling presence inside your mind. Your mental attunement to this divine reality will sweep-away all fears and doubts that block your full consciousness of Truth, thereby eliminating the necessity for *"hoping."* As of this day forwards, view hope for what it really is: a result of intellectual and spiritual indolence. It is hardly a real virtue.

On the other hand, unlike hope that suggests passivity and weakness, *knowing* is affirmative, confident and powerful. Passive energies are always detrimental to the creative imagination; they reduce the spiritual forces that energize the will to create.

Creating Your Reality

There are practically three main components in the material self, which are indispensable to the process of creating your reality: [1] consciousness; [2] willpower; [3] imagination. To our understanding, concisely, this is how it works: after visualizing in your mind's eye your intended design, you must also feel that that thought form or image is indeed real and does exist in some higher dimension; though yet inaccessible physically, but real and capable of materialization.

Actually, this is your opportunity to transcend all fears and doubts for good, because your chance of successfully doing this consciously is squarely dependent on the strength of your faith and confidence that this is indeed possible. Your human pragmatism, local perception and intellectual understanding of reality do not apply in this subtle but powerful method of creation. For remember, it is the vibrational level of your entire being that ultimately determines the quality of your experiences.

But the question is: *are you aware that you are constantly creating realities by simply being, or by the mere acts of observing, thinking, imagining and choosing?*

Yes, creating your reality is truly that easy. However, it can also be difficult if you cannot keep the simplicity of it in mind. Do not doubt or deny this because you feel that you are not in control of many actualities that surround you. This is as it should be. Spiritually speaking, you certainly cannot nor should you aspire to control other beings. As individuals, you have very little to no power over the vast web of realities, which bind and connect all of us together, e.g., nature and the cosmos. However, you can control your own mind and direct your personal thoughts and feelings in this infinite network of possibilities to the extent that you may lead an exemplary life, and are a model of inspiration to others in their quest for Truth and spiritual emancipation. It is only a choice and you can make it, even now!

In effect, it is a well-known and documented fact in your world's scientific community today that mortals are literally reality-producing creatures. This is not just by your whole personalities, but also by each part—from the cellular to the organismic levels. There is a permanent organic process that provokes, crystallizes, and sustains reality throughout your bodies completely independent of the involvement of your personal action. For instance, besides distributing blood to your arteries and nervous system, the heart automatically regulates and balances the flow of energy throughout the body. This single organ not only ensures the physiological functions of the others throughout the body, but it also maintains your material existence with little to no effort, on your part. This incessant upholding of life by this unique organ is similar to what many of you; call a *hand-free or automatic process*. Yet, it is not magical. It is a natural phenomenon that triggers many other biological operations, new realities within your bio-chemical system—your mortal tabernacle.

The supreme purpose of your whole ascension careers from time to eternity is to find the Primordial Source and Architect of your personalities on Paradise – your Eternal Creator and Cosmic Benefactor. And…that parcel of Him which indwells each of you, even now, is the pure energetic force that empowers your creative mind and helps you create your reality. While those divine gifts spring from God the Father with definite plans for your short existences on earth, your choices to embrace their programs are indispensable for them to elevate and spiritualize you. And... doing so is the secret to unleashing the full potentials of your creative personalities. This is why we cannot urge each of you enough to go in stillness and find that Mighty I AM Presence that lives within your soul and speaks to your minds constantly, albeit, normally most of its kind messages are usually unheard.

The human identity, which you are now experiencing, is obviously a transient phenomenon of selfhood – a passing biological construct. In all its beauties and sorrows, this temporary self is highly serviceable to both, God's personality and yours. For it offers you the opportunity to fuse with the Father's Spirit, while he enjoys the sublime satisfaction of bringing back another evolving soul from the animal-origin homo sapiens of time to Himself. And... the entire journey of your spiritual elevation to the First Source and Center is essentially a creative process between you and your Thought Adjusters. Thus, again, please learn to make time for regular communion with your Higher Selves, for this is the key element to your full empowerment as an inspired faither; to become a wise and thoughtful creator.

Remember, the Correcting Time Plan itself is a co-creative endeavor between humanity and divinity. This essentially means, as we have said before, that the overall outcome of this cosmic enterprise is fundamentally dependent upon your choices and the qualities of the experiences you create. Hence, we admonish and caution you to create wisely, to reflect deeply upon your thoughts and examine your emotions as you imagine what must come to be.

It has been a wonderful occasion for us to impart our two cents on this rather complex subject for some of you, concerning your personal power to generate reality. This is a very broad topic that cannot be fully covered and elucidated in a single short transmission. And so, we believe it is best to think of and pose related questions to stimulate us, as that will widen the dialogue on the theme and provide us with greater opportunities to disclose more Truths regarding this extraordinary faculty that each of you possesses individually.

This is something I encourage you to do personally my friend in order to continue to increase the frequency and enhance the quality of our communications. As you know, in and of itself, this very contact between us is entirely a co-creative experience. The entire work that you are about to conclude the first volume, is essentially a creative expression of your mind directed and filtered through *spirit*.

We have now arrived at the end of the last Paper to finalize this initial volume of the Great Correcting Time Plan trilogy. As an unfolding recovery project that continuously fluctuates in response to a variety of changing worldly circumstances, all the details of its numerous activities cannot be provided at one time, in a single book. Thus, we concluded that our narratives of this cosmic undertaking to salvage the rebellion stricken worlds of Satania must be presented in a sequel of at least three volumes. We know that you did not imagine this dear friend, but we did, and your Higher Self also knew.

Does that inspire you to carry on in creating this experience with us? We certainly hope so. Please continue to approach and stay ever closer to your Inner Guide. I will now bid you farewell for a short season of rest and rejuvenation - good evening.

WE'VE NOW ARRIVED AT THE end of the first chapter of our voluntary efforts to assist our celestial helpers and friends in the propagation and implementation of the programs of the Great Correcting Time Plan on Urantia. As you probably just read in the final lines from the last Paper, this is not necessarily the conclusion of our co-creative work in the proceedings of the Creator's design for our badly ill planet. We have committed ourselves to pen two more books to cover the full spectrum of all the matters that are involved in this comprehensive inter-planetary project. And these texts will also be published as soon as they are complete.

A true leader is one who seeks to inspire and guide others to lead themselves. Thus, it should be noted that we are willfully engaged in this process not only because of our unconditional love for God, but also because of our desire to see our fellow men wake up to the full realization of who they truly are spiritually. We are not expecting any personal rewards from this effort as we have already been immensely blessed by our commitment to this task.

Because our main objective is to share channeled informations with all open-minded truth-seekers, respectfully without any persuasion, and knowing that Truth always speaks for itself in the heart of all sincere souls, we find it rather inconsequential and irrelevant to reveal in whose name, or by what authority, we are doing this. Nevertheless, we are concerned about the curiosity of any sincere inquirer who has genuine and thoughtful questions about our work.

And now, I want to thank all the celestial personalities who are attached to the service of Urantia, notably the angels and midwayers, for their tireless efforts in the vast ministry to assist mankind in correcting the manifold problems that beset this world. Although, unfortunately, many of your colleagues were led astray during the planetary revolt of the traitorous Prince Caligastia, it is in record that the recent corps of spirit helpers has been true to its trust since the momentous triumph of Christ Michael's incarnation as Jesus of Nazareth.

It is a fact that since your appointment to this realm, you have toiled continuously to upgrade the social and spiritual status of mankind. Most of you have remained truthful and loyal to your assignments throughout the long ages of evolution here. I honor and love all of you dearly just as you are all appreciated and beloved by our divine parents. I reverently marvel at your patience, wisdom and compassion for humanity; and, on behalf of all my fellow mortals, with favor and grace, please receive our thanks and gratitude.

In addition, I want to thank my personal celestial teacher, Abomaly, [the main voice of this text], for your relentless support and encouragement. You have been a wonderful counselor, a sympathetic friend and a tolerant mentor. I strongly anticipate the moment in time, when we will join in spiritual embrace on the mansion worlds of Satania to continue our long ascent to Paradise. Although I'm not usually conscious of your actual presence, but I know you are always near, and I'm deeply comforted when I remember the prospect of our long cosmic journey together.

Furthermore, I send my greetings and somewhat late welcome to the present acting Governor General representing Christ Michael on the planet for this century. It is unfortunate that your presence must currently remain a secret to humanity because of our superstitious tendency to worship supernatural personalities.

I also want to acknowledge the Vorondadek Son, who is in a stationary supervision on Urantia. Since you were dispatched by the Most Highs of Norlatiadeck after the Caligastia betrayal for such an irregular assignment on this rebellion-stricken world. You've been a patient, sympathetic, and wise leader. Age after age, you have remained always true and loyal to your great responsibility to oversee the political and social affairs of planetary evolution here, and whenever necessary, to intervene in the kingdom of men. Yet, you never abuse your authority. Although your invaluable service focuses on the collective of the human race, but your presence also inspires and provides great comfort to every oppressed and dejected soul on this planet.

Moreover, I praise and glorify Nebadonia, the Holy Mother Spirit of this universe who constantly overshadows us with her boundless affection as she quickens our minds and renews our dispositions to confront and cope with the many unpredictable vicissitudes and difficulties of life. Regardless of our shortcomings, doubts or virtues, your gracious ministry is steadfast and always dependable. Indeed, you embrace all of us in your infinitely kind nature irrespective of our personal circumstances, for your wisdom and understanding are magnificent as your love is divine and perfect. Although I will probably not see it in the flesh, but I pray for the arrival of the great age of enlightenment, when all men shall know the truth of your actual presence within themselves through their diverse heavenly ministers, i.e., the adjutant spirits, the angels, the midwayers, and many others.

Growing and expanding the horizon of humanity's collective consciousness by refining and elevating the quality of our thoughts, values and understandings, is one of the main goals of the Great Correcting Time Plan, which is presently enfolding on earth. And I am extremely happy and grateful to You, Father, and all other concerned celestial personalities for allowing me to participate in this magnificent supernatural project. Though I aspire to be of greater service to you in the future, but for now, I am fully content and satisfy with my simple and somewhat obscure assignment to fulfill this extraordinary cosmic undertaking. Knowing my honest efforts to execute it will delight You, even in the smallest capacity such as writing this book; I shall faithfully remain true to my task until I depart from this world.

This ends the preliminary phase of the work you have given me to accomplish on Urantia. I will consider this book to have attained its purpose if every person who reads it becomes a zealous truth seeker with a passion to serve and be about your business and thus, contribute something to attain the goals of the Great Correcting Time Plan. After all, the eternal Truth, which declares that God is love, is the greatest revelation regarding your benevolent and merciful nature to mankind. And finally, let us all embrace this sacred knowledge wholeheartedly as we once again reiterate and confirm for ourselves the amazing declaration of Christ Michael: *"Every human being is a unique and beloved planetary child of God—the Father of all."*

Appendix

Brief Descriptions of Unusual Celestial Names, Titles, Places, and Other Terms Used Throughout this Book

Celestial Teacher: Abraxady – Channel: Joseph Elie 2-21-2013

ONE OF THE MAIN THEOLOGICAL problems that provoke serious confusions among religionists on Urantia is their ignorance of the correct names and proper universe functions of different celestial personalities mentioned in their scriptures. Throughout history, many and diverse orders of spirit intelligences have ministered to this world, and most of their inspired messages were all attributed directly either to angels or to God Himself.

This confusion has grossly distorted the meanings attached to many revelations that were communicated to humanity, and thus, has deeply bewildered and misguided scores of believers for generations. Consequently, in our effort to elucidate the matter, we want to share here a brief description for each of the few, which are commonly known and several others that were recently revealed to humankind and cited throughout this book.

The Universal Father—is the One and only True, Primal and Eternal God of all creations—the First Source and Center of reality—the Great, Absolute and Infinite I AM. We refer to His Presence in the human mind as the Mystery Monitor, Thought Adjuster, Divine Gift, Inner Voice, Pilot Light, the Divine Presence, Inner Guide, the indwelling Spirit, and Father fragment.

The Eternal Son—is the Second Source and Center of reality—the Absolute Personification and expression of the Father's perfect thought into the Divine Word—His original and Eternal Son. Hence, He possesses all the transcendent qualities and attributes of the Universal Father save a few factors such as the ability to fragmentized Himself and indwell the minds of mortals or the power to bestowal personality.

Paradise—is the central Isle of all cosmic actualities—be they material or spiritual – temporal or celestial. It is the everlasting source of energy, the geographic center of infinity, the original pattern of absolute perfection, and the official residence of God the Universal Father with His vast hosts of co-ordinate associates. Paradise is an eternal reality; it is existential with God.

Immanuel—was confounded with Christ-Michael by biblical writers during the latter's last bestowal mission as a mortal on Urantia. Immanuel is a Union of Days—a highly distinguished class of trinity origin personalities functioning on behalf of the Paradise Father in the evolutionary universes of time and space. He is the elder brother and mentor of Christ Michael. Immanuel is not the Creator of Nebadon. He is a Paradise ambassador to this universe, representing the voice and wisdom of the Father—the supreme and personal counselor of the Creator Son. Until recently, subsequent to the publication of the Urantia Book, the order of Days was never revealed on earth.

Among other probable but yet unrevealed reasons, there are two main ones that explain why Immanuel was so closely connected with the bestowal mission of Christ Michael on Urantia. First, he was the divine counselor of the Creator Son prior and throughout the whole incarnation period. Second, He was temporarily invested with the authority of Nebadon by the superuniverse rulers—the Ancients of Days—during the thirty-six years Michael was absent from His usual administrative headquarters on Salvington. Every evolving local universe receives the blessing of Paradise by the divine presence of a Union of Days as an observer, ambassador, and counselor in the courtship of the Creator Son of that particular creation. However, such a Paradise minister never participates in the administrative procedures of His assigned universe unless a request is made directly by the Creator Son. These Sons are the personal representatives of Paradise and exclusively act on behalf of the Universal Father in the finite experiential creations of time and space.

Christ-Michael—is the name of the Creator Sons of the evolutionary universes of time and space. The Michaels are perfect creator personalities who spring from the union of the Universal Father and the Eternal Son. Each is truly a divine and only-begotten Son of these two existential Deities. There can never be a duplicate of such a being throughout all eternity. Even though these Sons are equal in every respect concerning their divinity and perfection, nonetheless, each is an entirely original individualized Personality. But they do enjoy a unique relationship with their Paradise Parents. Since they are dual in origin, being from the Universal Father and the Eternal Son, the Creator Sons may reflect the character of one or both of their Parents. For example, the personality of Michael of Nebadon—the Creator of our universe—mostly reflects the personality of the Eternal Son.

To all extents and purposes, a Christ Michael represents God in the universe of his making. He is the personification of the Father for the evolving creatures in his creation. In fact, Michaels possess an extra power as they represent and act in the stead of both of their Paradise Parents. However, prior to their seven bestowal missions as creatures of the realms of their own universes, these Creator Sons rule their creations in the name of the Paradise Father.

After his seventh incarnation experience, a Creator Son practically becomes the incontestable Sovereign Lord and Chief of his universe. A Son of this status is usually denominated as a Master Christ-Michael. Though the Michaels create the local universes of time, but before the completion of their seven incarnations in creature likeness, they never rule alone. Only after fulfilling the bestowal requirements of the Paradise Trinity, can it truly be said of such a Son *"all powers in heaven and on earth are given into his hands."*

Nebadonia—is the name of the Mother-Spirit or Holy Spirit of this universe, which bore the name Nebadon.

Gabriel—is the firstborn of Christ-Michael and Nebadonia. He is the eldest of all the created intelligences in this universe, and the only of his kind in the entire creation. He is the Chief Executive and Administrator of Nebadon. Every universe possesses just one of such a unique and versatile being of matchless executive powers, exceptional intelligence and unimaginable wisdom. Their personal names may differ in each creation, but their order is universally known as The Brilliant Morning Stars.

Gabriel naturally embodies many characteristics and attributes of his divine Parents—Michael and Nebadonia. However, he is as well, in and of himself a unique Being and an original personality. Besides being the Prime minister of the universal government, Gabriel is also the Commander in Chief of the celestial army of Nebadon. Save for Immanuel and Christ Michael himself, all orders and classes of intelligences within the vicinity of this universe are under the immediate jurisdiction of this peerless and brilliant executive.

It was Gabriel and his loyal assistants who fought against Lucifer and Satan during their disastrous outbreak of rebellion in Satania.

Melkisedek—is mentioned twice in the Bible, but very little was revealed about this high order of celestial beings in the scriptures. Melkisedek is not a personal name, but that o f a divine order of universe sons of God. Although the Melkisedeks maintain the highest form of self-representative government in the universe, they are completely reliable and faithful to the Father's will. They have never been indicted for abuse of their privileges. They are naturally honest, loyal and true to their duties. Although they were created fully capable to assume almost any cosmic responsibility, they also gain more experiences in their diverse self-imposed services. The autonomy of the Melkisedeks is not an arbitrary act of the Creator. Two factors contributed in the qualification of this superb order for self-governance: First, the firstborn of this order—the Father Melkisedek—participated in the creation of the whole order. Second, they are among the most trustworthy and reliable group of universe intelligences. They are trusted by all imaginable types of celestial beings.

The Name of the Melkisedek Son who incarnated on Urantia about two thousand years before the bestowal of Christ Michael as Jesus was Machiventa. Machiventa was a member of the twelve Melkisedeks, who were on duty as the supervising council of Urantia's celestial government during humanity's earliest days of evolution. After the Adamic default, the world's condition had rapidly deteriorated to the point that it became necessary for this council to take serious measures to prevent mankind from sinking completely into an ocean of darkness. Consequently, a petition to the Most-High for some unusual act to uplift the world spiritually was made, and permission was granted to him [Machiventa] to incarnate as a mortal of the realm on Urantia.

Machiventa's mission in the flesh was not typical of his order because the Melkisedeks seldom incarnate on the evolutionary realms of their assignments. During his sojourn here, he was widely known as the "Sage of Salem" for there was the headquarters of his religious activities.

Machiventa remained here for ninety-four years. He vigorously ministered to uphold and advance truth in the religious mentality of practically every culture on Urantia by sending his well-trained and organized emissaries throughout the world in preaching tours. Unlike Caligastia and Adam, Machiventa's mission was a complete success. He wisely led his followers into the worship of a unique God, which he denominated as *El Elyon*—the Most-High. Upon the termination of his mission, Machiventa returned to his primal state as a Melkisedek Son, but he remained fully attached to the circumstances of Urantia's spiritual evolution.

Two thousand years ago, he was appointed by Christ Michael as the vice-gerent Planetary Prince of Urantia, and was given a seat in the council of the twenty and four elders [also appointed by Michael] to supervise the affairs of this and the other troubled worlds of Satania. He is currently serving here in this capacity, overseeing the development of Michael's Correcting Time Plan to retrieve this lost planet.

Vorondadeck: The Most Highs—are the highly exalted rulers of a universe's Constellations. Typically, every evolving universe of time is comprised of one hundred Constellations [there are exceptions]. A Constellation normally contains one hundred thousand inhabited worlds of diverse types of living organisms and intelligences. Each is presided over by three Vorondadeck Sons—the Father, the Junior, and the Senior Most Highs. However, not all of these brilliant beings serve in this capacity. Like their elder brothers, the Melkisedeks, their ministry is broad and various.

The Most Highs or Constellation Fathers constitute the highest committee of the legislative body of the Creator Son. They assume great responsibilities in the managerial procedures and in maintaining stability of purpose in the universe. They exercise complete jurisdictions over the administrative affairs of the Constellations. Their wisdom of leadership and loyalty to the plan of the Deities are practically matchless and incomparable to any subordinate order of Sons.

They were created by Christ Michael in liaison with the Divine Mother Spirit of the universe following the creations of Gabriel and the Melkisedeks.

APPENDIX

Nebadon—is the cosmic name of our universe as revealed by celestials.

Urantia—is the cosmic name of the planet earth as revealed by celestials.

Lanonandek—is the fourth order of Local Universe sonship, which is specialized in three different categories of cosmic services. As the first order of divine origin that is required to undergo an educational training before their classifications for administrative duties, the Lanonandeks are a very peculiar type of personalities who bridge the inconceivable gap between the highest and the lowest forms of intelligent existences in the universe. The numbers of these Sons are stationary for they do not procreate or reproduce themselves. Following their relatively short course of evaluation in the Melkisedek universities, they are usually classified as Primary, Secondary and Tertiary graduates. Each of these distinct groups is then qualified to function in three major domains of the universe's administration, but they are not specifically limited to these special assignments.

The Primary Lanonandeks are usually designated as System Sovereigns. Those of the Secondary level are normally appointed as Planetary Princes to the evolutionary worlds of time, whereas the Tertiary alumnae are commissioned to assume several miscellaneous tasks throughout the creation.

Lucifer—is vaguely known on Urantia since he delegated his first lieutenant, Satan to defend his cause on this bewildered world following his open defiance against Michael's authority. Until recently in history, very little was ever revealed about this wayward personality here.

Lucifer is a Primary Lanonandek Son of great intelligence, abilities, and wisdom. He was created by Christ Michael in union with Nebadonia—the Mother Spirit of this universe. For over three hundred thousand years prior to his rebellion, he reigned as the Chief Executive and ruler of Satania – a large planetary system comprises of more than six hundred inhabited worlds. His brilliance sagacity and charming character earned him the respect and loyalty of virtually all the resident creatures within the domains of his jurisdiction. He was an extraordinary figure and a distinguished member of his order.

As a Primary Lanonandek Son of divine origin, Lucifer belongs to the fourth order of the series of universe sons of God created to assume many formidable tasks in the administration of the universe. Although they may serve in different capacities on various universe levels, the Lanonandeks are, however, especially preoccupied with the administrative affairs of their native creations - the local universes. They usually serve as System Sovereigns and Planetary Princes on the evolutionary worlds of time. They were created with exceptional executive talents and administrative skills to carry out their duties effectively. And...they also acquired additional experiences that improve those natural faculties, which render them even more competent and serviceable as expert rulers of the numerous planetary systems of the universe. They were intentionally designed for a closer approach to the physical realms of time, to better serve the lower orders of evolving creatures, such as the angels, the midwayers, and the mortals. They are technically indispensable to the ascension of the evolving souls of time.

Although they were created a little inferior to the Melkisedeks and the Vorondadecks, and notwithstanding they normally function under the supervisions of these Sons, the Lanonandeks, however, are not considered as entirely subordinate to these classes of universe dignitaries. The highly created sons of God always stand on equal footing with their brethren irrespective of their differential levels of divine origins or cosmic services. God is no respecter of persons, celestial or mortal.

From the universe's standpoint, the attenuation of the divine word in the creation of the Lanonandeks is more or less a form of technical adjustment to the lower creations of the universe rather than an actual diminishment of the spiritual status of these personalities. It is a sad history that since their registration as living beings in Nebadon, scores of these marvelous sons have succumbed to pride, that so many have allowed the sophistries of their exalted egos to lead them into sin and darkness.

After his graduation from the Melkisedek universities, Lucifer was selected as one of the most brilliant personalities of his order. Before his revolt and apostasy, he was the chief administrator of the Local System of Satania—one of the one hundred clusters of inhabited worlds that make up the constellation of Norlatiadeck for over three hundred thousand years. He had sat in council with the Most Highs in many occasions during his universe career, and was highly praised and respected throughout the System.

Departing from that eminent and honorable status, he embraced sin, degraded his mind, and tarnished the beautiful name of his order. His delusions of self-importance blinded his spiritual understanding. Around two hundred thousand years ago of Urantia time, he orchestrated a furious and widespread rebellion against the universal government of the Creator Son in Nebadon. Though this revolt was not the first of its kind in the universe, it was, however, the most disastrous and far-reaching. It provoked the greatest cosmic upheaval to have ever so dogmatically challenged the divine authority of the Creator Son since the birth of this creation. Among the many deplorable losses and casualties of this catastrophic insurrection, earth and 36 other evolving worlds in the Local System of Satania were largely thrust into spiritual chaos and confusions by their apostate Planetary Princes who fully embraced the cause of Lucifer.

After Christ Michael's bestowal on Urantia, this archenemy of the universe was incarcerated by decree of the Ancient of Days of Uversa. He was held in isolation for almost two thousand years until his recent annihilation following the adjudication of his rebellion.

Satan—has been seriously mischaracterized on Urantia. Few scriptural accounts have accurately described this nefarious personage. Besides his iniquity, very little to nothing is known about Satan's personality on this planet.

Like his chief Lucifer, Satan was a primary Lanonandek Son created by Christ Michael in harmony with Nebadonia—Mother Spirit. Before he espoused Lucifer's manifesto, he was a veteran administrator with an enviable record of long experiences in the managerial affairs of Nebadon. Prior and during the rebellion, he was Lucifer's lieutenant, serving as the official representative in the Local System of Satania [not to be confounded with his name]. He paid frequent visits to the evolving worlds to confer with their Planetary Princes. As we saw in Paper 2, it was he who informed Caligastia about Lucifer's secret plan to revolt against the universe government during one of his regular periodic inspections on Urantia.

Soon after the rebellion was announced, Lucifer invested him with authority to represent and defend the cause on earth and the other apostate worlds. This is why he and not Caligastia became the planetary icon of that cosmic revolt on Urantia. As we said, some religious records do fairly portray his deceiving character, which is virtually typical of all the rebels. However, they poorly characterized this fallen Son in their caricatures of his majestic personality. Not that it is important to know what he actually looks like, but it is nonetheless, true that Satan himself is a Lanonandek Son of great brilliance.

During Michael's bestowal as Jesus, Satan with Caligastia and Lucifer were in a league to thwart the Lord's mission. But they were emphatically defeated. Finally, Michael officially terminated their rebellion in the Local System of Satania. Individual isolated worlds like Urantia may continue to suffer the casualties of the rebellion. However, as a whole, the Local System was delivered from the strains of doubts and confusions of this sinful insurrection after Michael's incarnation on earth as Jesus of Nazareth.

Caligastia—prior to the revelation of the Urantia Book, Caligastia was practically never mentioned or figured anywhere in the world's diverse religious annals. However, every generation that has ever lived on the surface of the earth symbolically knows this nefarious celestial personage as the *"devil or the evil One."*

Like Lucifer and Satan, Caligastia is a defiant Lanonandek Son, who succumbed to the illusions of self-pride and betrayed his sacred pledge as Planetary Prince of this world. But unlike them, he was a secondary member of his order. Before he was appointed as the Principal of Urantia, he had a long desirable career in many governmental departments of the local universe, during which he displayed efficiency as a leader and a talented administrator. Besides the highest rulers of creation, probably no one could have predicted that he would so quickly and shamefully betrayed the trust invested in him by the Constellation Fathers when they commissioned him with his staff to assume authority on earth. Though his real name receives little to no publicity throughout history, the effects of his sinful act of betrayal have largely remained since he plunged humanity into spiritual darkness during your earliest and most vulnerable days of planetary evolution. His imminence and influence in global affairs may have been deeply obscured and concealed, but the presence of this apostate and fallen Prince was nonetheless, real up until the recent final adjudication of the Lucifer rebellion. These sworn adversaries of the universe, symbolically represented by the dragon, were utterly destroyed and erased from the memory of the cosmos at the onset of the 21st century of Urantia's time. Now they have become as if they had never been.

Beelzebub—is the chief commander of the rebellious Midwayers, who joined Caligastia in his insurrection on earth. He is a secondary Midway creature. Following the outbreak of Caligastia's revolt, Beelzebub rapidly became the icon of personified wickedness throughout the world because the Prince's Lieutenant, Daligastia, designated him as commander to oversee the activities of the rebel creatures of his order.

He was figured as the devilish prince himself in several religious records primarily because of the strong influences his emissaries were exerting upon some feeble minded and degenerated humans—a title which should have been reserved expressly for

Caligastia. But the latter [Caligastia] desired that the world mostly remain ignorant of his existence. So, very few humans of those epochs knew anything about the true identity of the apostate Prince.

Instead, Beelzebub was chosen, groomed, and deceitfully implanted as a decoy to impersonate Caligastia, the real mastermind behind the unwarranted revolution against God on earth. For a time, he was feared, exalted, and even revered like a god by many misguided souls during the dark periods following the rebellion. This miscreant and his subordinates used to roam the earth to propagate the deceptions of his chief, Caligastia. Under his command, the rebellious midwayers worked incessantly to incite global discords, provoke confusions, and draw the human mind further away from the indwelling presence of God.

However, on the day of Pentecost, after the pouring out of the Spirit of Truth upon all flesh, he and his throng were interned. Prior to the final verdicts in the case filed by Gabriel against Lucifer on Uversa, which was only recently announced, for over 250,000 years no one could accurately forecast the future of these unruly personalities.

Uversa — is the Capital of Orvonton, one of the seven superuniverses comprising the totality of the evolutionary creations of time and space. This supernal abode is presided over by three Ancients Of Days.

Norlatiadeck — is the name of one of the 100 major organized divisions of the Local Universe of Nebadon.

The Mystery Monitors **[Thought Adjusters]** — are the fragmentized indwelling spirits of God the Father bestowed upon each mortal creature with the mental capacity to love and worship. These marvelous divine presences are perfect and infallible guides. They never fail to attain the heights of the most glorious values conceivable in the universe. In essence, they are God.

The Spirit of Truth—is a bestowal gift from Christ Michael to all receptive and teachable souls on earth. It is the divine counselor and comforter Jesus had promised to send to his loyal followers and Apostles. On the eventful day of Pentecost, this Spirit was imparted unto all Adjuster indwelt mortals on Urantia, to facilitate their communication with the Universal Father and realize the sublime truth of their sonship with Him.

Ancient of Days—is a Paradise order of Trinity origin personalities, which were created since near eternity. Like most of the highest orders of universe intelligences, they are stationary in number for they do not reproduce themselves. Their creation dated as far back to the origin of matter itself; hence their name. Three of those super personalities preside over the capital of each of the seven superuniverses, which constitute the totality of the evolutionary creations of time and space.

Forthcoming Titles From Paradise Press

The Great Correcting Time Plan—Vol. 2 & 3

The Cries of the Forgotten

Sonship With God IS A Personal Reality

My Interviews with God: *an Unusual Conversation*

A Mastery Course of Occult Philosophy

The Last Agondonters : End of the Age of Faith

A Glimpse Into the Times that will Precede the Ages of Light and Life on Earth

The Coming Grand Collision & Collapse of Synthetic Civilization

Evolution over Revolution : How to Subdue the Mind to the Leadings of the Indwelling Spirit

The Firewalls of the Matrix : How to Break Free

Discovering The Mysterious **'I AM'**: the Creator, the Observer, & the Experiencer

Picture by © Khaalid Yaqoub

About the Author

Joseph E. Jean-Phillippe is a spiritually rehearsed personality, who functions as a channel [Transmitter/Receiver or TR] for transcendental communications under the guidance of the celestial agencies overseeing supernatural services on planet earth. Penetrating the profound mysteries of life and finding the *Primordial Ancestor* of all creations, are his ultimate purposes in this journey. Thus, he fully commits himself to these objectives.

Joseph fervently believes that all persons who gracefully receive the glad tiding of *Sonship with God* are entrusted with an enormous sacred responsibility to become emissaries of this sublime message themselves—even as this was recommended by Christ Michael during his short sojourn here. He is convinced that by virtue of the Divine Spark within each of us, we possess sufficient spiritual powers and creativities to overcome all temporal challenges-- including transcending the perceptions of our 'human or mortal identities,' and turn our fears into love and confidence.

His commitment to this ministry is voluntary, but he trusts that his faith and determination are inspired by his indwelling Guide. Being entirely dedicated to complete this peculiar assignment successfully, Joseph personally chooses to 'socialize' merely to stimulate others' appetite for Truths. He invites all honest and thoughtful truth seekers to join him in spirit to propagate the inspiring news of *The Great Correcting Time Plan*, and lay the foundation for an emerging transformational, spiritual renaissance on earth. He strongly believes that a new era of formidable and magnificent changes is truly upon us.